TOO BIG TO FAIL

Too Big to Fail
The Hazards of Bank Bailouts

WITH A NEW PREFACE

Gary H. Stern
Ron J. Feldman

BROOKINGS INSTITUTION PRESS
Washington, D.C.

Copyright © 2004
First paperback edition copyright © 2009
THE BROOKINGS INSTITUTION
1775 Massachusetts Avenue, N.W., Washington, D.C. 20036
www.brookings.edu

The Library of Congress has cataloged the hardcover edition as follows:
Stern, Gary H.
  Too big to fail : the hazards of bank bailouts / Gary H. Stern,
Ron J. Feldman.
    p. cm.
  Includes bibliographical references and index.
    ISBN-10: 0-8157-8152-0 (cloth : alk. paper)
    ISBN-13: 978-0-8157-8152-3 (cloth : alk. paper)
    1. Bank failures—United States. 2. Bank failures—Government
policy—United States. 3. Banks and banking—State supervision.
4. Intervention (Federal government) I. Feldman, Ron J. II. Title.
  HG2491.S74 2004
  332.1'2—dc22   2003026258
    ISBN 978-0-8157-0304-4 (pbk. : alk. paper)

        9 8 7 6 5 4 3 2

The paper used in this publication meets minimum requirements of the American National Standard for Information Sciences—Permanence of Paper for Printed Library Materials: ANSI Z39.48-1992.

Typeset in Minion

Composition by Cynthia Stock
Silver Spring, Maryland

Printed by R. R. Donnelley
Harrisonburg, Virginia

Contents

Foreword

Paul A. Volcker

From this perspective, there is still unresolved controversy about the cascading bank failures and the Great Depression of the 1930s: Which was cause and which effect? But of one thing there can be little doubt. The coincidence of those events had an enormous and long-lasting impact on the thinking of government and monetary authorities—and of bankers themselves—on the risks posed by bank failures for economic activity.

In most advanced countries, commercial banks had long been subject to some regulation and official oversight. While limited, that approach reflected a general view that banking stability and continuity, more than other areas of businesses, rested on a sense of mutual trust and confidence and that a breakdown of that perception would pose great risk for the economic system generally. However, it was not thought appropriate or anticipated that depositors or other creditors of failed or failing banks be protected by an official "safety net."

To be sure, central banks had come to be looked to as "lenders of last resort," able to provide liquidity to the banking system and individual banks in time of crisis. But accepted central banking doctrine would limit that support to solvent institutions able to provide solid, and rather narrowly defined, collateral.

In the midst of depression, that rather passive approach could not stem the tide of failures and restore confidence. Consequently, after intense debate about the implications for moral hazard, the United States decided on explicit legislation to protect only small depositors of failed banks. While a formal system of deposit insurance was not common in other countries, there wasn't much doubt that governments generally would be prepared to be more activist in dealing with the threat of a banking crisis.

The Federal Deposit Insurance Corporation and the new attitude were not tested for decades. The scars of the Great Depression and banking failures led to a more conservative, risk-adverse approach by bankers themselves. For almost a half century, the United States was free of significant bank failures, remarkable in the light of the many thousands of individual institutions.

All that changed, beginning in the mid-1970s. Memories of financial crisis had faded for a new generation of commercial bankers. They were faced with intense new competitive pressures. Ready to challenge established practices and regulatory restraints, they moved more aggressively into new lending areas and international markets.

At the same time, other events roiled markets and amplified risks. The repeated oil crises, accelerating inflation, more speculative real estate markets, and a massive buildup of debt by developing countries in Latin America and elsewhere were capped by an unanticipated squeeze on money markets as anti-inflationary monetary policies took effect.

While not the first banking failure to test the willingness of governments to respond more actively, the demise of the Continental Illinois Bank, one of the largest American commercial lenders and one of the most important major correspondent banks, marked a watershed. Strong intervention by the Federal Reserve and a critical decision by the Federal Deposit Insurance Corporation to recapitalize the bank from its own resources moved beyond the narrow and explicit legal requirement to reimburse "small" depositors for loss.

In the surrounding disturbed financial circumstances of the time, with a strong sense of financial fragility, there was relatively little controversy about those decisions. Subsequently, nearly all depositors in the long string of failures of thrift institutions were protected by enlarged Federal Deposit Insurance Corporation and Federal Savings and Loan Insurance Corporation insurance. With few exceptions, governments around the world have, by one means or another, protected depositors of regulated commercial banks from the consequences of failure when the institution involved was judged to be of "systemic" importance, that is, to present a risk to the stability of the banking and financial system as a whole.

Obviously, that judgment is difficult, and it has come to invoke strong controversy and debate.

One consequence has been a sense of unfairness, particularly voiced in the United States, where there are many small institutions clearly not of "systemic" importance. They feel they are put at a distinct competitive disadvantage. They want less ambiguity and judgment and more certainty of protection for their depositors.

The broader concern is the perceived sense of growing "moral hazard," specifically the possibility that confident expectations of creditor "bailouts" will dull normal market discipline. Inherently, a protected creditor will have less incentive for "due diligence," with the perverse result of encouraging excessive risk-taking and failure itself. Japan, where successive governments have confirmed a blanket guarantee of commercial bank liabilities, is pointed to as an extreme example of encouraging imprudent banking practices, misallocating financial resources, and prolonging structural weaknesses.

The extent to which the shift in public policy—the reputed doctrine of "too big to fail"—has in fact had damaging repercussions in the United States is much more difficult to judge. Gary Stern and Ron Feldman, in writing *Too Big to Fail: The Hazards of Bank Bailouts*, clearly take the view that the need for reform and clarity in U.S. practice is evident and urgent. Equally plainly, they are not in the school that minimizes the risks and sees official attitudes as dominated by private and ulterior motives.

Stern and Feldman are cognizant of one important aspect of reality. Faced with the clear and present danger of a severe fallout from a large bank failure, on the one hand, against the more amorphous and certainly more distant risk of losing market discipline, on the other hand, official judgments may be biased toward the "not on my watch" syndrome. The basic Stern and Feldman approach, as I see it, is to build barriers to deal with the bias to protect depositors and creditors.

The implications of their work go beyond the world of commercial banking. Witness the officially encouraged (if not officially financed) rescue a few years ago of Long-Term Capital Management, a large but unregulated, secretive, speculative hedge fund. The fact is the relative importance of commercial banks in the United States has been diminishing steadily. Consequently, the lessons and approaches reviewed in *Too Big to Fail* have wider application.

All of this justifies the kind of objective, analytic approach that makes *Too Big to Fail* an important contribution to a vexed subject.

Preface to the Paperback Edition

In 2004, in the first edition of *Too Big to Fail*, we argued that the "too big to fail" (TBTF) problem was serious, was getting worse, and needed immediate attention, particularly given the advantages of addressing TBTF in relatively tranquil times. We were right: 2008 and 2009 have seen the targeted multibillion-dollar rescue of several large U.S. financial institutions, including Citigroup, AIG, and Bear Stearns (with similar, sometimes more expansive, actions taken in other countries). The same period has also seen a massive across-the-board expansion of financial institutions' safety net more generally, including the opening of the Federal Reserve's discount window to select investment banks, the provision of guarantees to money market mutual fund investors, and full insurance for business deposit accounts.[1]

Some observers initially suggested that these actions would not excessively increase moral hazard and future expectations of TBTF support,

---

This preface draws heavily on our recent analysis of the "too big to fail" problem. In particular, see remarks by Gary H. Stern, "Too Big to Fail: The Way Forward," a speech delivered at Winona State University, November 13, 2008 (available online at minneapolis fed.org/news_events/pres/stern11-13-08.cfm). See also Stern's "Limiting Spillovers through Focused Supervision," in the September 2008 issue of *The Region*, published by the Federal Reserve Bank of Minneapolis (minneapolisfed.org/publications_papers/pub_display. cfm?id=4043); and Gary H. Stern and Ron J. Feldman, "Managing the Expanded Safety Net," in the May 2008 issue of *Federal Reserve Bank of Minneapolis 2007 Annual Report* (mineapo lisfed.org/publications_papers/pub_display.cfm?id=4014).

1. More precisely, the unlimited insurance covers non-interest-bearing deposit transaction accounts.

which ultimately encourage financial institutions to take on excessive risk. They argued after the rescue of Bear Stearns, for example, that the imposition of losses on equity holders and management would counteract to some degree the ill effects of supporting a wide range of fixed-income creditors. Those who made this argument failed to appreciate that only the creditors the government supported—not equity holders—typically have incentives to check firms' risk taking; protecting these creditors from loss defines the expansion of the TBTF problem. But as the range of government support for financial institutions grew—and as policymakers relaxed some of the initial costs they put on some creditors—arguments downplaying the TBTF issue lost force. Indeed, policymakers began to acknowledge, at least implicitly, their previous underestimation of the TBTF problem; TBTF now rests at the very top of the mountain of financial ills elected officials, policymakers, and bank supervisors must deal with.[2]

Timely and accurate identification of the severity of the TBTF problem is not, however, the primary justification for reissuing this book now. Instead, the framework we provide to deal with the TBTF problem and the specific recommendations suggested by that framework to better reduce the TBTF problem in the future are the reason. We think the framework and recommendations in this book should constitute a core part of any new approach to managing TBTF. Ignoring this framework and recommendations would constitute a major policy error, perhaps a more costly mistake than ignoring our warnings about TBTF in the first place.

Our framework emphasizes the importance of so-called spillovers in explaining why governments protect the creditors of large failing banks and other systemically important financial firms. As we emphasize in the book, "Policymakers should give highest priority to reforms limiting the chance that one bank's failure will threaten the solvency of other banks." As a general rule, policymakers should try to fix the TBTF problem by better managing the risk of spillovers: creditor expectations of government support will diminish—-and market discipline will increase—-when policy-

2. Policymakers have made this point directly. See, for example, Kate Gibson and Greg Robb, "Bernanke Sees Long Slowdown, but Still Confident," *Market Watch*, PBS, October 15, 2008. In addition, see Eric S. Rosengren, "Some Principles to Consider in Future Regulatory Reform," speech given at Global Risk Regulation Summit, Geneva, Switzerland, December 8, 2008 (www.bos.frb.org/news/speeches/rosengren/2008/120808.htm). Press accounts also highlight the importance of TBTF. For example, see Cheyenne Hopkins, "Big Policy Choices Face New President," *American Banker*, November 5, 2008. See also Bob Davis, Jonathan Weisman, and Timothy Aeppel, "New Economic Ills Will Force Winner's Hand," *Wall Street Journal*, November 4, 2008.

makers take on the underlying spillover threat that leads them to support creditors.

We have seen policymakers begin to adopt the TBTF framework. Consider comments from former Secretary of the Treasury Henry Paulson:

> In an optimal system, market discipline effectively constrains risk because the regulatory structure is strong enough that a financial institution can fail without threatening the overall system. For market discipline to constrain risk effectively, financial institutions must be allowed to fail. Under optimal financial regulatory and financial system infrastructures, such a failure would not threaten the overall system. However, today two concerns underpin expectations of regulatory intervention to prevent a failure. They are that an institution may be too interconnected to fail or too big to fail. We must take steps to reduce the perception that this is so—and that requires that we reduce the likelihood that it is so.[3]

But it is not enough for policymakers to rely on our general policy approach; such a framework may be consistent with a large number of specific reforms. We think policymakers should begin their quest to rein in TBTF by starting with the reforms we articulated. Indeed, we think the reforms we proposed in 2004 would have been of appreciable benefit if they had been implemented prior to the 2008 turmoil. Of course, we cannot truly know what might have ameliorated the many spillovers, particularly from one financial institution to another, that followed the collapse of the subprime lending market. But awareness of these recommendations would have left policymakers better prepared for the fallout that accompanied the weakening of systemically important financial firms. Such preparation may not have prevented the need for safety net expansion, but it would have improved the chances that more limited financial support for creditors would have sufficed to address the spillover threat. (We discuss this point in more detail later in the preface.)

This line of argument naturally leads to a more basic question: If our reforms were so on-target, why were they not adopted in the first place? We will answer that question first and then turn to why we think our reforms would have made the 2008 crisis less severe.

Some may have viewed TBTF reforms as a poor use of scarce resources.

3. See U.S. Treasury Secretary Henry M. Paulson Jr., "The United States, the World Economy, and Markets before the Chatham House," press release, July 2, 2008 (treas.gov/press/releases/hp1064.htm).

Policymakers always have a large number of initiatives under way, but they can give priority to only a select few. In this context, recall that by virtually all measures, most of the largest financial institutions seemed to be in excellent condition prior to the start of the turmoil in 2007. So, ex ante, other issues may have reasonably seemed more important even if, ex post, TBTF is now viewed as paramount.

In other cases, the answer lies at least partly in the belief that previously enacted reforms would make it both exceedingly difficult and unnecessary for policymakers to support uninsured creditors. Observers seemed to believe these reforms put creditors at risk of loss and obviated concerns about TBTF. In particular, we heard from many that the regime created by the 1991 Federal Deposit Insurance Corporation Improvement Act (FDICIA) to limit TBTF support rendered our concerns about the scale and persistence of TBTF moot. Adherents of this view would not be expected to put efforts to fix TBTF at the top of the "to do" list.

Suffice it to say that we had a different view of this topic, one that is explained in detail in appendix A of this book. We did not think that FDICIA reforms, when push came to shove, would act as an effective limit on creditor expectations or on policymaker actions, and the events of 2008 and 2009 in large part bear this out. Why? Simply because these procedural changes did not address the underlying reason policymakers provided support in the first place. Consider that the intervention with Bear Stearns involved the type of on-the-record support and consultations across agencies that FDICIA mandated. In another, more recent, example, policymakers invoked FDICIA's so-called systemic risk exception when they greatly expanded select deposit insurance at all banks.[4] In light of this, we see little promise of effectively containing the expanded safety net by increasing the coverage of FDICIA-like regimes.

Other observers may have thought that existing or enhanced supervi-

4. Policymakers invoked the so-called systemic risk exception of FDICIA in creating the FDIC's Temporary Liquidity Guarantee Program and in the context of the proposed acquisition of Wachovia Corp. by Citicorp Inc. See FDIC, "FDIC Announces Plan to Free Up Bank Liquidity," press release 100-2008, October 14, 2008, and FDIC, "Citigroup Inc. to Acquire Banking Operations of Wachovia," press release 88-2008, September 29, 2008. In contrast, policymakers did not invoke the exception in the failures of IndyMac Bank, F.S.B., and Washington Mutual Bank, despite the large size of these two depositories. See FDIC, "FDIC Establishes IndyMac Federal Bank, FSB as Successor to IndyMac Bank, F.S.B., Pasadena, California," press release 56-2008, July 11, 2008, and FDIC, "JPMorgan Chase Acquires Banking Operations of Washington Mutual," press release 85-2008, September 25, 2008. Links to all FDIC press releases, listed chronologically, can be found at www.fdic.gov/news/news/press/2008/index.html.

sion and regulation would appropriately curtail financial firms' risk taking. We were skeptical of this claim, too. As discussed in appendix C, although supervision and regulation have an important role to play, these tools may not adequately restrain the risk taking encouraged by TBTF. For example, supervisors with discretion cannot easily limit risk taking by firms before the damage is done. Minimum capital rules also seem one step too slow; that is, regulators cannot readily institute capital rules that link minimum capital levels to current bank risk. In short, we would not view increased reliance on the supervision and regulation basket, at least not as has been described to date, as the linchpin of better TBTF management.

In answer to the second question, "Would our reforms have made a difference?" we point to some representative examples suggesting that the reforms we recommended in 2004 would have contributed to better preparation prior to the crisis four years later.

One recommendation that would have increased preparedness for events in 2008 and 2009 concerns what we called scenario planning. We described key aspects of this reform in the book as follows:

> Policymakers could reduce the uncertainty that they face when a large bank fails by knowing the potential exposures other banks have to the failing institution in advance and practicing their response to such failures. . . . [Supervisors should examine] how the failure of one institution would affect the solvency of [other large banks]. . . . This amounts to checking out how much one bank . . . owes the others at a point in time—say, at the end of a business day. . . . [T]he government would focus on spillovers and cross-institution exposure. . . . Supervisors should develop detailed plans for addressing the failure of a large bank, test those procedures in simulations, and revise the procedures to account for test results. Supervisors should repeat the cycle regularly, given the rapidly changing operations of the largest banks. . . . [S]upervisors must identify the documents and data they will need to determine a bank's solvency and the exposures it would present to other banks at the time of failure. . . . Ultimately, supervisors must identify the gaps between what institutions can provide and what supervisors require. *We view it as of the highest priority for supervisors to eliminate such gaps.*[5]

5. See pages 112 and 114 in this volume. We explain our broad definition of the term "bank" and our use of it on pages 14–16.

This approach would have been of considerable value when determining potential responses to the illiquidity or insolvency of specific large financial institutions in 2008 and 2009. To be sure, such preparation may not have ultimately changed the need for significant policy action, but policymakers likely would have had a better understanding of the specific "interconnectedness" of large financial firms, suggesting that responses to the outcomes could have been more timely and better focused.

In particular, if policymakers had grasped the net of connections of large financial firms in, say, 2006 instead of 2008, they might have taken steps to figure out how to contain the ability of this network to spread risk. For example, policymakers have now identified the absence of an effective resolution scheme as a major weakness in dealing with the spillovers created when large nonbank financial firms get into trouble. This absence and a desire to contain these spillovers explain, in part, the extraordinary support such firms ultimately received. It is likely that the type of exploration we advocated would have raised the visibility of this problem.

In a second recommendation, we emphasized the importance of communicating and signaling to creditors policymakers' intent to impose losses in the resolution of institutions they might consider TBTF. We have been clear that policymakers need to "anchor" the expectations of these creditors to avoid surprising them, particularly if policymakers have taken actions to reduce the chance that they will provide support. Some observers have attributed the deterioration of credit and financial market conditions in the fall of 2008 to surprises that creditors of large institutions experienced.[6]

In a third example, we encouraged policymakers to consider new capital regimes that would have enhanced bank capital positions in bad times by locking in the ability to raise capital in the future. At the time we highlighted it, we noted that this proposal may not have been practicable, and it still might not be. But certainly many observers have concluded that a more "procyclical" capital regime would have provided a better response to the 2008 turmoil than the one currently in place.[7]

6. For our suggestions, see Gary H. Stern and Ron J. Feldman, "Constructive Commitment: Communicating Plans to Impose Losses on Large Bank Creditors," in *Systemic Financial Crises: Resolving Large Bank Insolvencies,* edited by Douglas D. Evanoff and George G. Kaufman (Hackensack, N.J.: World Scientific Publishing, 2005).

7. For an example of an extension of the capital proposal we highlighted, see Anil K. Kashyap, Raghuram G. Rajan, and Jeremy C. Stein, "Rethinking Capital Regulation," paper prepared for the Federal Reserve Bank of Kansas City symposium Maintaining Stability in a Changing Financial System, Jackson Hole, Wyoming, August 21--23, 2008 (kc.frb.org/pub licat/sympos/2008/KashyapRajanStein.08.08.08.pdf).

There are other recommendations we could mention. For example, we identified the benefits of increasing the use of centralized clearinghouses for derivative markets and stressed the importance of resolution schemes that could quickly make payments to uninsured creditors of the funds owed them by the failing institution.

In sum, the answers to these two direct questions indicate that our previously articulated reforms clearly have merit and deserve a second look. So where should policymakers start?

We would begin the effort to manage TBTF with an approach, based solely on reforms in this book, that we now call systemic focused supervision (SFS).[8] In general, SFS attempts to focus supervision and regulation efforts on reduction of spillovers, and it rests on three pillars: early identification, enhanced prompt corrective action (PCA), and stability-related communication.

Early Identification. This is a process to identify and, where appropriate, respond to the material exposures among large financial institutions and between these institutions and capital markets. This process relates closely to our scenario-planning recommendation. The goals of the exercise we described are (1) to give policymakers a sense of which events are not likely to severely impair a large financial institution, thus permitting them to avoid providing support, and (2) to identify those exposures that might bring down the firm, and thus are deserving of closer policy scrutiny and, most important, an effective and timely response.

Enhanced Prompt Corrective Action. PCA works by requiring supervisors to take specified actions against a bank if its capital falls below specified triggers. Closing banks while they still have positive capital, or at most a small loss, can reduce spillovers in a fairly direct way. If a bank's failure does not impose large losses, by definition it cannot directly threaten the viability of other depository institutions that have exposure to it. Thus, the PCA regime offers an important tool to manage systemic risk. However, this regime currently uses triggers that do not adequately account for future losses and gives too much discretion to bank management. We would augment the triggers with more forward-looking data outside the control of bank management to address these concerns.

Communication. The first two pillars of SFS seek to increase market discipline by reducing the motivation policymakers have for protecting cred-

8. See Gary H. Stern, "Limiting Spillovers through Focused Supervision," *The Region,* Federal Reserve Bank of Minneapolis, September 2008.

itors. But creditors will not know about efforts to limit spillovers, and therefore will not change their expectations of support, absent explicit communication by policymakers about these efforts.

Despite what we see as a compelling case, we know that others continue to have real doubts about our approach. These observers tend to focus on the inability of our recommendations, or any recommendations for that matter, to anticipate the source of the next major disruption. These observers argue that the idiosyncratic nature of each financial disruption means that policymakers can at best fight the last war and cannot take steps to limit future spillovers. Who could have foreseen, critics might ask, that losses originating in subprime mortgages would ultimately lead to a freeze in the secured-funding markets on which investment banks and other failed firms have relied? The manner in which AIG and other large firms imploded certainly caught most observers and market participants by surprise. But it was no surprise that the collapse of very large financial institutions posed spillover risks or raised TBTF concerns.

Moreover, we do not need to forecast the event that brings down systemically important firms to make progress against TBTF. Instead, we need to consider the spillovers such a failure might cause. For example, would such a failure eliminate the availability of important clearing and settlement services? If so, what can we do today to facilitate continued provision of those services? Would that failure impose large losses on other firms potentially seen as TBTF? If so, what actions today would help policymakers quickly quantify potential exposures and assess counterparties' management of that risk? Though not perfect, this approach is superior to efforts that do not focus on spillover potential or that react to instability only after a firm fails. Policymakers will not stop the next flood, but that is no reason for them to situate themselves at the lowest point in the flood plain.

April 2009

Preface to the First Edition

In late 2001, following the tragic events of September 11, a medium-size broker-dealer firm headquartered in Minneapolis—MJK Clearing (MJKC)—experienced severe financial difficulty. It was alleged to the Federal Reserve Bank of Minneapolis that the failure of MJKC would spill over and severely impair around 200,000 retail customers, several brokerage firms involved in the stock-lending deal that initially caused the problems, and a variety of small brokerage houses throughout the Midwest for which MJKC provided back-office services. MJKC's lawyer argued that the firm was too big to fail (TBTF), that its failure would disrupt economic activity in the Midwest, and, therefore, that the Federal Reserve should provide assistance to it. Indeed, the leader of a second Reserve bank in the Midwest called Minneapolis to inquire about the possibility of spillover effects.

The largest liquidation of a securities broker by the Securities Investor Protection Corporation was hardly a trivial event.[1] However, the initial claims of financial and economic disruption were thought at the time, and later demonstrated, to be exaggerated, and no assistance was provided. The fact that MJKC's well-respected representative raised TBTF concerns shows

1. Securities Investor Protection Corporation, "2001 Set Record for Number of Customers Paid, Amount of Advances," news release, March 13, 2002.

how deeply the ethos of creditor protection in the name of financial stability permeates the financial environment. More important, if TBTF arguments are advanced in a case with only a hint of regional complications, they certainly will present themselves in almost any failure of significance. Indeed, a local newspaper columnist and a national banking association seemed to find examples of contagion in the MJKC failure.[2] Left to their own devices, policymakers could protect creditors even when other options would prove superior and reforms to prevent this undesirable outcome were available. Thus we viewed the events as a warning: Too big to fail is no theoretical problem, but rather a central public policy dilemma. This conclusion confirmed earlier concerns.

Before the MJKC failure, in mid-2000 to be precise, we presented options for addressing the TBTF problem at a conference held at the University of Chicago Business School. Michael Mussa, then the research director for the International Monetary Fund, dismissed our options out of hand. He argued that governments cannot convince creditors of large banks that they will take losses if their bank fails. In short, too big to fail is an unsolvable problem. We later heard from equally distinguished audience members that, in fact, there was not a TBTF problem in the United States. Legislation passed in the early 1990s had eliminated the problem, and other countries could easily adopt the same reforms. In either case, the message was the same: policymakers and the public should not spend much time worrying about how to address too big to fail.

We left the conference convinced that our previous, abbreviated work had failed to make our case. We had not adequately conveyed how policymakers could enact reforms that reduce creditors' expectations of a bailout. Moreover, we had not sufficiently established that earlier legislation had failed to fix the problem.

From such events came the impetus for a book-length treatment of the TBTF problem as well as the book's organization. In the first part, we warn readers that the TBTF problem is real, costly, and becoming more severe. In the second, we provide policymakers with options to address it. Too big to fail is not unsolvable, and this is the right time to address the problem—waiting for the next banking crisis can hardly improve our lot.

We thank three anonymous reviewers, Richard Todd, and David Mayes for providing comments on the entire manuscript; Robert Eisenbeis,

2. Ed Lotterman, "Stockwalk Situation Shows How Quickly Failure Can Spread," *St. Paul Pioneer Press*, October 7, 2001; Stone (2002).

William Isaac, George Kaufman, and Larry Wall for providing comments on our discussion of the Federal Deposit Insurance Corporation Improvement Act of 1991; Karen Hovermale, Therese Maroney, and Janet Swan for reference assistance; Jason Schmidt for research assistance; Doug Clement, David Fettig and Julie Randall for editorial assistance; and Barb Pierce for her considerable support of the entire project.

The views in this book are not necessarily those of the Federal Reserve Bank of Minneapolis or the Federal Reserve System.

January 2004

TOO BIG TO FAIL

1

Introduction:
Our Message and Methods

Summarizing the warnings and options of this book requires a little background for the uninitiated. We start with the trivial observation that banks fail.[1] Some banks fail without notice. Other failing banks capture the attention of policymakers, often because of the bank's large size and significant role in the financial system. Determining the appropriate policy response to an important failing bank has long been a vexing public policy issue. The failure of a large banking organization is seen as posing significant risks to other financial institutions, to the financial system as a whole, and possibly to the economic and social order. Because of such fears, policymakers in many countries—developed and less developed, democratic and autocratic—respond by protecting uninsured creditors of banks from all or some of the losses they otherwise would face. These banks have assumed the title of "too big to fail" (TBTF),[2] a term describing the receipt of discretionary government support by a bank's uninsured creditors who are not automatically entitled to government support (for simplicity we use creditors and uninsured creditors synonymously from here on).[3]

1. We use the term bank broadly to describe depositories whose liabilities are backed by implicit and explicit government support as well as their holding companies.
2. Although TBTF terminology has been applied to nonfinancial firms and subnational governments, we focus on banks and explain this decision in chapter 2.
3. Too big to fail is a misleading term in several ways—which we describe in chapter 2—but we continue to use it because it is established in the policy debate.

1

To the extent that creditors of TBTF banks expect government protection, they reduce their vigilance in monitoring and responding to these banks' activities. When creditors exert less of this type of market discipline, the banks may take excessive risks. TBTF banks will make loans and other bets that seem quite foolish in retrospect. These costs sound abstract but are, in fact, measured in the hundreds of billions of dollars of lost income and output for countries, some of which have faced significant economic downturns because of the instability that too big to fail helped to create. This undesirable behavior is frequently referred to as the "moral hazard" of TBTF protection. Such behavior wastes resources.

Our Message

Despite some progress, our central warning is that not enough has been done to *reduce creditors' expectations of TBTF protection*. Many of the existing pledges and policies meant to convince creditors that they will bear market losses when large banks fail are not credible and therefore are ineffective. Blanket pledges not to bail out creditors are not credible because they do not address the factors that motivate policymakers to protect uninsured bank creditors in the first place. The primary reason why policymakers bail out creditors of large banks is to reduce the chance that the failure of a large bank in which creditors take large losses will lead other banks to fail or capital markets to cease working efficiently.

Other factors may also motivate governments to protect uninsured creditors at large banks. Policymakers may provide protection because doing so benefits them personally, by advancing their career, for example. Incompetent central planning may also drive some bailouts. Although these factors receive some of our attention and are addressed by some of our reforms, we think they are less important than the motivation to dampen the effect of a large bank failure on financial stability.

Despite the lack of definitive evidence on the moral hazard costs and benefits of increased stability generated by TBTF protection, the empirical and anecdotal data, analysis, and our general impression—imperfect as they are—suggest that TBTF protection imposes net costs. We also argue that the *TBTF problem has grown in severity*. Reasons for this increase include growth in the size of the largest banks, greater concentration of banking system assets in large banks, the greater complexity of bank operations, and, finally, several trends in policy, including a spate of recent bailouts.

Our views are held by some, but other respected analysts come to different conclusions. Some observers believe that the net costs of TBTF protection have been overstated, while others note that some large financial firms have failed without their uninsured creditors being protected from losses. However, even analysts who weigh the costs and benefits differently than we do have reason to support many of our reforms. Some of our recommendations, for example, make policymakers less likely to provide TBTF protection and address moral hazard precisely by reducing the threat of instability. Moreover, our review of cases where bailouts were not forthcoming suggests that policymakers are, in fact, motivated by the factors we cite and that our reforms would push policy in the right direction.

A second camp believes that TBTF protection could impose net costs in theory, but in practice legal regimes in the United States—which other developed countries could adopt—make delivery of TBTF protection so difficult as to virtually eliminate the TBTF problem.

We are sympathetic to the general and as yet untested approach taken by U.S. policymakers and recognize that it may have made a dent in TBTF expectations. In the long run, however, we predict that the system will not significantly reduce the probability that creditors of TBTF banks will receive bailouts. The U.S. approach to too big to fail continues to lack credibility.

Finally, a third camp also recognizes that TBTF protection could impose net costs but believes that there is no realistic solution. This camp argues that policymakers cannot credibly commit to imposing losses on the creditors of TBTF banks. The best governments can do, in their view, is accept the net costs of TBTF, albeit with perhaps more resources devoted to supervision and regulation and with greater ambiguity about precisely which institutions and which creditors could receive ex post TBTF support.

Like the third camp, we believe that policymakers face significant challenges in credibly putting creditors of important banks at risk of loss. A TBTF policy based on assertions of "no bailouts ever" will certainly be breached. Moreover, we doubt that any single policy change will dramatically reduce expected protection. But fundamentally we part company with this third camp. *Policymakers can enact a series of reforms that reduce expectations of bailouts for many creditors at many institutions.* Just as policymakers in many countries established expectations of low inflation when few thought it was possible, so too can they put creditors who now expect protection at greater risk of loss.[4]

---

4. Mayes, Halme, and Liuksila (2001) and Mayes and Liuksila (2003) recommend a series of steps similar to our own to put creditors at TBTF banks at credible risk of loss.

The first steps for credibly putting creditors of important financial institutions at risk of loss have little to do with too big to fail per se. Where needed, countries should create or reinforce the rule of law, property rights, and the integrity of public institutions. Incorporating the costs of too big to fail into the policymaking process is another important reform underpinning effective management of TBTF expectations. Appointment of leaders who are loath to, or at least quite cautious about, providing TBTF bailouts is also a conceptually simple but potentially helpful step. Better public accounting for TBTF costs and concern about the disposition of policymakers could restrain the personal motivations that might encourage TBTF protection.

With the basics in place, policymakers can take on TBTF expectations more credibly by directly addressing their fear of instability. We recommend a number of options in this regard. One class of reforms tries to reduce the likelihood that the failure of one bank will spill over to another or to reduce the uncertainty that policymakers face when confronted with a large failing bank. These reforms include, among other options, simulating large bank failures and supervisory responses to them, addressing the concentration of payment system activity in a few banks, and clarifying the legal and regulatory framework to be applied when a large bank fails.

Other types of reforms include reducing the losses imposed by bank failure in the first place and maintaining reforms that reduce the exposure between banks that is created by payment system activities. These policies can be effective, in our view, in convincing public policymakers that, if they refrain from a bailout, spillover effects will be manageable. Such policies therefore encourage creditors to view themselves at risk of loss and thus improve market discipline of erstwhile TBTF institutions.

We are less positive about other reforms. A series of reforms that effectively punish policymakers who provide bailouts potentially also could address personal motivational factors. However, we are not convinced that these reforms are workable and believe that they give too much credence to personal motivations as a factor to explain bailouts. The establishment of a basic level of supervision and regulation (S&R) of banks should help to restrict risk-taking, although we view S&R as having important limitations.

Finally, policymakers have a host of other available options once they have begun to address too big to fail more effectively. For example, policymakers could make greater use of discipline by creditors at risk of loss. Bank supervisors could rely more heavily on market signals in their assessment of bank risk-taking. Deposit insurers could use similar signals to set their premiums.

One may agree with our arguments in concept but find them lacking in real-world pragmatism or realpolitik. A compelling case for relying on analytical rather than political principles in addressing the failure of large banks was made nearly thirty years ago—a full decade before the term too big to fail became commonplace:

> To many practical people the suggestion that a large bank be allowed to fail may seem to represent dogmatic adherence to standard economic doctrine, a victory of ideology over pragmatic common sense. A pragmatic position is to argue that, yes, business failures do serve a useful function, but in the specific case of a large bank, the costs of allowing failure outweigh the costs of supporting it. After all, the social costs of failure are immediate, while the advantages of permitting failure are indirect and removed into the future. But this pragmatic position should be rejected because it ignores externalities over time. If we prop up a large bank because the direct costs of doing so outweigh the cost of allowing it to fail, then the next time a large bank is in danger of failing it is likely to be propped up too. But in the future the same benefit will then probably be accorded to medium-sized banks. And from there it is likely to spread to small banks, to other financial institutions, and ultimately to other firms. When one includes the cost of moving down this slippery slope in the cost of saving a large bank, then the costs of allowing it to fail may seem small by comparison. At a time when devotion to pragmatism is so much in the air, it is useful to consider also the benefits of sticking to one's principles even in hard cases.[5]

Our Methods

Describing an author's approach runs the risk of self-indulgence. After all, the reader can judge the product on its merits. But a brief description of what we hope to accomplish might help prospective readers to set their expectations. The types of arguments made in this book and the evidence on which we rely reflect our target audience and what we perceive to be our comparative advantages. Fortunately, there is a large degree of intersection between these two rationales.

In terms of audience, we intend this book to help the wide range of staff practitioners, as well as the policymakers they support, to confront the

5. Mayer (1975, pp. 609–10).

TBTF problem. Although such an audience has a growing appreciation for concepts like moral hazard and the reasoning of economists, it is unlikely to find a treatment of the relevant issues that is suitable for academic journals to be approachable or convincing. Instead, it is likely to value clarity, concreteness, and conclusions that can be internalized.

In terms of our comparative advantages, they are twofold and relate to our interests and experience. We have policy experience—most notably Stern's eighteen years of service as a Federal Reserve Bank president, making him the most senior, active U.S. central banker. We both have spent a good part of our careers trying to explain the central findings of technical experts to an interested but frequently lay audience. Typically, we have tried to move from general findings to policy recommendations. Although this book contains some new analysis of data and, we hope, an insight or two that others have not made or stressed, it is not a source for mathematical models or sophisticated uses of empirical methods.

Many in our target audience of practitioners would just as soon skip empirical models in the first place. An explanation for our strategy is unnecessary for them. But given the central role that economists have played in highlighting the TBTF problem, it is worth considering the merits of an approach that relies on deductive reasoning and economic logic rather than academic research. We have already argued that a simple and direct approach is likely to be more influential with the target audience than the converse. But what is influential could very well be wrong. We have persuaded ourselves that another rationale justifies our approach: namely, that policymakers must make decisions based on the best available information, and what is known today about too big to fail frequently requires reasoning and exposition to fill in substantial analytical gaps.

The truth, as demonstrated by rigorous analysis and derived through consensus, does not exist when it comes to many of the issues related to too big to fail. For some issues, the relevant data have not been collected and perhaps cannot easily be collected in any reasonable time period. For example, there is no comprehensive list of countries in which uninsured creditors of banks have received government protection. Records describing the size and type of bailouts that creditors have received are not readily available. Simply put, the basic facts are elusive. More generally, data on and applied analysis of too big to fail are made quite difficult by the implied nature of the support. To be sure, some data have been collected and some analysis completed. Such work is often based on an after-the-fact review of a single event with real limitations because of a lack of scientific controls.

There is also theoretical work, but it often abstracts so far from institutional detail as to provide little guidance. These models do not let policymakers know if they should support creditors of one large bank but not another.

As a result, the environment for policymakers is characterized by opaqueness and uncertainty. Policymakers and their staffs could wait until a long-term research program is complete before they take action. Acting today with sub-par information could actually make things worse, and history is replete with such cases. But waiting for a final answer does not seem realistic to us. A recent conference on the Great Depression revealed strong disagreement on the underlying causes of an event that is more than seventy years old.[6]

Policymakers frequently play the role of emergency room doctor. Their actions should be informed by basic research, but they cannot wait for final results from exhaustive laboratory experiments before operating. Given that policymakers will often act sooner rather than later, it seems reasonable to try to take the best available information and combine it with economic reasoning that has passed the tests of time and experience. We hope the result assists staff and policymakers sort through the options that await them in triage.

Reliance on a more informal methodology certainly has downsides, particularly the chance that one may speak too authoritatively given the data at hand. The ambiguity surrounding the TBTF issue means that we must be careful and note where our information is incomplete, where others disagree with our views, and how we come to our conclusions. Incomplete information also suggests that we take a measured approach to reforms, and, as noted, that is our approach. At the end of the day, however, we clearly do not think that incomplete information should lead to inaction. The "do nothing" strategy could very well impose the most sizable costs of all.

6. Fettig (2000); Rolnick (1999).

P A R T *One*

Warnings

This first section explains why we think creditors' expectations of
TBTF coverage is a serious problem and sets up how we think policymakers should respond. We begin by explaining the nature of the TBTF
problem more precisely (chapter 2). We establish that too big to fail is a
problem of credibility: Creditors of large banks do not believe that the government will make them bear all their losses from bank failure.

We follow with two chapters on the costs of too big to fail. Chapter 3
explains the costs in a general way, focusing on how expectations of
bailouts lead to wasted resources. Chapter 4 reviews the empirical evidence,
suggesting that expectations of TBTF coverage are real, pervasive, and
potentially quite costly. We also explain how our concerns jibe with findings that creditors at large banks have at least some doubt about receiving
government protection.

Chapter 5 analyzes policymakers' motivations in bailing out creditors.
Balancing out the chapters on cost, these motivations reflect the benefits
that policymakers believe extralegal coverage of creditors provides. Establishing these motivations is key to our analysis. The only way to credibly
reduce expectations of TBTF coverage is to address the underlying rationale for them.

We then describe (in chapter 6) why expectations of TBTF coverage are
likely higher today than they were roughly a decade ago. Clarifying the

trends that make the TBTF problem more severe should help policymakers to determine their responses. Our view that too big to fail is an increasingly important problem runs counter to sentiments that legal fixes have eliminated it. We summarize in this chapter, and detail in appendix A, the inadequacies of these legal reforms.

Finally, we test our analysis in chapter 7. We want to see if our story about why TBTF bailouts occur also helps to explain some prominent cases where creditors of large financial firms did not receive bailouts. The absence of the general factors we identify as motivating bailouts at TBTF banks—particularly concern over spillovers—appears to have influenced the decision not to bail out creditors in these cases.

2

What Is the Problem?

The roots of the TBTF problem lie in creditors' expectations. The problem arises when uninsured creditors of large, systemically important banks expect to receive government protection if their bank fails. Government financial support shields these creditors—who are not covered by explicit government protection—from losses they otherwise would incur. These expectations lead banks that creditors consider too big to fail to take on too much risk and waste resources (this concept is developed in more detail in chapter 3).

The underlying source of the TBTF problem is a lack of credibility. Policymakers have not convinced uninsured creditors of TBTF banks that governments will minimize the financial support they receive. Governments must reform institutions and policies to put creditors of TBTF banks at credible risk of loss. Policymakers must do more than simply pledge to end bailouts if they hope to achieve consistency between actions and words over time.

Because our discussion of what motivates TBTF bailouts relies on a comparison of costs and benefits, we conclude with a general discussion of them. We think that the costs of TBTF protection exceed the benefits it provides. But even those who come to the opposite conclusion have reason to seriously consider our analysis and recommendations.

What We Mean by Too Big to Fail

Governments typically treat banks and the creditors of banks differently than most other firms and creditors, reflecting the perceived uniqueness of bank services and the chance that one bank's failure can spill over and threaten the viability of other banks.[1] Banks, for example, face unusually comprehensive and stringent government direction and review of their activities. In addition, an insolvent firm can file for liquidation or reorganization in the United States under the bankruptcy code, which sets parameters for the treatment of creditors. In contrast, the government takes over insolvent banks, and a bank-specific legal regime governs the fate of creditors of such failed banks. Formal programs protecting bank depositors from loss—often called deposit insurance—constitute a critical part of bank insolvency regimes. Protection offered under deposit insurance is normally capped at some maximum amount (for example, $100,000 per account in the United States).

Explicit insurance and caps, however, do not always govern the protection that bank creditors receive. For example, between 1979 and 1989, when roughly 1,100 commercial banks failed, 99.7 percent of *all* deposit liabilities were fully protected through the discretionary actions of U.S. policymakers.[2] Beyond depositors who have been protected, uninsured creditors include short-term funders (for example, sellers of overnight funds), holders of longer-term senior and subordinated debt, and equity holders, among others.

Protection of uninsured creditors of banks is one major feature that underlies any description of too big to fail. The second feature is bank size. As the figures for the U.S. banking crisis imply, policymakers can decide to protect uninsured creditors at nearly all failed banks whether they are big or small. Our focus is on special protection for creditors at big banks. Big in this context does not refer solely to size. Rather, it refers to banks that play an important role in a country's financial system and its economic performance. A bank that is not the largest in the country could be important if it processes many payments or securities transactions, for example.

Treatment of the uninsured creditors of failed large banks raises issues not present in the failure of a small bank. The failure of a large bank raises

1. This special nature of banks is discussed in more detail in chapter 5 and appendix C.
2. Moyer and Lamy (1992) and the Federal Deposit Insurance Corporation's historical statistics on banking, available at www2.fdic.hsob/index.asp [October 23, 2003].

concerns for policymakers about the potential failure of other banks, the inability of the financial system to carry out its functions, and a diminution in economic activity. Policymakers think that protecting uninsured credi-tors can mitigate these spillover effects by keeping the operations of the failed bank afloat and creating a climate conducive to financial stability.

The components of (1) a policy of protecting uninsured creditors at banks from the losses they might suffer and (2) a definition of big bank come together in our use of the term too big to fail. A TBTF regime is a policy environment in which uninsured creditors expect the government to protect them from prospective losses from the failure of a big bank; big banks are said to be too big to fail in countries following such a regime. Box 2-1 discusses our focus on banks and explains why we use the term too big to fail even though a literal reading of it is misleading.

Our use of the term too big to fail with regard to government banking policy is closely associated with the failure of Continental Illinois in 1984. Continental Illinois was the seventh largest bank at the time of its failure, and its uninsured creditors received what many observers considered exceptionally generous government protection.[3] At a minimum, the treatment was seen as setting a new precedent.[4] During questioning of the comptroller of the currency during congressional hearings, Congressman McKinney asserted that, with the bailout of Continental Illinois,

> we have a new kind of bank. And today there is another type created. We found it in the thrift institutions, and now we have given approval for a $1 billion brokerage deal to Financial Corporation of America. Mr. Chairman, let us not bandy words. We have a new kind of bank. It is called too big to fail. TBTF, and it is a wonderful bank.[5]

The amount of protection that uninsured creditors expect to receive, and have received, under a TBTF regime has been higher than Continental Illinois in some cases and lower in others. The methods by which governments support uninsured creditors can also vary a great deal; support can be very subtle and hidden. There has been some documentation of coverage for uninsured creditors. For example, a review of twelve banking crises reported eleven where the government provided a "blanket government

3. Davison (1997) discusses Continental Illinois.
4. Golembe (1999) puts the treatment of Continental Illinois in the context of the previous policies of the Federal Deposit Insurance Corporation.
5. Inquiry into Continental Illinois Corp. and Continental Illinois National Bank (1984, p. 300).

Box 2-1. *The Use of "Too Big to Fail" Inside and Outside Banking*

Our use of "too big to fail" raises two issues that require additional explanation. First, we restrict its use to banks even though it has been used to describe other firms. Second, we use the term even though it is misleading if taken literally.

Use of too big to fail in the banking context. Although many attribute the genesis of the term too big to fail to congressional hearings on Continental Illinois, this was not the case. The print media had used the term in the context of the Continental bailout even before the congressional hearings.[1] That said, late 1984 appears to be the starting point for more frequent use of the term. Since that time, too big to fail has become rooted in the popular debate, being used about 900 times over the past fifteen years in fifteen major dailies and business magazines (see figure 2-1).[2] The peak usage of the term with reference to banking organizations occurred in the early 1990s, reflecting congressional activity to limit protection of uninsured creditors, a development we discuss in later chapters.

Too big to fail has also spread from banking to the nonbanking sector. In fact, the media used the term to describe protection of uninsured creditors

Figure 2-1. *Use of "Too Big to Fail" in U.S. Print Media, 1984–2000*

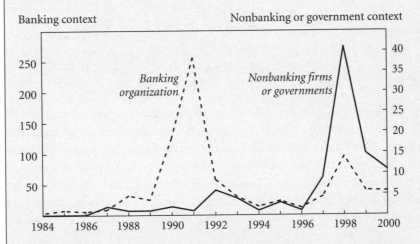

Source: Authors' calculations based on data from Dow Jones.

1. Eric Gelman and others, "The Continental Bailout," *Newsweek*, July 30, 1984, p. 86.
2. Based on a computer search of major publications contained on Dow Jones.

at industrial firms at least a decade before the hearings on Continental Illinois. In 1975 an article in a business magazine used the term to describe "corporations [that] have become so important to the U.S. economy that government does not dare let one go under."[3] The article referred to the 1971 government loan guarantees for Lockheed and government support for railroads and even hinted at government support for Chrysler, a policy action that came to fruition several years later.[4]

We focus on the banking sector in our discussion of too big to fail despite its occurrence elsewhere for several reasons. First, in at least some cases, the protection of creditors of commercial firms had the ultimate intent of protecting the creditors of banking organizations. For example, the Korean government rescued Hanbo Steel to prevent the failure of its creditor banks, and the Japanese government supported the real estate market in part to preclude the failure of financial institutions holding real estate assets.[5] The bailout of creditors of at least some large commercial firms was a tool to protect bank creditors rather than a separate policy.

Several important cases of too big to fail in the context of subnational governments have a similar story. Consider the case of Brazil in the mid-1990s:

> Intergovernmental fiscal relations in several Latin American countries such as Argentina and Brazil are similarly characterized by problems of financial solvency for state and local governments leading to stopgap lending or grants from higher-level governments. In the Brazilian case, for example, a number of the country's major commercial banks are owned by state governments, and the states themselves have borrowed heavily from these banks to finance their public expenditures. . . . In order to avoid a general financial crisis, the central bank of Brazil is assuming control of these banks and, in the process, may end up absorbing large amounts of state government debt.[6]

3. John Cobbs, "When Companies Get Too Big to Fail," *Business Week*, January 27, 1975, p. 16.
4. U.S. General Accounting Office (1984a) discusses bailouts of large firms and municipalities in the United States.
5. Gup (1998, p. 8).
6. Wildasin (1997, p. 2). See also Litvack, Ahmad, and Bird (1998); Rodden (2000b); and Rodden, Eskeland, and Litvack (2002) discuss subnational government borrowing and bailouts.

(Box continues on the following page)

Box 2-1 *(continued)*

Extraordinary support for local governments and state-owned banks in Germany also appears related.[7]

We also focus on banks because many of the policy prescriptions we and others have suggested, which are discussed in the second half of this book, would apply to bailouts of creditors of commercial firms and subnational governments as well. Most important, policymakers trying to reduce expectations of TBTF bailouts must rely on the same foundation: making ex ante commitments of no bailout more credible to creditors.

Analysts and policymakers have also expressed concern about the effect that implied government guarantees have on the risk-taking, resource allocation, and systemic risk potential of government-sponsored enterprises, particularly Fannie Mae and Freddie Mac.[8] On the one hand, we do not discuss government-sponsored enterprises—very large U.S. financial firms that are owned by private investors but operate under unique federal government charters—for some of the same reasons that we do not discuss TBTF municipalities or commercial firms. On the other hand, we exclude government-sponsored enterprises from our discussion because their government guarantee, while not legally binding, seems closer to explicit support than does the more conjectural TBTF protection we examine. The issues raised by government-sponsored enterprises might be analyzed more appropriately in a review of explicit government guarantees than in a review of too big to fail.

Using too big to fail even if it is misleading. We have already noted that a TBTF bank need not always be the very biggest in a country. There are other ways that a literal reading of too big to fail would be misleading. The creditors and not the bank receive government protection, governments have let large banks fail, and some creditors of TBTF banks, particularly equity holders and employees, typically do not receive government protection and suffer losses. Because of these drawbacks, other policymakers and observers have used terms such as "too big to liquidate quickly" to describe banks where uninsured creditors expect government protection.[9] But because the term TBTF is so firmly ensconced in the public debate and the alternative terms seem cumbersome, we continue to use the original, warts and all.

7. Rodden (2000a, p. 17).

8. U.S. Office of Federal Housing Enterprise Oversight (2003) discusses government-sponsored enterprises and systemic risk. Feldman (2001) discusses concerns about government-sponsored enterprises more generally.

9. Kaufman (2000); Poole (2003); U.S. House of Representatives, Committee on Banking and Financial Services (1998, p. 62).

guarantee" covering deposits and potentially other bank liabilities.[6] However, this list is far from exhaustive. Unfortunately, there is no readily available list of, nor potentially tractable method for, determining the types of TBTF protection that governments have supplied to date. Our impression is that coverage tends to be fairly extensive for depositors, less extensive for holders of other fixed-income securities or money market instruments, and rare for equity holders, although there clearly are notable exceptions to these generalizations.

Why a TBTF Policy Is Problematic

TBTF coverage is problematic and costly because bank creditors who do not face the full cost of the failure of their bank lose some of their incentive to monitor and assess its riskiness. Risk assessments influence the prices creditors require before they will turn over their funds to a bank. Higher-risk banks should face higher prices from creditors. Prices, in turn, influence the decisions of banks. Projects that might have made sense if funding were inexpensive may not go forward with higher prices. In addition to prices, risk assessments influence the quantity of funds that creditors provide a bank. A creditor believing a bank poses a high chance of failure may provide less funding or, perhaps, no funding at all. Lack of funding directly limits the ability of banks to carry out their operations.

The price and quantity signals from creditors that previously would have constrained bank activities are muted by the expectation of TBTF protection. The more confident creditors are about receiving protection and the greater is the level of protection they expect, the more muted are their price and quantity signals. If creditors have only a faint inkling about receiving government support, the changes to their decisions regarding pricing and quantity could be slight. At the other extreme, if creditors are 100 percent sure of receiving 100 percent protection without any disruptions, they would fund even the most risky TBTF bank as if it were as safe as the central government providing the implicit support.

The change in behavior induced by the TBTF guarantee is just one example of so-called moral hazard. Every insurance policy creates a moral hazard, in that the insured have less incentive to monitor risks than they would in the absence of coverage. Consider a family with insurance against flood damage. They would have an incentive to locate their house closer to a river than a family who would have to bear the entire cost of a flood. Too

6. Kane and Klingebiel (2002).

big to fail expands insurance coverage and therefore exacerbates moral hazard.

The excessive risk-taking by banks is costly due to resource misallocation. We cannot say with confidence how excessive risk-taking will manifest itself in a specific case, although it probably has assumed all the possible forms over time. Banks might, for example, buy financial assets with a chance of default that exceeds the standard they would maintain in the absence of TBTF protection. Or banks might make bets on interest rate movements that they would avoid otherwise.

Excessive risk-taking also manifests itself in the provision of loans that would not be made if bank creditors bore the risk of bank failure. In this case, the loan decisions made by the banks with TBTF protection could lead to the financing of projects with limited potential to increase economic output. A review of bank lending in Japan, for example, finds that government bailout policies gave banks an incentive to misallocate credit to weak borrowers who actually became weaker after receiving the credit.[7] Not only may banks take riskier actions, but they also may assume excessive risk by growing faster than they would otherwise. In total, these actions misallocate resources to lower-value uses and, if done on a large scale, can retard current and future economic growth.

We have discussed the problem of too big to fail, moral hazard, and misallocation of resources with many policymakers and analysts. Some find the story compelling and intuitive, while others find it hard to believe. Skeptics usually tell us that bankers would never knowingly take on too much risk for the purpose of receiving government support. Bankers find concern about moral hazard particularly offensive, often responding as if their integrity had been impugned. However, we do not view bankers as sitting in a back room scheming to defraud the government. Instead, we view bankers as rational actors who respond to the signals they receive from markets. In terms of the risk-reward calculations they perform, given the prices and quantity of funding they receive, bankers are making optimal decisions: the problem is that the prices and quantities confronting them do not fully reflect the risk of their institutions or of their activities.

Consider the case of a TBTF bank on the brink of failure. Without expectations of TBTF protection, creditors would pull more of their funds from the bank or at least restrict the inflow of funds and charge a higher price for those funds. With expectations of protection, they do not take

7. Peek and Rosengren (2003).

such remedial steps. As a result, funds continue to flow into projects that appear reasonable to bank management but that brought the institution to near failure in the first place. Alternatively, owners and managers looking to keep their bank open might fund those projects already under consideration that have the highest prospective short-term return. By definition, these projects have the highest risk. Neither creditor nor banker has acted unethically in these cases, and yet the result is that TBTF guarantees led resources to high-risk opportunities.

Time Inconsistency

The essence of the TBTF problem is that creditors believe they will receive protection on the failure of their bank despite not having an explicit right to it. Indeed, creditors can develop expectations of government protection even when policymakers have in the past committed to no-bailout policies. The problem is that such pledges are not time consistent. When the time comes to enforce their commitment, policymakers discount or ignore long-run concerns and focus exclusively on the perceived short-term benefits of their actions, specifically the ability to prevent the failure of one bank from spilling over and leading to the failure of other banks, weakening the economy as a whole.[8] As a result, they violate their earlier commitment; they behave in a time-inconsistent fashion. Creditors recognize that policymakers will encounter this same set of short-term benefits, costs, and incentives each time a potential failure forces them to contemplate a bailout.

The problems of time inconsistency and credibility have received extensive analysis and discussion in the setting of monetary policy, and we believe that experience sheds light on the link between credibility and too big to fail.[9] The key lesson from the experiences of monetary policy—which we develop in chapter 8—is that policymakers can make credible commitments in the face of much skepticism. Policymakers can take actions to put uninsured creditors at large banks at credible greater risk for loss.

A second observation is that monetary policymakers clearly weighed costs and benefits and engaged in policy trade-offs when deciding whether to inflate. A similar assessment of benefits, costs, and policy trade-offs

8. Brock (1998) documents the pressure put on governments in Central and South America to bail out creditors, for example.
9. Kydland and Prescott (1977) discuss time inconsistency and the setting of monetary policy.

characterizes the bailout decision. When the benefits of policies that lead to bailouts of the uninsured seem high relative to costs, such policies receive support. Concluding that policymakers act rationally means that reforms which reduce the benefits of TBTF coverage and increase its costs make such coverage less likely. Reduced incentives for policymakers to provide coverage would, in turn, affect the perception of creditors, making them less likely to expect protection. Creditors would then more fully include risk assessments in their price and quantity decisions, which, in turn, would improve decisionmaking by banks.

Because policymakers weigh costs and benefits, we find it difficult to imagine that their behavior will change without addressing underlying incentives, hence our discounting of reforms that simply pledge not to bail out creditors. Low absolute caps on deposit insurance or plans that ostensibly eliminate government support for all depositors, for example, fall into this category of reforms that are not credible or time consistent.[10] There are also more specific reasons to doubt the credibility of a no-bailout pledge.

A credible policy is one that policymakers have little desire to change when the pressure is on. A credible policy with regard to TBTF protection must also be difficult to evade. In fact, policymakers will still fear the economic and political consequences of failure of a large firm if a no-bailout rule exists and will have considerable incentive to eviscerate the rule. A fair number of options are available to policymakers for circumventing outright prohibitions, including emergency legislation, lending from the central bank, and resolution techniques that accomplish the economic substance of a bailout without violating the legal restriction.[11]

Our rejection of no-bailout pledges and their equivalents helps to explain the organization of this book. In the rest of the first half we discuss the costs and benefits of TBTF protection in greater detail, while in the second half we discuss reforms that go beyond rules prohibiting coverage of the uninsured.[12] In our view, the costs of TBTF protection are large and growing, and we spend the next several chapters developing this point. But before we initiate that discussion, we briefly discuss our general treatment of these costs relative to the benefits of TBTF coverage.

10. For examples of such reforms, see Bank Administration Institute (1996); Bankers Roundtable (1997).

11. Gup (1998) discusses about twenty ways for governments to intervene to address large bank failure.

12. Litan and Rauch (1997, pp. 97–134) also focus on underlying sources of systemic risk and reforms to address them.

Costs and Benefits

Concluding that TBTF coverage has large costs puts a burden on those who do not take the downsides of bailouts seriously. But it is not equivalent to proving that the cost of a TBTF policy regime exceeds its benefits. Developing incontrovertible proof about the costs and benefits of too big to fail is not realistic given the available information and the exceedingly complex nature of the costs and benefits. At best, quantification of costs and benefits will remain at the general, impressionistic level for some time. However, policymakers must act in the here and now. For better or worse, policymakers and advisers have to rely on general perceptions in comparing the benefits and costs, and our impression is that the costs exceed the benefits.

Given the subjective nature of our conclusions, it is not surprising that others disagree. The disagreement reflects their own general impression; more formal, but still incipient and very subjective, analysis of costs and benefits; and theoretical models that could justify a bailout but are so stylized and simplified that they cannot guide the bailout decisions policymakers will face.[13] We would not expect those with a different weighing of costs and benefits of TBTF protection to support all of our analysis or recommendations. That said, there are several reasons why even those who disagree with us on benefits and costs could support many of our suggested reforms.

—Existing policies affect the potential for spillovers from the failure of a large bank. That is, the potential for spillovers is not fixed and immutable. Because the potential for spillovers motivates the decision to bail out creditors, policies that reduce the threat of spillovers should make bailouts less likely. We recommend several types of policies that we think make spillovers less of a threat and would expect those worried about spillovers to support such recommendations. With a reduced threat of spillovers, policymakers should be more willing to let uninsured creditors suffer losses, which, in turn, should help to address the moral hazard problem.

—Policies that reduce moral hazard can reduce the threat of instability. In this sense, a credible TBTF policy leads to a "virtuous circle," an outcome we discuss in chapter 8. Because banks do not take on too much risk, they have a lower chance of failure, therefore providing policymakers with fewer opportunities to provide TBTF protection.

13. See Frydl and Quintyn (2000) for a comparison of costs and benefits of government intervention in response to a banking crisis, including government guarantees to bank creditors; Cordella and Yeyati (1999) and Freixas (1999) for models of bank bailouts.

—The provision of bailouts may not end the suboptimal use of resources associated with moral hazard or reduce instability. For example, government actions consistent with TBTF protection actually raise the cost of financial crises, a point we return to later. Additionally, if governments do not combine large bank bailouts with other reforms of banking organizations, their actions could allow banks to repeat risky practices, waste resources, and make additional bailouts a possibility. Alternatively, a bailout may not be sufficiently large or credible to prevent creditors from pulling funds or taking other actions that could increase financial instability.[14]

—Creditors of some banks whose failure would yield negligible spillovers might believe they will benefit from TBTF protection. Policymakers typically have not taken steps beyond general statements to convince these creditors that they are at risk. Altering these creditors' expectations will require policymakers to take actions—and we suggest several—signifying a more credible commitment to impose losses.

—Some observers have argued, based on historical cases, that even very large bank failures and panics yield small costs. We do not think this view will persuade policymakers to drop the bailout option and explain this position later in the text. Nonetheless, this view suggests that one can overstate the threat of spillovers and hence the benefits that bailouts provide.

—Although addressing instability is the primary motivation for bailouts, there are others. These alternative motivations suggest that bailouts might be provided even if the costs of the bailout in the form of increased moral hazard exceed the benefits of stability. Some of the recommendations we make do not try to reduce the threat of spillovers but instead seek to reduce these other motivations and thus should enhance benefit-cost trade-offs.

Finally and most generally, we do not seek to eliminate all TBTF bailouts. Instead we recommend policies that encourage policymakers to give TBTF protection a harder, more skeptical look than it might receive now. After instituting our recommendations, we hope that policymakers will provide the minimum support—zero in some cases—to uninsured creditors at large banks that is consistent with stability. This outcome will not prevent bailouts where the benefits to society far exceed future moral hazard costs. But it should help to reduce resource misallocation, a topic we discuss in the next chapter.

14. Klingebiel and others (2000) discuss market responses to government restructuring of banking systems, including government guarantees for creditors.

3

Why Protection Is Costly

Expectations of TBTF coverage are costly because they lead to a wasting of resources and a reduction in the welfare of the citizenry. Some of the wasted resources arise because TBTF banks take on too much risk. Wasted resources also result because banks whose creditors expect TBTF guarantees are more likely to operate inefficiently than banks without such protection. The potential costs of poor resource allocation become most apparent in the extreme cases: TBTF policies seem to have played a role in the collapse of the financial systems and economies in a number of developing countries over the last decade or so.

Excessive Risk-Taking

Discussions of the costs of too big to fail and banking crises tend to focus on fiscal and accounting costs incurred by the government as it funds bailouts. These costs have reached up to the mid-double digits of gross domestic product (GDP) in some countries (although estimates for the same crisis can vary depending on the source, suggesting that such estimates are not entirely robust).[1] The U.S. government raised $153 billion, or about 2 percent of U.S. GDP, from the banking industry and taxpayers to

1. Frydl (1999).

fund losses associated with the savings and loan debacle.[2] While spectacular in some instances, these fiscal transfers do not measure the economic costs associated with government guarantees. Instead, these flows capture the payment of funds from taxpayers to creditors; one party benefits from the flow, and one party loses.[3]

Rather than focusing on flows, policymakers should be concerned about the types of resource misallocation induced by expected government support. Unlike a transfer, the wasted investment encouraged by government guarantees benefits no one. The costs of lost output can dwarf the transfers from financial losses. While the fiscal flows of the savings and loan bailout in the United States equaled $150 billion, lost output from the savings and loan crisis—largely attributed to moral hazard and poor resource allocation—was on the order of $500 billion.[4] Measuring poor resource use is quite difficult, and the estimate we cite here is illustrative only. Even if off by 50 percent, it still suggests that poor resource allocation associated with suboptimal banking decisions imposes a huge cost.

Why Countervailing Forces to Moral Hazard Fail

There are countervailing pressures on banks that, in fact, limit incentives for risk-taking. Government intervention, such as safety and soundness regulation, can reduce bank risk-taking, but potentially more important is the fact that failure can impose a large cost on bank owners and managers. Equity holders, potentially including employees of the bank, could lose much of their wealth if the bank fails. Managers also might find it difficult to obtain a new job at their former salary.

The extent of the costs of failure depends on the ability of the bank to generate future profits as a going concern (often called the franchise value of the bank). When franchise value is high, owners and managers have something to lose, and they should take steps to make failure less likely. Banks with high franchise value, for example, diversify their loan portfolios to a greater extent than weaker banks.[5] Franchise value depends, in part, on the level of competition in the relevant markets. Because competition in

2. Curry and Shibut (2000).

3. It is worth noting, however, that the taxation required to pay off TBTF debts distorts the behavior of the taxpayer, imposing losses on society. The costs of taxation are not unique to too big to fail, and thus we do not delve into them. Suffice to say that the costs of taxation can be quite high. See Ballard, Shoven, and Whalley (1985); Feldstein (1997).

4. U.S. Congressional Budget Office (1992).

5. Demsetz, Saidenberg, and Strahan (1996).

banking is often limited by regulation, banks could have an easier time generating future profits than firms in other, more competitive industries.

However, high franchise value has proven insufficient as an absolute bulwark. This failure reflects, in part, the fact that the conditions under which franchise value limits risk-taking may not exist when needed. Those holding substantial equity positions in the largest banks could have a small portion of their wealth in bank stock, or they could have the ability to dispose of their equity before it declines in value.[6] Under certain conditions, a bank with extensive government guarantees for creditors has a strong incentive to take on significant risk.[7]

Factors that formerly generated unusually high franchise values in banking also have abated. Governments have relaxed some of the regulations that limited the ability of banks to enter a market and compete with established firms, for example. New financial technologies, such as asset securitization and the development of substitutes for deposits, also have raised the level of competition banks face. Analysts have identified such changes as contributing to the excessive risk-taking by financial institutions.[8] (Shocks to an economy could reduce franchise value as well.)

More important, too big to fail corrodes disciplinary forces precisely when franchise value is low and cannot limit poor allocation of resources. A TBTF policy is most valuable to creditors when a bank's risk-taking makes insolvency increasingly likely. Market incentives would lead those providing cash to banks to raise the prices they charge weak institutions, tighten other terms of funding, or reduce the amount of funding they provide. Finding its access to cheap funds curtailed, the bank would have to slow its activities and maybe wind down its operations. Government policy, like potential TBTF support, circumvents market forces by allowing a bank to attract funds and grow even as it heads toward insolvency.[9]

The ability of TBTF protection to facilitate additional risk-taking by weak banks points to an important difference between economic and fiscal costs. Accounting systems record the initial estimates of fiscal flows when banks fail (or when failure is considered imminent), but the final tabulations can take many years, as the government sells the assets of failed institutions.

---

6. Haubrich and Thomson (1998) examine a case where a shareholder with a significant ownership stake imposed discipline on a large bank but note that such concentrated ownership or actions are not typical.

7. Kareken and Wallace (1978).

8. Keeley (1990).

9. Kane (1989) discusses the risk-taking and growth of insolvent thrifts.

However, the economic costs accrue long before failure. The meter starts running when weak market discipline associated with too big to fail induces banks to make suboptimal decisions. Perhaps it is not surprising that costly banking crises have a strong association with domestic credit booms.[10] In other words, the costs pile up when credit growth makes the banking system seem strong.

Why Resource Misallocation Spreads to Other Banks

Although our focus is on large banks, a tally of the costs imposed by too big to fail should recognize that it encourages resource misallocation across the banking system. Policymakers face charges of unfairness if they support extraordinary coverage for creditors of large banks and not for those of smaller institutions. The chairman of the Federal Deposit Insurance Corporation (FDIC) argued during the U.S. banking crisis, for example, that policymakers could not effectively limit TBTF coverage and therefore should expand coverage to smaller banks. He noted that too big to fail "puts small banks at a competitive disadvantage that can only be compensated for by fairly extensive deposit insurance coverage. Without it, funds will flow from the small to the large institutions because too-big-to-fail is still a possible event."[11]

Similar arguments have been made more recently in support of expanded explicit government insurance for bank deposits. The small bank trade association argued in congressional testimony that "an adequate level of deposit insurance coverage is vital to community banks' ability to attract core deposits, the funding source for their community lending activities. Many community banks face growing liquidity problems and funding pressures. It is harder to keep up with loan demand as community banks lose deposits to . . . 'too-big-to-fail' banks. . . . Federal Reserve spokesmen reject the notion that any bank is too-big-to-fail. The historical record, however, is to the contrary."[12]

Internal Inefficiency and Lack of Innovation

Besides encouraging excessive risk-taking and wasting resources, there is a second manner in which expectations of TBTF coverage could lead to

---

10. Eichengreen and Arteta (2000).
11. Seidman (1991, p. 4).
12. Gulledge (2001, p. 4).

inefficiency. Not only does the protection from market forces by a TBTF policy lead to inefficient credit decisions, but it also can lead the firm to operate in a cost-inefficient manner relative to firms subject to competition. Public support for firms appears to explain their inefficiency better than formal ownership by government.[13]

In a similar vein, for more than 100 years, analysts have also associated government ownership of, and influence on, firm behavior with a lack of innovation. More recent work continues to cite this effect on innovation as one of the most damaging aspects of government control or influence of private sector firms.[14] Although it is surely speculative, one might posit that TBTF firms similarly have less reason to innovate.

In total, there are several ways in which a TBTF policy leads to sub-par use of society's resources.[15] Although some of the figures we have mentioned sound large, the connection between the conceptual costs of too big to fail and actual harm to individuals may not be clear. As such, we conclude by pointing to a striking manifestation of wasted resources: the potential link between TBTF coverage and the virtual collapse of a country's financial system and economy.

Collapse of Financial Systems

A number of prominent analysts believe that expansive government protection of bank creditors has played a major role in recent financial crises. Essentially, TBTF-type commitments have weakened confidence in countries' long-run solvency. To provide a sense of the role of too big to fail, we summarize here one model that puts extensive coverage of bank creditors and moral hazard at the center of its explanations for recent financial crises.[16] In response to the likelihood of government protection, creditors reduce discipline and banks take on excessive risk. High-risk behavior increases the chance of bank failure and bailouts by the government. The high fiscal costs of bailouts require the government to raise a massive amount of funds. The income that governments earn by printing money is

13. Bartel and Harrison (1999).
14. Shleifer (1998).
15. A TBTF policy also represents an excessively costly means of transferring a subsidy, especially relative to a direct cash payment. A direct subsidy to a targeted population would reduce the administrative costs of providing the benefit, lower the government's exposure to loss, and increase the satisfaction of the recipient.
16. See the papers of Burnside, Eichenbaum, and Rebelo (2000, 2001a, 2001b).

one source of funding for future transfers. Fearing potential inflationary pressure from such a strategy, financial market participants act in a manner that puts the country's currency at risk of steep depreciation. The resulting currency and related financial crises trigger a severe recession with significant social costs.

Some other models do not rely on moral hazard to explain financial crises, and there is surely no single cause of the collapse of the financial sectors in numerous countries over the last decade and a half. And although our understanding of what causes such collapses has improved, the tentative conclusions drawn to date could be found lacking in the future. One must therefore be leery of putting too much importance on any single factor when explaining these crises. That said, the model we have summarized is not the only one of its ilk. Other analysts view policies that are tantamount to too big to fail as important drivers of recent financial crises.[17]

And although we have focused on implicit guarantees in the formal models of financial crises, we should not lose sight of the judgments of those operating in and supervising key financial markets. According to some observers, for at least twenty years participants' incentive to monitor and respond to each others' risk-taking in the international interbank market was dulled by implied guarantees.[18] Similar sentiment was expressed by the Basel Committee on Banking Supervision with regard to Asia: "Almost all observers agree that East Asian financial institutions, prior to the crisis, took on what turned out after the event to be excessive risk, in part due to implicit government guarantees given to or perceived by investors."[19]

17. See McKinnon and Pill (1999) and Krugman (1998) for other models emphasizing the moral hazard of government guarantees for banks. See Chang (1999) for a nontechnical summary of the literature and Kaminsky and Reinhard (1999) for the link between currency and banking crises.

18. Bernard and Bisignano (2000).

19. Basel Committee on Banking Supervision (1999c, p. 57).

4

How Pervasive Is TBTF?

Although largely conceptual, chapter 3 presents figures implying that the costs of too big to fail could be large. Unfortunately, direct estimates of the net cost of expected TBTF protection do not exist, and producing anything too specific seems doubtful. So instead we focus on indirect measures. Specifically, we examine evidence on the existence and scope of TBTF protection. That is, we ask whether the universe of banks where uninsured creditors might reasonably expect government support is large or small. This discussion has a practical purpose. Without a sense that the TBTF problem is large, policymakers have no incentive to manage it.

In our view, the scope of too big to fail is large, and the cost is likely to be quite high. We base this conclusion on evidence from estimates of the subsidy provided by government guarantees, from so-called event studies, from reviews of the data of credit rating agencies, from lists of banks considered too big to fail, and from the costs of recent banking crises.

Given the large costs of too big to fail, we want policymakers to put creditors of large banks at real risk of loss. Part of our support for recommending greater reliance on market forces is evidence that uninsured creditors of banks can price the risk-taking of banks. Some analysts have argued that evidence of risk-based pricing indicates that uninsured creditors of large banks do not believe they will benefit from government protection. Because this evidence appears to conflict with our central premise, we conclude this chapter with an explanation of how these arguments can coexist.

What Subsidy Estimates and Event Studies
Say about Too Big to Fail

A TBTF policy provides valuable insurance for bank owners and creditors. Creditors benefit from the potential for protection. Owners also benefit because insurance for creditors allows the bank to raise funds at more favorable terms than otherwise. As a result, too big to fail should manifest itself in two types of market prices. First, TBTF banks should pay less for funding than they would otherwise. Second, the insurance policy should increase the wealth of shareholders.

Some analysts try to tease out the cost of government insurance policies by treating the insurance as if it were a financial instrument, specifically a security called an option. They then value the government insurance as if it were an option, using fairly standard analytical techniques.[1] Estimates using this approach can reflect, at least in part, the subsidy provided via a TBTF policy, although teasing out the specific costs of too big to fail is not possible. Recent calculations find that government guarantees for bank liability holders generate very large subsidies in developing countries; the subsidies in developed countries like Japan are not trivial either.[2] They also find that the higher are the estimates of the implied subsidy, the more likely is the country to experience a financial crisis and the bank to require government support.[3]

Most reviews of too big to fail take another approach to using market prices to explore the existence and size of TBTF guarantees. Instead of using a financial valuation methodology, analysts examine how changes in market prices correlate with specific events that they would expect to change creditors' expectations of receiving TBTF protection. These events create natural experiments to test the existence and value of TBTF status. Most of these so-called event studies examine either (1) policy actions or statements that might capture a moment where the probability that creditors will receive TBTF coverage changes or (2) mergers among the largest banks.

Event Studies Based on Policy Actions and Statements

As noted in chapter 2, Continental Illinois was the first banking organization publicly labeled by supervisors as too big to fail in the United States.

---

1. Whalen (1997) provides an example of this technique.
2. Kaplan-Appio (2001).
3. Kaplan-Appio (2002); Laeven (2002a).

During congressional hearings on the failure, the comptroller of the currency agreed that policymakers would treat creditors of the eleven largest banks in the country in a similarly generous fashion if those banks were to become insolvent. The financial press, particularly the *Wall Street Journal*, focused on this statement, reporting that "U.S. won't let 11 biggest banks in nation fail . . . Testimony by comptroller at House hearing is first policy acknowledgment."[4] The reporting went on to highlight the statement of policymakers "who said the government had created a new category of bank: the 'TBTF bank,' for Too Big to Fail."

The original policy statement and the resulting news stories could have led creditors to believe that they would benefit from TBTF coverage or to solidify their expectations of such coverage. Either result would increase returns to, and the wealth of, shareholders of TBTF banks. O'Hara and Shaw examine stock returns for banks immediately before and following the comptroller's announcement.[5] They compare the returns for banks the comptroller said would receive Continental Illinois–like coverage to the returns of banks not viewed as too big to fail by the comptroller. They find that banks deemed too big to fail by the comptroller had higher returns than other banks. Moreover, greater returns accrued to the largest banks on the TBTF list. Policy statements and news reports establishing or confirming TBTF status had the predicted effect of increasing shareholder wealth.

O'Hara and Shaw set a standard that other analysts have followed with some modification. By and large, this body of research confirms the initial conclusion that too big to fail exists and transfers wealth from taxpayers to shareholders. Three findings from this literature are of particular interest:

—Too big to fail could be broader and have a longer history than the findings of O'Hara and Shaw indicate. Using a somewhat different focus, some analysts find that the comptroller's original pronouncement has spread TBTF coverage beyond those banks on the top-eleven list. Shareholders of banks on the list as well as those not on the original list also appear to have lowered their expectations of suffering loss after the announcement.[6] An analysis using short-term debt and deposit prices

4. Tim Carrington, "U.S. Won't Let 11 Biggest Banks in Nation Fail," *Wall Street Journal*, September 20, 1984.

5. O'Hara and Shaw (1990) argue that the comptroller meant the eleven largest national banks even though news reports focused on the eleven largest banks. Swary (1986) finds that the bailout reduced wealth for equity holders of banks with Continental Illinois–like portfolios and funding practices.

6. Black and others (1997).

suggests that creditors expected TBTF coverage even before the failure of Continental Illinois.[7]

—The role played by the Federal Reserve System in coordinating the privately funded bailout of Long-Term Capital Management (LTCM) reinforced and expanded TBTF protection for the largest banks. An analyst has determined that the banks deemed by the Federal Reserve to be large complex banking organizations (LCBOs)—a term we discuss in more detail shortly—that were not creditors of LTCM experienced a reduction in their cost of raising funds in the overnight market following the bailout of LTCM. According to this argument, the Federal Reserve's role in the bailout confirmed its concern about spillovers. As a result, uninsured creditors of banks whose failure could have spillover effects increased their expectations of receipt of government protection.[8]

—It is not clear whether legislation passed in 1991 achieved the goals of reducing the cost of bank failures and government coverage of uninsured creditors in general and, more to our point, of making TBTF protection less likely. Event studies of this legislation are mixed. One such study finds that the legislative action lowered large banks' costs of funds, while others find that it decreased shareholder wealth.[9] We discuss aspects of this legislation at greater length.

Event Studies Based on Mergers

Analysts do not believe that enhanced efficiencies or revenue production can easily explain mergers between the largest banking organizations (a point we discuss in more detail in chapter 6). This result has led them to ask whether a desire to reach TBTF size or grow beyond minimum TBTF levels explains mergers. In these cases, mergers are the "events" facilitating the testing of hypotheses about too big to fail.

In general, analyses of mergers also support the existence of expectations of TBTF coverage. For example, only mergers undertaken by the very largest banks show an increase in stock market value for shareholders. Such a research finding stands out, given previous conclusions that mergers rarely create long-term value for shareholders. The largest banks appear to benefit from increased government support.[10] In addition, bank size helps

7. Johnson and Lindley (1993).
8. Furfine (2001b).
9. Angbazo and Saunders (1996); Athavale (2000).
10. Kane (2000).

to explain the increase in wealth that holders of bank debt realize when mergers are announced (other factors remaining equal). The gains in wealth from mergers are particularly noteworthy when the resulting banking organization has more than $100 billion in assets.[11]

In addition, analysts have used the tools associated with measuring cost economies to evaluate the role of too big to fail in mergers. These efforts suggest that TBTF protection benefits larger banks by lowering their costs of raising deposits.[12]

Analysis by Credit Rating Agencies

Firms that assess the ability of banks to repay their debt—credit rating agencies—provide assessments useful for identifying those institutions likely to have creditors expecting TBTF coverage. We first provide a brief background on credit rating agencies and the widespread use of their assessments in regulatory processes. We then turn to their views on the existence and scope of TBTF guarantees.

Credit rating agencies assess the likelihood that issuers of debt will make full and timely payment of their obligations. The major agencies in the United States, and some other countries, are Moody's, Standard and Poor's, and Fitch. Credit rating agencies assign ratings, typically on an alpha or numeric basis (for example, 1–5 or A–E), indicating the relative likelihood that an obligor will pay off its debt.

Although the credit rating agencies are private firms, their output has become increasingly intertwined with government regulation, suggesting that supervisors and legislators view their output as credible. Bank supervisors, for example, make extensive use of credit ratings in determining the amount of capital banks must hold when they retain some exposure to the potential risk of loss on an asset and sell the rest.[13] Credit ratings play a role in determining the types of activities some large banks can carry out under financial modernization legislation passed in the United States.[14]

---

11. Penas and Unal (2001). Boyd and Graham (1991) also raise the possibility of TBTF motives for mergers. For alternative views, see Benston, Hunter, and Wall (1995); DeLong (2001).

12. Hughes and Mester (1993).

13. Board of Governors of the Federal Reserve System (2001b).

14. Board of Governors of the Federal Reserve System and U.S. Treasury Department (2001b).

Given their extensive use of credit rating output, supervisors and policymakers appear to attach significant importance to the information contained in credit ratings (even if others have questioned their value).[15] As a result, we view data on the extent of TBTF guarantees from credit rating agencies as having the potential to convince supervisors and policymakers of the widespread nature of the guarantees. To use credit rating data in this fashion requires us to make an important distinction. Some credit ratings do not separate the inherent ability of an obligor to repay debt from the potential support it might receive from the government. For example, Moody's issuer credit rating is used to implement aspects of the financial modernization bill.[16] Moody's defines the bank issuer rating as the "opinions of the financial capacity of a bank to honor its senior unsecured financial contracts." In general, these ratings are similar to Moody's bank deposit ratings. Moody's defines deposit ratings as "opinions of a bank's ability to repay punctually its foreign and/or domestic currency deposits. . . . Moody's bank deposit ratings do not take into account the benefit of deposit insurance schemes that make payments to depositors, but they do recognize the potential support from schemes that may provide direct assistance to banks."

In contrast to the deposit or issuer ratings, Moody's provides bank financial strength ratings, which exclude potential external credit support. Such ratings are intended to elaborate on and explain Moody's bank deposit ratings, which incorporate and reflect potential government support. The bank financial strength ratings, according to Moody's, "can be understood as a measure of the likelihood that a bank will require assistance from third parties such as its owners, its industry group, or official institutions." (Fitch has an even older rating system that captures government support. Until recently, Standard and Poor's did not make this distinction in its ratings.)[17]

In contrast to supervisors, we focus on bank financial strength ratings because they try to remove protection provided under TBTF policies from their assessment and, as a result, help to gauge the size of TBTF guarantees at a point in time. We first examine a recent distribution of bank financial strength ratings (see figure 4-1).[18] Roughly a third of the institutions with

15. Partnoy (1999) is critical of rating agencies.

16. Definitions of the various types of Moody's ratings are from "Ratings Definitions" (www.moodys.com/moodys/cust/ratingdefinitions/rdef.asp [December 2001]).

17. Fitch IBCA, Duff, and Phelps (2001); Standard and Poor's (1999, 2002).

18. Moody's Investors Service (2001).

Figure 4-1. *Distribution of Moody's Bank Financial Strength Ratings, as of December 2001*

Percent of all ratings

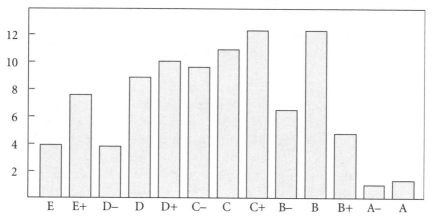

Source: Authors' calculations based on data from Moody's Investors Service (2001).

such ratings fall into the D and E categories. We cite Moody's definition of an E rating to provide a sense for the condition of such banks: "Banks rated E display very modest intrinsic financial strength, with a higher likelihood of periodic outside support or an eventual need for outside assistance. Such institutions may be limited by one or more of the following factors: a weak and limited business franchise; financial fundamentals that are materially deficient in one or more respects; or a highly unpredictable or unstable operating environment." This distribution of ratings indicates that, from the view of Moody's, many rated banks have a significant chance of requiring government or other third-party support if their operations are to continue.

Other rating agencies come to the same general conclusion. Fitch provides support ratings that "do not assess the quality of the bank. Rather, they are FitchRatings' assessment of whether the bank would receive support should this be necessary."[19] As of March 2002, 41 percent of the 1,259

19. "Financial Institutions: Banks and Securities Firms" (www.fitchratings.com/credit-desk/ratings/definitions/index.cfm?rd_file=bank [March 2002]). Fitch IBCA, Duff, and Phelps (2001) also discuss ratings.

banking organizations with support ratings were in categories 1 through 3. Fitch believes that creditors of these entities would receive government or other third-party support if the institution fell into financial trouble. Another 30 percent of the institutions had a support rating of 4, defined as a "bank for which support is likely but not certain."

Comparing institutions that have a high long-term bank deposit rating and a low bank financial strength rating is another way of identifying firms whose creditors could benefit from TBTF-type protection. As of December 2001, nearly a third of the 106 banks with a bank financial strength rating of E or E+ had an investment deposit grade rating (that is, the rating was above junk bond status). Another 30 percent of the institutions with the lowest bank financial strength rating had a deposit rating that fell just below investment grade. Moody's officials seem to support this approach to determining the level of government support: "Our ratings do not ignore the role that implicit support plays in terms of reducing credit risk. Our bank ratings are often higher than would be justified on the basis of stand-alone financial strength. Deposit ratings and BFSRs [bank financial strength ratings] can diverge quite widely. For example, we rate the three Mizuho bank's deposits at A3 (medium grade), but their FSRs [financial strength ratings] are rated E+, signaling a potential solvency problem."[20]

But the gap between ratings with and without potential government support is not a phenomenon unique to Japanese banks or the current period. For example, during the early 1990s both Citibank and Chase Manhattan Bank had noticeable gaps between their Fitch individual rating, which does not account for external support, and their Fitch long-term rating, which does consider such support. Chase had an individual rating of C and a long-term rating of A as of 1990. Citibank had an individual rating of C as of October 1991; its earliest available long-term rating was A as of August 1993.

Certainly comparisons between ratings are illustrative of TBTF guarantees but are not a precise measurement. There has been very little rigorous analysis using rating agency judgments as to the TBTF status of a bank.[21] Nonetheless, ratings data suggest an important role for government support

20. Mahoney (2000, p. 6).
21. Soussa (2000) also compares such credit ratings. He finds that banks perceived as too big to fail have lower funding costs but may not take on excessive risk. In contrast, Nier and Baumann (2003) find that banks judged by a credit rating agency to have a high chance of receiving public support assume greater risks—by assuming riskier loans and holding less capital—than other banks, holding other factors equal.

in market participants' perception of the creditworthiness of large banking organizations. Those responsible for providing ratings confirm this view: "No major bank in any developed country has ever been allowed to default upon any rated or unrated deposit or debt obligation. . . . Consequently, as a general rule, the historical credit risk associated with OECD [Organization for Economic Cooperation and Development] banks approaches zero, and that associated with emerging market banks (excluding external payments crises) also approaches zero. . . . The reason, of course, is official support popularly known as 'Too-Big-To-Fail.'"[22]

Lists of TBTF Banks

Perhaps the most simple method of measuring the scope of TBTF guarantees is to list those institutions whose uninsured creditors will likely receive government protection. Naming names does not quantify poor resource allocation, nor does it indicate the extent of potential TBTF coverage (for example, will coverage of the uninsured equal 100 percent or 20 percent?). But such exercises help to provide an upper bound on the creditors potentially affected by too big to fail.

Our discussion of credit rating agency data has provided one type of list. In chapter 6, we provide such lists through (1) measures of the increasing concentration of large bank assets throughout the world, (2) an update of the comptroller's original TBTF list, and (3) a supervisory estimate of U.S. banks whose payment system activities make them "systemically important." These lists imply that a substantial majority of bank assets in the United States and in other developed countries are held by institutions whose uninsured creditors, we reasonably believe, expect to benefit from government guarantees.

In a similar vein, in this section we try to determine which institutions could potentially be designated large and complex banking organizations by the Federal Reserve's Board of Governors. Listing large complex banking organizations can help to clarify the scope of TBTF coverage because the Federal Reserve views them as posing significant risks to the financial system and subjects them to a specialized supervisory regime. As Board of Governors' staff have argued, "By paying special attention to LCBOs, supervisors aim to minimize significant adverse effects on the public, on financial markets and the financial system in the United States and abroad, and

22. Mahoney (2000, pp. 3–4).

on taxpayers, who provide the ultimate resources behind the bank safety net."[23] Although we would not claim that LCBO designation equals TBTF status, this description, the need for special supervisory regimes, and the criteria used to define LCBO status suggest a strong overlap between the two concepts.

The Federal Reserve does not provide outside parties a current list of institutions deemed large complex banking organizations. However, we can guess—and we must stress that any list of potential LCBOs will be extremely imprecise—which institutions would make an LCBO list using information that is available to the public. For example, in the past, the Federal Reserve published some of the names of large complex banking organizations.[24] The Federal Reserve has also published the general criteria used to determine which institutions have LCBO status. The criteria used to determine institutions with LCBO status include size along with other factors that we think policymakers would link to the potential for spillovers. Finally, the Federal Reserve has indicated what would be the typical number of large complex banking organizations and revealed the typical breakout of the total LCBO population by domestic and foreign institutions.[25]

Based on this publicly available information, the institutions that could potentially have LCBO status are listed in box 4-1 (which also notes our admittedly crude methodology in a bit more detail). The banking organizations on our list of likely LCBOs are very large, holding the vast majority of U.S. banking system assets. That said, the list also has many specialized, nontraditional banks. Of the nineteen domestic banking organizations, at least one-fifth concentrate their activities in processing, trust, and asset management activities.[26] It is important to note that the LCBO list is fluid and that our guesses may not accurately reflect current or past membership. In that sense, our list is certainly illustrative. Nonetheless, this list and the others we discuss later suggest that the scope of expected TBTF coverage is very wide.

23. DeFerrari and Palmer (2001, p. 50).
24. Study Group on Subordinated Notes and Debentures for the Federal Reserve System (1999, p. 172) published the names of some large complex banking organizations.
25. DeFerrari and Palmer (2001).
26. For characterization of these banks' core business, see Catherine Murray, "U.S. Banking Industry: Remain Cautious on Bank Securities Services," J. P. Morgan, November 14, 2001; Diane Glossman, "State Street Analyst Day Upbeat," UBS Warburg Global Equity Research, December 10, 2001; Diane Glossman, "Trust Banks: Downgrading Mellon and State Street to Hold from Buy," UBS Warburg, November 27, 2001.

Box 4-1. *Organizations Potentially Considered Large Complex Banking Organizations*

Staff of the Board of Governors of the Federal Reserve System note that roughly twenty-five to thirty banking organizations are considered LCBOs.[a] Institutions that could potentially be designated this way are listed below and meet one of three criteria:

—Identified already as an LCBO in a publication of the Board of Governors, specifically, Study Group on Subordinated Notes and Debentures for the Federal Reserve System (1999), or

—Fell within the top fifteen matching at least four of the criteria that DeFerrari and Palmer note are reviewed by the Board of Governors in determining which organizations should be designated LCBOs,[b] or

—Was among the ten largest foreign banking organizations.[c]

Institution	Assets as reported to U.S. banking regulators in billions of U.S. dollars	Institution	Assets as reported to U.S. banking regulators in billions of U.S. dollars
Citigroup	1,068	SunTrust Banks	103
J. P. Morgan Chase and Company	799	Société Générale	99
Bank of America Corporation	640	National City Corporation	97
Deutsche Bank AG	514	Bank of Montreal Holdings	91
Mizuho Holdings	422	Royal Bank of Scotland Group PLC	91
Stichting Prioriteit ABN AMRO	382	Bank of New York Company	90
UBS AG	357	KeyCorp	84
Wachovia Corporation	326	Toronto-Dominion Bank	76
Wells Fargo and Company	298	State Street Corporation	73
Bank One Corporation	270	PNC Financial Services Group	72
Credit Suisse Group	255	Mellon Financial Corporation	43
MetLife	252	Royal Bank of Canada	41
HSBC Holdings PLC	240	Bayerische Hypo-und Vereinsbank AG	40
FleetBoston Financial Corporation	202	Dresdner Bank AG	40
U.S. Bankcorp	168	Charles Schwab Corporation	37
BNP Paribas SA	119	Countrywide Financial Corporation	36
Mitsubishi Tokyo Financial Group	114	Northern Trust Corporation	35

a. DeFerrari and Palmer (2001, p. 50).

b. We chose four of the criteria as a cutoff, because numerous organizations were in the top fifteen for four or more of the criteria while relatively few were in the top fifteen for less than four. Moreover, we reviewed data only for the criteria that were readily quantified from regulatory reports as of September 30, 2001.

c. We chose ten because DeFerrari and Palmer (2001) note that about one-third of LCBOs—whose total is typically around twenty-five to thirty—are foreign bank organizations.

Analysis of Banking Crises

Too big to fail likely has played a role in the spate of banking crises over the last two decades. The entire magnitude of output lost or social costs associated with a banking crisis cannot be attributed to moral hazard in general and the risk-taking associated with the TBTF problem more specifically. Nonetheless, these events provide an indirect measure of the potentially staggering costs of expected TBTF protection. Much attention has focused on the costs of crises in emerging markets such as Russia, where the financial crisis "resulted in a sharp decline in household incomes, rising unemployment, and increasing poverty rates."[27] But the costs of crises in developed countries—our major focus—appear to be as high or higher than in emerging markets perhaps because the crises in developed countries last long. A systematic review of banking crises puts the lost output on the order of 15 percent of annual gross domestic product.[28]

More specifically, analysts have tried to explain the cross-country variation in the costs of a banking crisis. Some of the policies used to provide TBTF protection significantly increase these costs. "Unlimited deposit guarantees, open-ended liquidity support, repeated recapitalization, debtor bailouts, and regulatory forbearance" are associated with a tenfold increase in the fiscal cost of banking crises.[29] Other cross-country reviews find that government bailouts in response to banking crises do not increase and may reduce economic output.[30]

What Prices of Uninsured Liabilities Tell Us about the Scope of TBTF Coverage

We began this chapter by noting that TBTF status should manifest itself in market prices. Creditors who think they will benefit from TBTF status, all else equal, will demand a lower return on their funds. If the creditors were 100 percent confident that they would receive 100 percent protection, they would view their investment as risk-free. Therefore, the degree of so-called risk-based pricing by uninsured bank creditors could suggest the level of TBTF coverage.

When analysts examine the links between market prices and bank risk-taking, they typically focus on fixed-income instruments, such as certificates

27. Lokshin and Yemtsov (2001, p. 1).
28. Hoggarth, Reis, and Saporta (2001) and citations within.
29. Honohan and Klingebiel (2000).
30. Boyd and others (2000).

of deposit (CDs) or debt that has the next-to-last priority on failure (so-called subordinated notes and debt, or SND). In the United States, some basic measures of risk-taking by a bank help to explain the rates that institutions pay on CDs. Measures of risk include, for example, asset quality metrics (for example, number of loans not currently receiving repayment) and measures of capital. To be more precise, these measures of bank risk are statistically significant when regressed against a measure of CD rates and yields.[31]

A second market-based analysis examines the shift in the quantity of uninsured CDs that banks issue. After banks in the United States become more risky, for example, they appear to increase their use of insured deposits at the expense of uninsured deposits.[32] Such a response is consistent with an attempt by banks to evade creditors who charge more for their risk-taking. (This behavior also has implications for incorporating market discipline in a supervisory regime, discussed in appendix D).

Recent reviews of SND pricing find a relationship between risk characteristics of the banking institution and yields. Specifically, analyses of data from 1983 to 1991 find evidence of risk-based pricing, with the results driven by the last three years of the sample.[33] Analysis of more current data confirms this result, establishes a link between the riskiness of assets that banking organizations hold and the initial price they pay to issue SND, and finds that risk characteristics influence the decision of a banking organization to issue SND.[34]

Analyses in the same vein have been conducted on changes in the pricing and quantity of deposits outside the United States. This work yields a similar conclusion. Depositors and SND holders take into account measures of risk.[35]

Analysts have drawn at least two conclusions from analyses of market prices. The first, and one with which we agree, is that policymakers can make progress in reducing TBTF expectations. The finding that SND

31. For summaries of the empirical work, see Gilbert (1990); Study Group on Subordinated Notes and Debentures for the Federal Reserve System (1999). Ellis and Flannery (1992) review pricing of uninsured deposits at large banks. Furfine (2001a) also finds risk-based pricing in overnight lending markets.

32. See Billett, Garfinkel, and O'Neal (1998); Jordan (2000) in general; and Marino and Bennett (1999) for the case of large banks. Penas (2001) discusses how the change in the mix of uninsured and insured liabilities affects bank risk-taking under a TBTF policy.

33. Flannery and Sorescu (1996).

34. Morgan and Stiroh (2001); Study Group on Subordinated Notes and Debentures for the Federal Reserve System (1999).

35. Barajas and Steiner (2000); Bartholdy, Boyle, and Stover (forthcoming); Demirgüç-Kunt and Huizinga (2000); Martínez-Peria and Schmukler (1998); Mondschean and Opiela (1999); Moore (1997); Opiela (2001); Sironi (2000).

spreads showed at least some pricing of bank risk-taking during the late 1980s and very early 1990s was novel. Prior analysis had not found risk-based pricing, suggesting that creditors felt at greater risk of loss starting in the late 1980s and early 1990s than they had before. Although we still believe that other trends suggest a worsening of the TBTF problem, we doubt that creditors are so sure that they will receive TBTF coverage that they have stopped pricing risk altogether.

The second conclusion, with which we disagree, is that TBTF guarantees cannot exist simultaneously with risk-based pricing. These analysts find the evidence just described as proving that "participants in the subordinated debt market . . . believe . . . that their investment is not protected by an implicit or explicit guarantee."[36] Risk-based pricing is certainly incompatible with creditor perceptions of a 100 percent guarantee that gives them access to their funds without delay.

But expectations of TBTF are not always going to be so solid, given its implicit nature. There will be some chance that the bailout will not occur, that the coverage will not be for 100 percent of a creditor's claim on his principal and interest, and that the funds will not be remitted to the creditor immediately. Even creditors with a strong chance of getting at least some coverage beyond that to which they are formally entitled have incentive to price a degree of risk. And, in fact, it is only by comparing existing prices to the prices that would occur in a world without TBTF protection that one can determine the existence and extent of such protection with this approach. The evidence we cited on risk-based pricing is not the same as these counterfactuals.

Even depositors with legal rights to protection in the United States and overseas are found to base their pricing of deposits on the level of risk-taking by banks.[37] If creditors have doubts about the government guarantee, even if it is a legal right, they will incorporate bank risk-taking into their decisions. This result illustrates why governments must develop credible policies putting creditors at risk if they hope to reduce the costs associated with too big to fail. The more that creditors believe they are at risk, the more effectively will they discipline banks and the more effectively will bank supervisors be able to rely on market data to assess bank risk-taking. We return to this subject in the second half of the book. But before doing so, we review the rationale for too big to fail and the expansion of TBTF protection.

---

36. Study Group on Subordinated Notes and Debentures for the Federal Reserve System (1999, p. 14).

37. Cook and Spellman (1994, 1996); Martínez-Peria and Schmukler (1998).

5

Why Protect TBTF Creditors?

Creditors' expectations of TBTF protection are costly. Simply announcing that fact and ignoring the incentives to offer TBTF protection will not persuade policymakers to tackle the problem head on. If policymakers act rationally and systematically in reaching decisions about TBTF support, as we think they do, they believe that the benefits of such support outweigh the costs. That belief implies that curtailing too big to fail requires reducing the perceived benefits or increasing the perceived costs and sets up the recommendations we make for addressing too big to fail.

We first describe the three major sets of incentives that could propel coverage for uninsured creditors of large banks, although this division reflects, to some degree, organizational convenience, as these incentives are not mutually exclusive. First, policymakers may view the costs of protection as smaller than the benefits that result when they prevent instability in the banking system from occurring and potentially spilling over to the rest of the economy. In short, policymakers believe that TBTF protection helps to preserve macroeconomic stability. Although we review the two other explanations, we believe that concern over spillovers is most often the best explanation for TBTF bailouts.

Second, policymakers may protect creditors of banks because doing so maximizes personal welfare. In this case, policymakers view the benefit and cost trade-off through their own lens, as opposed to the costs and benefits confronting society. Providing protection for the uninsured at large banks could, for example, advance the career of a policymaker even if such protection were not justified from the view of society.

Finally, policymakers may view government influence over the allocation of credit as increasing society's long-run welfare. To make such credit allocation viable, governments may have to protect creditors if the banks that finance state industrial policy cannot honor their obligations in full or on time. The long-run benefits associated with credit allocation and uninsured creditor protection exceed the costs of the moral hazard of such protection from the policymakers' perspective.

In the last section of this chapter, we argue that all three sets of incentives play at least some role in explaining coverage for uninsured creditors at large banks, depending on the time and place of the coverage. We make recommendations to address all three. However, we spend relatively little time discussing or addressing the credit allocation motivation, viewing it as part of a large set of issues raised by government central planning. And while the personal motivation could play a role in the protection of TBTF creditors, we think it is typically less important than the concern over spillovers. Governments will not, in our view, significantly reduce the likelihood of TBTF coverage unless policymakers believe they can impose losses on creditors of large banks without creating significant economic spillovers. We think they can, and the bulk of our recommendations aim to dampen moral hazard by reducing the threat of spillovers.

Economywide Consequences

In our view, policymakers typically bail out uninsured creditors at a failing bank to reduce the likelihood that creditor losses at one bank will spill over and significantly increase the chance of failure at other banks. Policymakers hope that by preventing spillovers in the financial system they can shield the economy from a significant decline in national output. In our experience, most policymakers believe that their concern about contagion is self-evident and well justified. Indeed, their views certainly adhere to well-known conclusions. However, because we want our reforms to link to and address underlying incentives, we provide additional details on the concerns of policymakers.

Some economists have argued that policymakers' concerns about spillovers are overblown on several counts and do not justify special protection for uninsured creditors. This alternative view raises important questions about the spillover justification, and for that reason we discuss it after reviewing policymakers' concerns. Furthermore, if it were compelling, the alternative view should convince policymakers not to bail out uninsured creditors at large banks in the name of preventing spillovers. However, after reviewing the alternative view, we do not think that policymakers would find it convincing. So instead we offer a series of recommendations that directly address policymakers' concerns about spillovers.

The Logic of Policymakers

Policymakers explain their fear of spillovers as follows (although we know they do not use the same terminology we have chosen). They begin by noting that even the largest, most well-respected financial institutions can run into such severe financial trouble that their chance of survival appears to be low. Not only can banks fail because of their weak condition, but they also are prone to runs capable of causing even a healthy bank to go quickly out of business. Policymakers recognize that banks cannot pay off all creditors in the short term—because banks' assets are difficult to dispose of quickly, while many of their liabilities can be retrieved on demand. As a result, creditors have an incentive to grab their funds before others can beat them to the punch. Creditors at the end of the line may get nothing. Policymakers frequently make mention of their commitment to bolster financial stability and avoid runs and panics when discussing their approach to bank failure.

Policymakers move on to argue that the failure of one bank might lead to the failure of others. Discussions among policymakers focus on several means of transmission. In the most straightforward case, institutions can have unsecured exposure to others, say, through federal funds sold or through positions in the payment system that do not settle until the end of the day. In the first case, if a large net purchaser of federal funds fails, the sellers of those funds may not get them back in a timely way, reducing their capital and possibly resulting in insolvency. In the second case, if an institution fails before settlement is effected, creditors in its payment system are left short, with similar hits to capital and the possibility of cascading effects to downstream creditors.

Further, public decisionmakers now have a better understanding, particularly following the September 11 terrorist attacks, that a small number of banks are responsible for processing a very large percentage of payments (particularly with regard to payments resulting from securities trades). The failure of a bank at the nexus of the payment system could leave other institutions in the lurch. The central bank could also fear the failure of a payment-oriented bank if fundamental aspects of monetary policy, such as the trading of treasury securities, rely on the central bank or treasury interacting with the bank.[1] That is, the central bank may face stiff challenges, at least in the short run, to intervene in the financial market and implement its monetary policy targets if banks key to implementing these financial transactions are allowed to fail. Creditors of such important banks might come to think that the central bank will protect them.

Policymakers also focus on the shared exposures of banks. Many banks could become weakened at the same time if they suffer losses from the same source. A number of large U.S. banks were believed to be near insolvency in the late 1980s due to their lending to developing countries. The problem with shared exposure is not just the actual losses that multiple banks could bear but also creditor uncertainty following news that a large bank is in trouble. For example, if a large bank becomes insolvent because of excessive exposure to, say, the energy sector or to Latin America, bank creditors are likely to become concerned about institutions with similar exposures. These institutions may well be healthy, but creditors may nevertheless quickly withdraw their funds (or run the bank), especially if their solvency is difficult to assess. It is generally accepted that the assets that banks hold, particularly their loans, are relatively opaque to outsiders, who may have difficulty determining their value or potential for repayment. In the mind of policymakers, panics are a real possibility.

Finally, the failure of a single very large or particularly important bank or multiple failures can spill over and depress real economic activity. Simply by looking at the important roles that banks play in the day-to-day functioning of the economy, policymakers come to the conclusion that their absence could lead to undesirable outcomes. If the banking system freezes up, lending, payment processing, and other aspects of bank operations may not operate anywhere near capacity. We have heard policymakers discuss the following examples. Many firms rely on banks for short-term funding by, for example, drawing down on backup lines of credit that banks provide.[2] A good deal of the oil that greases day-to-day financing (that is, short-term liquidity) could vanish if the banking system seizes. Likewise, banks play critical roles in markets that let nonfinancial firms manage their risks—for example, in the financial markets where many types of changes

---

1. Board of Governors of the Federal Reserve System and U.S. Securities and Exchange Commission (2002, p. 4).
2. Saidenberg and Strahan (1999).

in prices are said to be hedged. Banks also play key administrative roles in cash management, allowing firms to pay their bills efficiently. Banking failures can thus reduce or deny essential services to firms.

In this context, policymakers also note the effect that instability in the banking system may have on the availability of credit. Banks may respond to failures in the system and their own deteriorating position by curtailing the supply of new loans to businesses and households, calling in existing loans where possible, and generally tightening the terms and conditions of credit. This reduction in bank credit, in turn, forces small businesses in particular, which do not have ready access to alternate sources of financing, to defer expansion and, in at least some instances, to reduce production and employment. If these problems become sufficiently large and widespread, there can be major negative consequences for the economy.

The move from a concern about spillovers to protection of uninsured creditors is a short leap for policymakers. Protecting creditors at the first large bank near failure effectively signals creditors at other banks that they have far less reason to withdraw their funds. The protection of creditors also changes the nature of the overall response from the government toward the failing firm. Rather than seeking to liquidate it and allowing market forces to divvy it up, creditor protection reveals a commitment to maintaining something closer to ongoing operations. Government protection aims to continue the provision of the failing banks' key services.

Responding to the Logic of Policymakers

We see two potential ways to address policymakers' belief that bank instability can threaten the economy and therefore justify protection of the uninsured. Our approach takes these concerns at face value. We then focus on reforms that help to mitigate the means by which spillovers occur in the banking sector and from banks to the rest of the economy.

A second approach, adopted by a respected group of analysts, takes issue with the underlying story. The threat of spillovers, according to these analysts, has been greatly exaggerated. The implication is that one might change policymakers' behavior by explaining faults in their reasoning.

We find that the alternative view raises several useful issues. It provides specific examples of how the concern over spillovers could be overstated and throws some doubts on the amount of benefits that bailouts provide. In the end, however, we think that the alternative view does not present a persuasive enough case to convince policymakers to give up their concern about spillovers. Thus simply articulating the alternative view is unlikely to reduce the likelihood of TBTF bailouts.

The Alternative View

The alternative case is a coherent story. First, the failure of one bank hardly ever imposes significant enough losses to put creditors out of business. The prototypical case of TBTF coverage, Continental Illinois, illustrates this point. After-the-fact analysis of financial records indicates that the failure of Continental Illinois would not have wiped out the entire financial capital of any respondent banks (that is, banks that used Continental Illinois to manage their short-term funding and other operations) and therefore would not have led many of them to fail.[3] Yet policymakers at the time of the failure justified TBTF protection in part by pointing to the risk that Continental's collapse posed to roughly 200 respondents.[4]

Second, policymakers misread the historical record on financial sector contagion. Creditors pulled funds from banks during so-called panics because the banks were financially weak and deserved quick closure. Confusion about the condition of banks did not play the threatening role that decisionmakers attribute to it. There are numerous historical examples to make this point. For example, creditors of banks in Chicago during the Great Depression differentiated between those banks that were financially strong and those that were not.[5] The same was true of creditors during periods of banking panics in the nineteenth century in the United States.[6]

Claims of informed withdrawals also look to more recent times for support. Equity prices of banks with exposures to Long-Term Capital Management and to countries that suffered banking or currency crises change after bailouts. Equity values of banks without exposure did not change after bailouts, suggesting that market participants differentiate between banks during times of crisis.[7]

In sum, this aspect of the alternative view seeks to recast the costs and benefits of cases where many banks simultaneously go out of business

---

3. Wall (1993, p. 7). Wall's calculations account for recoveries from the assets of Continental Illinois after its failure.

4. Davison (1997, pp. 250–51); Silverberg (1985) also discusses policymakers' concerns.

5. Calomiris and Mason (1997).

6. For examples, see Benston and Kaufman (1995); Kaufman (1994). Rolnick (1987) finds that depositors in the 1920s factored in bank risk-taking when pricing deposits.

7. Bong-Chan, Lee, and Stulz (2000).

because of creditor action. Brief, rapid disruptions weed out poorly run or weak competitors and discipline banks as to future exposures. Banking panics are simply a form of the invisible hand.

Another aspect of the alternative view covers the potential for spillovers from the financial sector to the real economy. Advocates of this view often argue that the standard spillover story has its facts upside down. Shakiness in the real economy is what puts weaker banks over the edge; it is not that problems in banking wreak havoc on the economy. And even if financial instability came first, these analysts question whether bank failures were the proximate cause of subsequent economic contraction.[8]

Finally, the alternative view notes that, in cases where instability does occur, the policymaker has more effective tools than guarantees for the uninsured. Central banks can lend funds to otherwise healthy banks that suffer runs in an effort to staunch spillovers. If managed in accordance with prudent rules governing collateral and assessment of the condition of the borrower, banks should be able to repay discount window loans. Moreover, the moral hazard of discount window lending made under such conditions should not rise to the level created by guarantees of uninsured creditors. In addition, open market operations by the central bank can inject liquidity into the financial sector more broadly.

Failings of the Alternative View

We are sympathetic to several aspects of the "just teach policymakers the truth" approach. The historical analyses enlighten the debate and our proposals in several regards and support our impression of the net costs imposed by TBTF bailouts. Moreover, the notion that direct losses to bank creditors are relatively small suggests that advancing liquidity to creditors—repaid by the sale of assets of the failed bank—can help to address the routine threat of spillovers. We also strongly agree with the bottom line of these critics: Policymakers should be skeptical of coverage of uninsured creditors and ensure that it takes place only when there are significant threats to the economy from the failure of a large bank.

Nonetheless, we find that this approach fails the litmus test: it is unlikely to change the behavior of policymakers and thus the expectations of creditors. The problem is that, after reviewing the evidence that the critics provide, policymakers would almost surely, in our view, remain uncertain

8. Kaufman (1994, pp. 141–43).

about the potential macroeconomic effects of a large bank failure. After hearing a debate on the alternative view, most policymakers would still see the failure of a large bank as posing a significant threat to the economy.

The alternative would likely fail to convince policymakers on several levels. For example, policymakers' intuition has considerable similarity to the most frequently cited theoretical models of the banking system. Well-respected mainstream economic theory suggests that banking runs are possible, that these runs can lead to panics, and that widespread contraction of the banking system could impose significant costs on the real economy. Moreover, many of the economists who developed these models explicitly recommend government protection as a means of preventing instability.[9] More recent economic models of TBTF bailouts focus specifically on the potential for interbank exposures—the same ones that concern policymakers—to lead to spillover failures.[10] In another example, economic theory and empirical evidence suggest that some firms will be dependent on banks for their funding and could face significant difficulties in finding other sources of funds.[11]

The alternative view also runs into scholars who find evidence of contagion and spillovers in past banking crises. Their history lessons suggest that bank failures can impose significant costs on the macroeconomy.[12] A fairly recent, extremely thorough review of the vast economics literature on systemic risk does not support a "don't worry about contagion" view.[13] The authors conclude, for example, that existing research cannot determine if contagion in the financial system—whose existence seems supported in a broad sense—is caused by the fragility of the banking system or represents the effective weeding out of weak institutions. Moreover, they note that important potential means of transmitting shocks within the financial sector and from the financial to real sectors, such as foreign exchange or securities settlement systems, have not received adequate empirical review.

Even if analysts supporting the alternative view correctly assess what happened in the past, policymakers may not find it compelling today. The problem is one of sample size. There just have not been enough historical

---

9. Diamond and Dybvig (1983). See Wallace (1990) for an alternative view.

10. Rochet and Tirole (1996b). For recent models of banking where panics and runs can occur, see Allen and Gale (2003); Ennis (2003); Peck and Shell (2003).

11. Berger, Kyle, and Scalise (2001); Petersen and Rajan (1994) discuss the relationship between small firms and lenders, particularly banks.

12. For examples, see Greenbaum (1995); Temzelides (1997).

13. De Bandt and Hartmann (2000).

cases to give policymakers confidence that contagion is not a potentially serious problem. Moreover, policymakers can reasonably cite important differences between the financial institutions, legal environment, technology, and so forth currently prevailing and those in previous bailouts. The situations are always likely to vary in some important institutional manner.

A couple of examples of "new" sources of contagion may help. Post–September 11 decisionmakers have a greater appreciation of the threat posed by the very small number of banks that play key roles in completing security trades in extremely large financial markets. And over the past decade or so, policymakers have become sensitive to the fact that several extremely large banks dominate the derivative markets. If one of these banks falls into financial trouble, derivative counterparties could have to liquidate positions and establish new ones. Liquidation of the collateral that supports the derivative contracts could lead to the dumping of assets, potentially in illiquid markets. The sale of assets would depress their value, raising the specter that many institutions with large holdings of this type of asset would suffer significant losses. Creditors of firms holding the faltering assets might seek to pull their funds in anticipation of such an event. The overall desire of the various market participants to bear risk could also fall precipitously.

We recognize that some analysts might object to our suggestion that a market like the one for derivatives poses "new" forms of systemic risk. Some experts argue that private mechanisms (such as clearinghouses) in markets for derivatives have proven adequate in managing concerns about systemic risk.[14] Again, however, the relevance of this historical example can be challenged.[15] If one expert lauds the historical role that coalitions of self-monitoring private firms play in insuring against failure, another notes that the Options Clearing Corporation in Chicago required central bank intervention to stay afloat during the 1987 stock market crash.[16] To a policymaker, the threats may appear new and claims to the contrary too uncertain to provide much reassurance.

Like advocates of the alternative view, we consider the discount window, and possibly open market operations, as potentially effective tools for managing the threat from a failing bank. Nonetheless, on several occasions in the past, policymakers did not avail themselves of such tools, and they are

14. Kroszner (1999).
15. Bordo (1999); Boyd (1999a).
16. Kroszner (1997); Litan (1997).

rarely touted by policymakers as serious replacements for TBTF coverage. So even if right in substance, we do not think this point will lead to a change in behavior. Why don't policymakers use these other tools in place of bailouts? One possibility is that even with the inside information generated by bank supervisors, the central bank may not have confidence in its ability to differentiate between solvent and insolvent banks or to value collateral when a large bank fails. The central bank may want to avoid lending to a failing bank whose collateral proves insufficient for repayment.

Policymakers may also want to respond to a large failed bank with a tool specifically aimed at keeping an insolvent bank alive, particularly if the bank offers a service, such as payment and settlement, whose absence would prove costly. The alternative tools of the central bank may not help in such cases. A similar problem may arise if several significant institutions become insolvent. The insolvency of several large institutions would likely prove disruptive to the economy, if only because of the time required for customers to make adjustments and find alternative sources of credit and services. More likely, simultaneous insolvency of several large institutions would severely undermine confidence and, therefore, would require extraordinary government support to reestablish stability.

Because of these failings of the alternative view, we take a second approach to addressing policymakers' concerns. Specifically, we work from the bottom up and suggest specific reforms that, if enacted, would reduce the chance of spillovers and make policymakers confident that such a reduction has occurred. After introducing such reforms, we believe that policymakers will be more likely to impose losses on uninsured creditors, because they will recognize that the threat of spillovers has diminished.

Although fear of economic instability is the primary motivation for TBTF coverage, there are other rationales as well. Some analysts believe that policymakers provide coverage because of their own concerns. In their view, personal motivations, rather than concerns about the costs and benefits facing society, are the drivers behind TBTF coverage.

Personal Rewards

Public decisionmakers act in the capacity of agents for others when they confront the failure of a large complex bank. Although it may appear of only theoretical interest, it is worth considering on whose behalf the government agent acts. Some argue that government agents represent the interests of the explicitly insured depositor, who is typically characterized as having limited sophistication and holding a small amount of assets. Because government protection for bank creditors is often more expansive, it affects the welfare of a group closer to society as a whole—that is, citizens or taxpayers. Ideally, policymakers act on behalf of this larger group.

At times, however, policymakers may act more like free agents.[17] In doing so, they may bail out creditors of large banks to maximize personal gain. Out of corruption, a desire to maximize their prestige or advance their own career, or a preference for a low-stress life, a policymaker may (deliberately) not act in the best interest of society as a whole. So, for example, the policymaker may try to curry favor with the supervised entity to facilitate later employment or simply to avoid conflict.

The fact that decisionmakers may seek to maximize their own gain makes TBTF coverage more likely.[18] Although we do not view this motivation as being as important as the concern over spillovers, it seems to play at least some role in bailouts. One reason why is forbearance—the practice of not enforcing standards of safety and soundness in a timely manner against banks. At the extreme, governments refuse to shutter insolvent banks and allow sickly institutions to continue the practices that put them in poor financial condition. If policymakers do not forbear and instead strictly enforce safety and soundness regulations, they might run afoul of powerful interests—including the regulated banks—which could retard efforts to maximize personal gains.

Decisionmakers who forbear can even appear more competent than decisionmakers who enforce the rules. Enforcement may mean that banks fail and are closed. Timely response to weak banking performance might lead to failures on a regular basis because problems are not permitted to build up. Because their jobs often have vague objectives and outsiders have limited ability to assess what they control, banking policymakers are often judged by externally visible outcomes, such as bank failures. The absence of failures in the current period may be interpreted as a job well done.

Perhaps the most well-known case of forbearance in the United States occurred during the savings and loan crisis.[19] Congress passed legislation that allowed insolvent firms to stay open; thrift supervisors did not close thrifts that were not viable. Hundreds of small institutions had their closings postponed because of forbearance.

---

17. Niskanen (1971).

18. The views summarized in this section are associated most closely with the works of Kane; see, for example, Kane (2001a) and citations to his previous work within.

19. Kane (1989).

The thrift crisis shows that forbearance is not necessarily linked to TBTF protection. That said, forbearance could make coverage of the uninsured at TBTF banks more likely by reducing the options available to policymakers at the time of a large bank failure. Although the attractions of forbearance are real, at some point policymakers realize that the banking problem is beyond repair, forbearance must end, and the large bank problem has to be resolved. That is, forbearance can buy time, but it rarely can buy sufficient time. A deeply insolvent bank imposes larger losses on creditors than a bank with more positive net worth. Policymakers typically view large losses imposed on uninsured creditors as a catalyst for instability in the banking system and the economy. To prevent such spillovers, policymakers may find bailouts the option they "must" take after extended periods of forbearance. Recent creditor bailouts of very large banks in Japan—including that of Resona Holdings in May 2003—are associated with both too big to fail and a policy of forbearance.[20]

By allowing big banks to stay open longer and to engage in excessive risk-taking, forbearance squanders the opportunity to protect taxpayers by closing the institution when it has positive capital. It also means that healthy organizations confront competitive pressures from banks that should have been closed. This exacerbates resource misallocation because failing institutions continue to operate, attract funds, and gamble on high returns. One head of a large bank described the U.S. banking crisis of the 1980s as "competition in laxity" with "the dumbest and weakest competitors in the marketplace set[ting] the basic standards of pricing and credit terms." Excessive government support for creditors of weak banks, in this banker's view, made such unfair competition possible.[21]

In addition to forbearance, a desire to increase personal gain also makes TBTF coverage more likely due to reputational effects. Decisionmakers may come to believe, as we have, that legislators and the heads of the executive branch of government expect containment of weakness in the financial sector. While elected officials recognize that instability may occur, they reasonably hope that it will happen infrequently and not on their watch. An inability to prevent or arrest instability may reduce the public decisionmaker to "damaged goods." Bailing out creditors at large banks and thus expanding the safety net and reducing market discipline may appear

20. Jason Singer and Martin Fackler, "Japan Sets $17 Billion Rescue of Ailing Big Bank," *Wall Street Journal*, May 19, 2003, p. A3.
21. Medlin (1997, p. 106).

insignificant when compared with the damage to reputation that could result if creditors were not protected and the financial sector were to appear unstable, even for a short period of time.

While we have tried to convey the essence of the view that personal gain matters in TBTF decisions, it is best summarized in the words of one of its major expositors:[22]

> The fundamental source of taxpayer losses does not lie in defects in the structure of the risk-management controls that have been written into deposit-insurance contracts. The critical defects lie instead in incentive conflicts that—in tough times and tough cases—lead government officials *not to enforce* the underwriting standards, coverage limitations, and takeover rights that are already included in existing contracts. . . .
>
> The roots of the spreading deposit-insurance mess lie in long-standing defects in political and bureaucratic accountability. The overriding problem is that, given the short horizons and narrow career interests of responsible politicians and bureaucrats, covering up troublesome evidence and engaging in regulatory forbearance is a rational response to the emergence of widespread industry insolvency. It pays regulators to use their discretion to cover up emerging problems and to put off painful adjustments to someone else's watch. . . .
>
> To put an end to the deposit-insurance mess, authorities have to "get real" about the temptations that high officials face and about the transactions that occur in the markets for *legislative and regulatory forbearances* in which temptations are offered and seductions completed. . . . In adopting forbearance policies such as too big to fail, authorities purport to fear contagious runs that produce macroeconomic damage. . . . I submit that what many government officials truly fear is losing "a right to deal" in influence.

How do these analysts support the claim that personal motivations explain decisions to bail out TBTF creditors? They focus largely on similarities between predicted and actual behavior of policymakers (as well as theoretical models of supervisory behavior).[23] In their view,

---

22. Kane (1991).

23. See Freixas and Rochet (1997) for summaries of more theoretical work; see also the material reviewed in appendix B of this book for more applied analysis.

—Forbearance appears to have played an important indirect role in coverage of the uninsured in the United States and, perhaps more prominently, in Japan.

—Discretion also appears to have played a significant role in subverting reforms in the United States designed to reduce forbearance, which some decisionmakers fought to prevent in the first place.

—Finally, some, and maybe most, of the public information about the size of banking crises in the United States and Japan appears to have been misleading.

Credit Allocation

Some countries have a tradition of government allocation of credit, either directly through government-owned and -operated banks or indirectly through encouragement of private lenders to finance particular enterprises. In some countries, this policy could contribute to the decision to bail out the creditors of large banks. However, we review this motivation only briefly because it seems linked to a host of issues that go beyond our focus.

Reflecting the potential role of the state in credit allocation, the World Bank recently noted banking regulation in many developing countries did not reflect a commitment to the safety and soundness of the bank but, rather, was a tool for forcing banks to make loans to targeted borrowers.[24] Policymakers may allocate credit to industries or firms believed important to the economic growth of the country that they think would be underserved by private markets.[25] Targeting may also serve a second, less noble, purpose if used for self-enrichment. Policymakers and their so-called cronies, including members of their families, might be the beneficiaries when credit is funneled to certain industries, perhaps through ownership stakes in the targeted firms.

Government credit allocation could require banks to take risks that they otherwise would not, particularly if the targeting is to benefit policymakers and cronies. If the risks inherent in credit allocation are sufficiently severe and mispriced, government industrial policy will lead to the potential for, or reality of, a high level of nonperforming assets on the books of the banks. The nonperforming assets will erode capital and reserves, with a real

24. World Bank (2002).
25. Tornell (2001) argues that "systemic bailout guarantees" can encourage economic growth under certain circumstances.

potential for insolvency and failure. Bank creditors who bear the losses resulting from a poorly run system of credit allocation will either become unwilling to bear additional losses in the future or require higher compensation for accepting them. Given the difficulty that creditors may face in judging the creditworthiness of loans in support of industrial policy, the option of withholding funds may seem compelling.

In this case, the government must either use taxes to fund credit allocation or find a way to get private funding to return. Protecting creditors from the losses they otherwise would suffer must strike many policymakers as a fairly straightforward way to ensure that the funding spigot stays open. Such protection encourages future funding of government credit allocation at relatively low direct cost. Even if it decides to end its policy of credit allocation, the government that previously pursued such a policy may have a difficult time avoiding bailouts for a combination of reputational and macroeconomic reasons. Policymakers put their names on the line when they commit themselves to credit allocation, and we suspect that officials will be loath to acknowledge failure and instead will find means to avoid closing insolvent institutions.

Assessing the importance of industrial policy and credit allocation to the protection of uninsured creditors of large banks is challenging because of the difficulty of measuring the existence and importance of policies such as credit allocation. In theory, it is also possible for government credit allocation to funnel money to industries that end up performing well and repaying their loans. That said, analysis that examines the history and economics of industrial policy suggests a fairly close relationship with TBTF protection in at least several countries. Most prominently, goals related to industrial policy help to explain the high level of protection that the uninsured receive in Japan.[26] Further, it appears that crony capitalism and centrally allocated credit played important roles in TBTF protection in the Southeast Asian Tigers.[27]

Conclusion: The Relative Importance of the Incentives

In this chapter, we have reviewed the three incentives we think lead policymakers to protect uninsured creditors at large banks. By identifying the

---

26. Fukao (2003); Hoshi and Kashyap (2001). Spiegel (1999) and Spiegel and Yamori (2000) discuss too big to fail in Japan.
27. Pomerleano (1998).

incentives that lead to the protection of uninsured creditors, we set the stage for identifying reforms that could make such coverage less frequent and less extensive. While some have tried to discredit the importance of some of these incentives, we believe that all of them play a role in bailout decisions. Therefore, the series of reforms we propose address, at least in part, all of these considerations. At the same time, we do not give each incentive equal weight when devising our reforms.

Credit Allocation

Although we have discussed industrial policy and credit allocation in the context of TBTF protection, we recognize that this is a narrow, and maybe even misleading, lens. We are more truly describing economies with meaningful amounts of central planning. TBTF protection is not the problem per se in countries that socialize not just the cost of bank failure but a whole host of other costs and benefits from economic activity. Advocating reforms specific to the management of too big to fail for (underdeveloped) countries adhering to central planning seems premature. Countries where official credit allocation routinely helps to explain TBTF coverage should consider basic reforms to establish viable, market-based systems (see chapter 9). We also feel comfortable in not taking on the credit allocation rationale for TBTF protection because of trends suggesting that such government intervention may die of its own failings (although we recognize that the transition from such systems could take decades). Over time, the view that directed credit almost always ends up imposing larger costs than benefits has come to dominate, particularly now that the East Asian experience with credit allocation looks less rosy.[28]

Personal Gain and Economic Implications

Determining the importance of personal gain in policymakers' decision-making also poses challenges because of the often subjective nature of the charge. In general, this incentive seems consistent with behavior in a non-trivial number of cases. Thus we support reforms that we believe will reduce the ability of policymakers to forbear and to maximize their own gains at the expense of society, including reforms that call for more accurate accounting of explicit and implicit guarantees in the federal budget

28. See Stiglitz (1993) for a defense of government credit allocation. For less positive views, see Caprio, Hanson, and Honohan (2001); Bruno and Pleskovic (1993), especially "Floor Discussion on the Role of the State in Financial Markets"; Jaramillo-Vallejo (1993); Vittas and Cho (1995); Vittas and Kawaura (1995).

(chapter 9) and limit the discretion of supervisors (chapters 10 and 11). However, exclusive reliance on personal motivation to explain TBTF protection seems excessive and unjustified. The notion that policymakers use systemic risk as a ruse to justify personal gain also seems extreme.

In fact, we believe that creditor expectations of TBTF coverage would impose real costs on society even if issues of personal motivation were addressed. In our view, policymakers have genuine concerns about spillovers disrupting the real economy, thereby reducing the level of business activity and employment, and view coverage of the uninsured as an effective means to stabilize the financial system and economy in the face of potentially disruptive threats. Although we recommend reforms to address all types of incentives, if we could manage only one, we would choose reforms that make policymakers less concerned about spillovers.

It is the scenario of banking problems spilling over to and depressing economic activity that keeps policymakers up at night and that is, in our judgment and experience, the single most important factor leading to TBTF protection. Admittedly, our ultimate justification for this relative weighting is "gut and experience" rather than empirical evidence. Nonetheless, we remain convinced that banking policymakers simply do not want responsibility for the possibility of banking sector problems contaminating the real economy and that they believe they have means at their disposal to prevent severe spillovers. We suspect that, in policymakers' calculations, the benefits of safeguarding economic activity loom exceedingly large relative to the long-run costs of exacerbating moral hazard and TBTF incentives. This imbalance has to be addressed if too big to fail is to be reined in. And action to limit TBTF expectations should be a high priority because the problem is getting worse, for reasons described in the next chapter.

6

The Growth of TBTF Protection

Three developments have increased the number of institutions whose creditors believe they will benefit from TBTF coverage and have strengthened creditors' belief that such coverage is forthcoming:

—Increased concentration of banking assets,

—Greater complexity of banking operations and activities, supervisory challenges, and concentration in payments-related activities due to new technologies, and

—Several policy decisions, such as a larger number of highly visible government bailouts.

Where we see growth of the TBTF problem, some observers look over the last fifteen years and find a reduction in expected TBTF protection. They typically point to the Federal Deposit Insurance Corporation Improvement Act of 1991 (FDICIA) as significantly reducing the chance that government can protect uninsured creditors at large banks, among other outcomes. FDICIA may have made a dent in TBTF expectations in the early 1990s, but we do not think its reforms will counteract the three developments nor that it will credibly address the TBTF problem in the long run.

Industrial Structure

The major trends characterizing bank structure are consistent with growing concern about spillovers and thus TBTF guarantees that are broader in

60

scope and less uncertain. First, the very largest banks are getting larger, forming a new class of mega-banks. Second, a growing number of banks appear to meet a minimum threshold at which policymakers are likely to view their creditors as potential recipients of TBTF protection.

The Very Largest Banks

The very largest banks in many developed countries increased their share of banking assets in their home country over the last decade (reversing what sketchy data suggest may have been a decline during the 1980s). The trend occurred even if the country already had a concentrated banking system (see figure 6-1).[1] The larger size of mega-banks could well make creditors more confident that their government will step in to protect them if their bank fails.

The distribution of asset holdings among the world's banks also supports the notion that the very largest banks hold a larger share of total assets than formerly.[2] The largest of these 100 banks control an increasing share of total group assets over time and have the largest increase in real assets (see figure 6-2). A final noteworthy trend among the asset holdings of the 100 largest banks concerns their home countries (see table 6-1). Countries with traditions of state ownership, government support, and TBTF coverage, such as Japan, seem to have gained asset share at the expense of countries with a less explicit history of guarantees. These trends may actually understate the concentration of assets in banking systems because our measures of size only count the exposure of banks to balance sheet assets. Large banks are heavily involved in off-balance activity as well.

Finally, as the number of large institutions has shrunk, the interdependence of the remaining firms likely has increased. To operate cost-effectively and take advantage of their size, large institutions may restrict themselves to large transactions, which effectively limits the number of institutions with which they will do business. This means that the failure of one large bank is more likely to have a (negative) effect on the solvency of other large banks. Consistent with that view, since 1995, investors appear to view the large complex banking organizations (LCBOs) as having greater links to one another.[3] Analysts argue that consolidation in the LCBO population

1. Group of Ten (2001, p. 447).
2. We base this conclusion on data from *The Banker* magazine, specifically its annual list of the 1,000 largest banking organizations in the world. We analyzed data on the 100 largest institutions for the years 1970, 1980, 1990, and 2000. Similar exercises with an alternative source of data, specifically the *American Banker*, generated similar results.
3. Group of Ten (2001, p. 137).

Figure 6-1. *Share of Bank Assets Held by Ten Largest Banks, 1990 and 1999*[a]

Percent

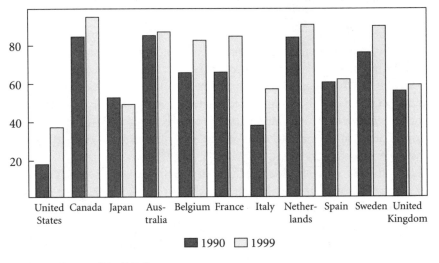

Source: Group of Ten (2001).
a. Data for Italy are 1992 and 1999. Data for United Kingdom, Sweden, and Spain are for 1990 and 1998.

Figure 6-2. *Relative Asset Holdings of 100 Largest Banks, 1970–2000*

Percent

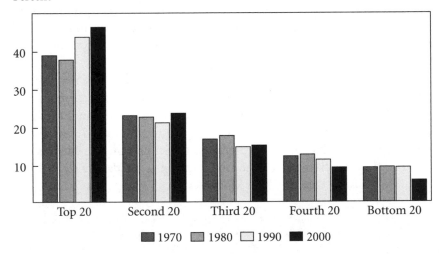

Source: Authors' calculations based on data from *The Banker*.

Table 6-1. *Home Country of 100 Largest Banks, 1970 and 2000*

	1970			2000	
Location	Assets (billions of U.S. dollars)	Percent-age of bank assets	Location	Assets (billions of U.S. dollars)	Percent-age of bank assets
United States	1,003	33	Japan	5,274.00	19
Japan	515	17	Germany	4,358.00	16
Germany	284	9	United States	3,966.00	15
Italy	280	9	United Kingdom	2,613.00	10
United Kingdom	262	9	France	2,441.00	9
Canada	182	6	China	1,511.00	6
France	160	5	Switzerland	1,268.00	5
Switzerland	84	3	Netherlands	1,204.00	4
Netherlands	58	2	Italy	969.00	4
Australia	40	1	Canada	825.00	3
Brazil	36	1	Belgium	789.00	3
Spain	36	1	Spain	605.00	2
Belgium	31	1	Sweden	530.00	2
Sweden	27	1	Australia	466.00	2
Hong Kong	18	1	Denmark	170.00	1
Yugoslavia	13	0.4	Ireland	74.00	0.3
			Brazil	71.00	0.3

Source: Authors' calculations based on data from *Banker.*

plays a role in this increase.[4] (Similar measures in Europe do not show a recent increase in interdependence among large banks, but this outcome may reflect already high levels of interdependence.)[5]

Growing Number of Banks Meeting Minimum TBTF Threshold

While the large banks are getting larger, we also believe that more banks have reached the minimum size necessary to be considered too big to fail by creditors. We recognize that such a claim is inherently qualitative and in many ways speculative given the implicit nature of TBTF guarantees. But the U.S. experience provides data to support our speculation. As noted in chapter 2, the comptroller of the currency's testimony on the failure of Continental Illinois indicates that creditors at the eleven largest banks

4. De Nicolo and Kwast (2001).
5. Group of Ten (2001, p. 156).

could expect expansive protection if their institution failed. A number of empirical studies, discussed in chapter 4, use this announcement and list of institutions to evaluate the presence of TBTF guarantees.

We use the same list of institutions to estimate the number of banking organizations whose creditors might believe they have TBTF protection. At the time of the comptroller's testimony, the smallest of the eleven institutions had assets of $43 billion (in 2001 dollars). We assume that this amount represents the minimum threshold at which TBTF guarantees begin to affect the behavior of creditors (see table 6-2). Under this assumption, creditors of twenty U.S. banks could believe that they would benefit from potential TBTF coverage as of the third quarter of 2001.[6] Another seven banks would have exceeded the cutoff with an acquisition of less than $10 billion. These twenty banks hold 54 percent of banking assets in the United States, while the eleven banks on the older list controlled 27 percent. One might argue that the trend toward more TBTF banks is uniquely a U.S. phenomenon, but this argument should provide little solace to policymakers. Most countries cannot accommodate additional TBTF banks simply because their level of asset concentration is already so high.

Why Larger Is Not Better

In contrast to our discussion, some analysts argue that the trend toward larger banking organizations makes TBTF coverage less likely. They argue that larger banks are less risky than their smaller predecessors because they have more diversified portfolios. In the United States, geographic restrictions on operations historically led to smaller institutions susceptible to downturns in a single industry or region. The new, larger banks have a lower chance of failure now that they operate without geographic restrictions. Larger banks could also pose a lower risk of failure if they operated more efficiently and had greater capability to generate revenue.[7] Managers of large banks and other observers have argued that revenue and cost factors explain the recent flurry of merger and acquisition activity among the largest banks.[8]

However, available empirical evidence does not support the contention that growth has reduced the risk-taking of larger banks. After becoming larger, banks "spend" their diversification benefit by taking on additional

---

6. Twenty-four banks actually exceeded the cutoff, but four of them are affiliates of other banks on the list and for simplicity's sake are combined under one name.

7. Saunders and Wilson (1999) argue that consolidation acts as a substitute for capital, allowing large banks to have lower net worth.

8. Stiroh and Poole (2000) discuss the role of mergers in consolidation.

Table 6-2. *List of TBTF Banks Based on the Comptroller's List for 1983 and an Updated List for 2001*

2001 U.S. dollars unless noted otherwise

		TBTF banks as of December 1983				TBTF banks as of September 2001		
Rank	Bank	1983 (billions of U.S. dollars)	2001 (billions of U.S. dollars)	Percent of all bank assets	Rank	Bank	2001 (billions of U.S. dollars)	Percent of all bank assets
1	Citibank	114	203	5	1	J. P. Morgan Chase[a]	711	11
2	Bank of America	110	196	5	2	Bank of America	575	9
3	Chase Manhattan	80	142	3	3	Citibank	424	7
4	Manufacturers Hanover	58	104	3	4	First Union NB	232	4
5	Morgan Guaranty	56	101	2	5	Fleet Bank	190	3
6	Chemical Bank	49	88	2	6	U.S. Bank	163	3
7	Continental	41	73	2	7	Bank One[b]	184	3
8	Bankers Trust	40	72	2	8	Wells Fargo[c]	176	3
9	Security Pacific	36	65	2	9	SunTrust Bank	99	2
10	First Chicago	36	64	2	10	Bank of New York	87	1
11	Wells Fargo	24	43	1	11	HSBC Bank USA	85	1
					12	Keybank	74	1
	Total	643	1,150	27	13	Wachovia Bank	73	1
					14	State Street	68	1
					15	PNC Bank	65	1
					16	LaSalle Bank	54	1
					17	BB&T	54	1
					18	South Trust Bank	47	1
					19	Bankers Trust	45	1
					20	Regions Bank	43	1
						Total	3,451	54

Source: Authors' calculations based on data contained in the consolidated reports of condition and income—commonly known as call reports—that banks file with regulators.

a. The assets of J. P. Morgan Chase are aggregated from three banks under the same holding company that all exceed the cutoff.

b. The assets of Bank One are aggregated from two banks under the same holding company that all exceed the cutoff.

c. The assets of Wells Fargo are aggregated from two banks under the same holding company that all exceed the cutoff.

risk. For example, larger banks hold assets in riskier categories, such as commercial and industrial loans, relative to smaller banks.[9] In fact, the mergers that generate the greatest wealth for shareholders actually concentrate the bank along geographic and activity lines.[10]

9. Akhavein, Berger, and Humphrey (1997); Demsetz and Strahan (1997).
10. DeLong (2001).

In addition, as a general matter, mergers of the very largest banks apparently are not the result of either cost efficiencies or revenue enhancements. The asset size believed to exhaust scale economies in most empirical analysis was on the order of $10 billion. The results hold across a wide range of studies, including those done for financial institutions outside the United States.[11] This minimum efficient size is much smaller than the institutions that have resulted from recent mega-mergers. While more recent analysis finds higher levels of minimum efficient scale, the gains to growing greater than $50 billion in assets appear small relative to growing in size up to that point.[12]

The New Technology of Banking

Developments in the technology of banking reinforce the growing concentration of banking assets. Changes in banking technology help to explain the dominant role that a few banks play in payments-related activity as well as the wider geographic reach of banking organizations. Uninsured creditors of both specialized banks and banks expanding their geographic footprint could have heightened expectations of government protection. Other technologically related trends that could increase the scope and strength of TBTF guarantees include growing dependence on capital market funding; a new range of highly sophisticated, complicated activities; and an overall increase in the complexity of large banking organizations. Increased complexity raises the uncertainty that policymakers confront in the case of large bank failure and therefore makes TBTF protection seem more attractive.

The Technology of Payments

Size is not the only factor that makes a bank too big to fail. An extremely large bank could engage in activities that pose very little threat of spillover effects and might rely almost exclusively on explicitly insured deposits for funding. Although few of the very largest banking organizations in a country might match this description, a number of large banks in the second tier could come close to being a big "community bank."

At the same time, creditors of a bank could have assets that fall below those of the top five or ten institutions in a country but still benefit from

11. Berger, Demsetz, and Strahan (1999); Group of Ten (2001, p. 253).
12. Hughes, Mester, and Moon (2001, p. 2200).

TBTF coverage because, for example, its failure would lead to significant spillovers. In the United States, for example, a group of institutions outside the very largest banks receive a significant portion of their revenue from payment-related activities.[13] Analysts have identified these payment system activities, which include processing of payments to holders of fixed-income securities or the settlement of capital market trades, as posing a significant threat of spillover. Without a bank to settle trades, important securities markets would not operate. Policymakers may want to mitigate fallout from the abrupt failure of such key settlement banks by protecting their creditors.

Banks, individually and in coalitions, have always been key processors of payments, and disruptions to the payment system have long posed a risk, but technology likely has heightened the risk. For one thing, more payments are being processed. While this trend is surely a function of economic growth, advances in computing and telecommunications were necessary to support the expansion. Moreover, the importance of computing and telecommunication investments has led observers to view payment processing as a business of scale and specialized skills. Both attributes could lead a relatively small number of banks to be particularly important in payment processing, meaning that their failure could be highly disruptive to the financial system.

Our discussion of large complex banking organizations has highlighted some of the payment-processing banks that rely heavily on technology. Draft guidance issued in 2002 in response to the effect of the September 11 attacks on the financial system provides a rough measure of the number of firms deemed important to operation of the payment network. In that guidance, U.S. supervisors identify banks that have to meet higher standards of business resumption or "sound practices" such as specific timelines by which they should recover and resume their activities and rigorous protocols for testing their recovery and resumption capabilities. Supervisors argue that the sound practices are "most applicable to organizations that present a type of systemic risk should they be unable to recover or resume critical activities that support critical markets. In this context, 'systemic risk' includes the risk that the failure of one participant in a transfer system or financial market to meet its required obligation will cause other

---

13. Radecki (1999) reviews payment-driven revenue at large banks and finds no clear correlation between size (measured by operating revenue) and percentage of revenue from payments. Rice and Stanton (2003) provide more recent evidence supporting the same point.

participants to be unable to meet their obligations when due, causing significant liquidity or credit problems and threatening the stability of financial markets."[14]

They go on to note that core clearing and settlement organizations could present such systemic risk, as could firms that play a significant role in critical financial markets. Critical markets include those for federal funds, foreign exchange, commercial paper, government securities, corporate securities, and mortgage-backed securities. In addition to the core organizations, between fifteen and twenty major banks and between five and ten securities firms play a significant role in at least one critical market. The final guidance on sound practices is largely consistent with the draft but provides more specific guidelines on what constitutes a firm playing a significant role in a particular critical market. The guidance notes, "The agencies consider a firm significant in a particular critical market if it consistently clears or settles at least 5 percent of the value of transactions in that critical market."[15]

Capital Market Funding

Over the past several decades, larger banks have made greater use of uninsured deposits and nondeposit sources of funds than smaller banks. This trend picked up as capital markets became more robust in the United States and other countries. Capital market funding for the largest twenty-five banks in the United States went from 36 percent of liabilities to 42 percent from 1985 to 2001 (we define capital market funding as total liabilities minus deposit funding). The increase was much greater for the larger banks in this cohort (see figure 6-3); for example, the five largest banks saw an increase of closer to 10 percentage points.

On the one hand, greater reliance on capital markets could reduce an institution's chance of failure. Capital market funding can be cheaper and allow for more effective and diversified management of liquidity. The more arenas in which a bank can raise funds, the more likely it can survive a cutoff from a single source. While observers have noted such benefits, an alternative view holds that capital market funding increases instability by quickening the pace of failure. Capital market participants, some argue,

14. Board of Governors of the Federal Reserve System, U.S. Office of the Comptroller of the Currency, and U.S. Securities and Exchange Commission (2002, p. 4).

15. Board of Governors of the Federal Reserve System, Office of the Comptroller of the Currency, and U.S. Security and Exchange Commission (2003, p. 7).

Figure 6-3. *Capital Market Funding as a Percentage of Liabilities for the Twenty-Five Largest U.S. Banks, 1985–2001*

Percent

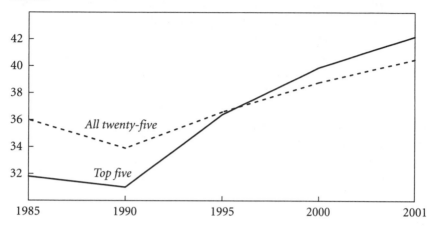

Source: Authors' calculations based on data contained in the consolidated reports of condition and income, known as call reports.

are quicker than other sources to restrict the quantity of funds they provide banks.

We are not aware of empirical evidence on the speed at which different funding sources react. However, there is a good reason for thinking that capital market funders might be quick to turn off the spigot. To greatly simplify, those who lend funds via the capital markets do not have much "private" information on the financial condition of their borrowers. Because of this information gap, they may be reluctant to try to mitigate the riskiness of a borrower by raising the price of credit. Instead, capital market participants may simply pull their funding from banks whose condition is not transparent or where they perceive a material chance of failure. Continental Illinois's quick demise, for example, was linked to its extensive capital market funding.[16] In a parallel case, observers also argue that commercial real estate development is more likely to be cut off quickly as funding in that arena moves from banks to capital markets.[17]

16. Davison (1997, p. 242).
17. Downs (2000); Thompson (2002).

Concern about capital market participants cutting off banks is particularly acute because a greater percentage of funding for the largest banks is short term. The share of the very largest banks' liabilities that are overnight borrowings, for example, has nearly doubled over the last fifteen years.[18] Quantity restrictions in short-term capital markets could generate a high degree of instability because banks rely on frequent and rapid replacement of such funding as it matures. For some institutions, no clear alternative exists to capital markets. Concern about the inability of a bank to raise funds in the capital markets becomes particularly acute if the bank engages in activities whose failure to proceed normally would generate spillovers (for example, securities settlement, trading, and payments). Also troubling is that much short-term funding provided to banks comes from other banks in the so-called interbank lending market. The increased reliance on short-term interbank lending has also been linked to the increased interdependence of large banks.[19]

Sophisticated and Complicated Operations

Advances in financial theory, telecommunications, and computing power have combined to foster new financial products, including a wide range of structured securities, derivatives, and securitized assets. Many large banks play significant roles in the construction, sale, and trading of these products. A high degree of involvement in these markets arguably makes it more likely that policymakers will provide TBTF coverage to the creditors of these banks.

First, the legal status of creditors under some of the new financial contracts remains unsettled.[20] This uncertainty increases creditors' incentives to seek protection against potential loss by trying to seize collateral, for example, or by refusing to enter into new transactions. Both responses could accelerate the decline of the bank on the other end of the transaction. A related concern is the documentation used in these transactions. Variation in documentation proved problematic during the 1998 period of bond market instability and continues to pose concerns.[21] Issues of documentation and legal status could collectively raise uncertainty about creditor status, which may present policymakers with the specter of financial panic.

---

18. Authors' calculations based on data from the reports of condition and income, known as the call reports, that banks file with regulators.

19. Group of Ten (2001, p. 139).

20. International Swaps and Derivatives Association (2000).

21. Crockett (2001); Financial Stability Forum (2001b).

Second, we believe the gap in knowledge between the banks and their supervisors and those responsible for resolving failed banks is growing, especially with respect to institutions that make extensive use of complex products. The gulf raises the level of uncertainty surrounding a large bank failure and likely induces policymakers to urge the provision of TBTF coverage. Certainly some in the supervisory world have a strong grasp of the nuances and details of newly complicated financial transactions. But our discussions with supervisors suggest that the number of staff with the experience and background to examine such activities is fairly small, although growing. Supervisors may well have a difficult time evaluating the potential for, and consequences of, spillovers, and thus they may opt for TBTF coverage as the "safe" solution.

Third, and closely related to the previous point, in the event of the failure of a large institution, policymakers are under pressure to act quickly and decisively. If the potential for spillovers from the resolution of complex financial instruments remains unclear, policymakers, fearing criticism for acting too slowly, have an incentive to provide creditor support. From the perspective of policymakers, the moral hazard costs of protection are intangible and occur in the future, while the instability could occur immediately. Thus we suspect that the greater is the use of the newer financial products, the greater is the incentive for policymakers to respond quickly with coverage for the uninsured.

Fourth, as mentioned, some new financial instruments are originated and traded in highly concentrated markets. We focus on derivatives to make this point, but the observations probably apply to other complex financial instruments and bank activities as well. The use of derivative contracts among banks has always been concentrated, but this concentration grew significantly over the 1990s (see table 6-3). In the United States the top four banks controlled about 50 percent of all bank-held derivative contracts in 1990 (measured in notional value). By 2000, the top four banks controlled 90 percent of all bank-held derivative contracts.[22] This degree of concentration suggests a significant potential for exposure among the largest bank users of derivatives. The failure of one leading institution could leave the others with substantial exposure to loss. Even analysts relying on public data have concluded that high levels of concentration in the derivative markets pose systemic risk.[23]

22. Authors' calculations based on quarterly fact sheets of the U.S. Office of the Comptroller of the Currency (various years).
23. Goldman Sachs (2002). They contrast systemic concerns with company-specific concerns.

Table 6-3. *Top Ten's Share of All Derivative Contracts Held by U.S. Banks, 1990–2001*

Cumulative percentage

Top ten banks	1990 (fourth quarter)	1995 (fourth quarter)	2001 (third quarter)
1	19	20	35
2	31	40	59
3	43	54	77
4	54	65	90
5	64	74	93
6	70	82	95
7	76	87	96
8	81	92	96
9	86	94	97
10	89	94	98

Source: U.S. Office of the Comptroller of the Currency (various issues).

Increased Overall Complexity

Many specific activities of the largest banks have become more complex because of the scale, scope, and technology underlying them. Each of these factors could, we believe, increase the potential of TBTF guarantees. Moreover, these factors interact to create organizations that are increasingly complex, which further solidifies TBTF guarantees. Complexity makes the resolution of the organizations more challenging in perception and practice. Faced with the prospect of a disorderly failure and the potential for spillovers, policymakers may elect to limit risk by providing support to uninsured creditors. Complexity reduces the quality of information, adding to the pressure on policymakers.

Four other aspects of complexity make policymakers more likely to offer TBTF protection. Because some of our later reform proposals respond directly to these characteristics, we list them here. First, as they have grown, the larger banking firms have developed extremely complex legal structures. Simply determining what activities the various legal entities engage in, not to mention their ownership structure, makes resolution difficult. The very largest U.S. banks, to use an extreme example, have hundreds of legal entities operating under their command. In addition, numerous partnerships, special-purpose vehicles, and other financial structures exist to facilitate complex financial transactions.

Second, the activities of large banks fall under the jurisdiction of many legal and supervisory regimes. These regimes might differ in important ways after failure. Banks typically come under the jurisdiction and rules of the deposit insurer. Securities firms in the United States are resolved under a legal regime specific to their organization and activities. Other legal entities of the firm, including holding companies, could face a standard bankruptcy code. The challenge of coordinating resolution under all of these rules and regimes could encourage creditors to race to protect their interests, even if that step makes resolution more difficult. The intersection of law and geography could also make resolutions more disorderly. The failure of a firm with operations in a number of countries may lead to unequal treatment of the domestic institution and its creditors vis-à-vis its foreign operations. Again, a lack of clarity in legal regimes could lead to actions that make it hard to resolve failures without government protection of creditors.

Clearly, the wide reach of large, complex financial institutions made possible by advances in technology requires cooperation among supervisors to avoid a disorderly resolution. In our experience, however, coordination among supervisors is challenging. In theory, the consolidation of supervisory powers in a single agency might mitigate such problems. In practice, regulatory consolidation requires significant reforms across a wide range of organizational and legal infrastructures. We simply do not have sufficient evidence to judge it a feasible option at this time.[24]

Third, and apart from the challenge of effective coordination in the resolution process, only a small number of firms could buy or even temporarily manage banking firms with a combination of highly technical operations and massive scope and scale. Yet the actual role that these firms play in payment and settlement combined with their symbolic stature likely make policymakers reluctant to allow their operations to fall dormant even for short periods of time. We cannot imagine policymakers allowing the secondary market for U.S. treasury securities, for example, to operate far below capacity for any length of time. Even if a firm is willing and able to assume key roles previously carried out by a failed bank, the successor may not have the resources (for example, computing or human)

---

24. Ferran (2002) discusses the United Kingdom's experience with a consolidated supervisor. De Swaan (2000) is skeptical of the consolidated model. Barth and others (2002) do not find a robust relationship between the organization of a supervisory agency and the performance of banks under its supervision.

or detailed knowledge of the failed firm's operations necessary to effect the transition.

Finally, the limited number of firms that operate in certain key financial markets and the relatively limited knowledge of supervisors mean that government officials likely will have to rely on parties with a conflict of interest (that is, a vested interest in the provision of TBTF protection) for expert advice. Only a small number of firms will have the expertise to determine whether the chance of spillover is real and significant or ephemeral and trivial. These are the same firms, however, that could well benefit from a bailout. At a minimum, the firms offering advice could use the information provided by the government to their competitive advantage. Both types of conflicts were observed in the treatment of Long-Term Capital Management.[25]

The combination of more complex operations and the overall increase in complexity has led some analysts to doubt the ability of policymakers to resolve the failure of a large bank without resorting to extraordinary actions, such as protecting uninsured creditors. One observer recently noted that, without some of the reforms we discuss in the second half of the book, "our financial institutions and markets operate in a world where the normal mechanisms for resolving insolvencies are wholly inadequate to cope with these systemically important institutions. Keep your fingers crossed."[26] To the degree that creditors have adopted a similar view of policymakers' intent and capabilities, the TBTF problem is becoming more severe.

Government Policies

Government policy may have increased the scope and strength of TBTF guarantees, although we believe this factor is less important than the structural and technologically driven changes just discussed. The significant number of bailouts of bank creditors over the last several years may have increased the expectations of bailouts. At the same time, we do not think that the reforms introduced by FDICIA, which some have hailed as making too big to fail a problem of the past, will put creditors at credible risk of loss.

25. Lowenstein (2000, pp. 170–76, 201–08). See Cai (2003) for a review of "front-running" during the Long-Term Capital Management crisis. Mayer (1999) discusses Long-Term Capital Management in the context of too big to fail.

26. Bliss (2002, p. 35).

Increased Bailouts

A number of analysts and policymakers believe that government has become more willing to protect bank creditors, particularly large bank creditors, over the last decade. The problem is one of precedent. An increase in protection for large bank creditors makes it more likely, all else equal, that creditors will expect such protection in the future. The United States provides an interesting example of the difficulty that policymakers face when trying to end even a minimal pattern of bailouts. The first cases in which the Federal Deposit Insurance Corporation (FDIC) officially sanctioned government support for uninsured bank creditors on an exception basis did not involve large banks. Instead, extra support was provided to creditors of small banks with African American ownership in the hope that the protection would prevent racial violence. However, an FDIC policymaker reports that these first exceptions set the precedent for bailing out creditors at larger institutions. It became harder to restrict such protection once it was provided.[27]

Unfortunately, data on the frequency of protection for uninsured creditors are incomplete, particularly with regard to protection for the largest banks most likely to be considered too big to fail. There certainly has been an increase in the number of banking crises over the past ten to fifteen years. Since the late 1970s, the World Bank reports 117 systemic banking crises in ninety-three countries.[28] One must go back to the 1920s and 1930s to find a period with as severe a set of events. Those finding that financial crises have become more frequent—although not necessarily more costly per crisis—over the last several decades view a TBTF-like policy of providing open-ended liquidity support for failing banks as one likely cause of the increase.[29]

Consistent with this explanation for a greater number of crises, the limited available data suggest that it is not uncommon for governments to protect uninsured creditors of banks. An examination of forty systemic banking crises found twenty-three countries where governments provided unlimited guarantees for bank creditors and twenty-three countries where governments provided emergency liquidity support for more than a year (the number of countries where both forms of protection was offered was not provided).[30]

27. Hetzel (1991, p. 6).
28. Caprio and Klingebiel (2003).
29. Bordo and others (2001).
30. Honohan and Klingebiel (2000, pp. 8–9).

In addition, various analysts have argued that the more expansive and frequent support for countries in financial crisis provided by the International Monetary Fund (IMF) in the 1990s, beginning with Mexico in 1994, created the expectation of future IMF "bailouts" among creditors.[31] The precedent set by the IMF, they claim, made later financial crises in Asia, Latin and South America, and Eastern Europe more likely.[32] Although concern about the precedent of IMF lending is not new to the 1990s, the scale of the rescue programs and role of the IMF in leading the rescues strike many observers as a departure from the past.[33] Anne Krueger—at the time an academic but currently the first deputy managing director of the IMF— has suggested, "It seems plausible that, especially after Mexico, bankers came to believe that the IMF would always bail them out and therefore they did not feel the need to concern themselves greatly with individual countries' economic policies. And, as contrasted with holders of equity or bonds, commercial banks do seem to have emerged with few losses."[34] Supporting the notion that IMF lending went "too far" in protecting creditors are the raft of reforms that the IMF is considering to put creditors at greater risk of loss.[35] Indeed, analysts with the IMF have argued that "limiting moral hazard to the extent possible" appears to have become an explicit policy objective of the International Monetary Fund.[36]

To be fair, the term bailout may not fully describe IMF rescue programs. Some analysts have noted that the IMF historically receives full repayment of its loans and that the interest rate subsidy provided by the IMF is relatively small. In this sense, the IMF loans are not bailouts akin to those provided by national governments to bank creditors. But for our purposes, this distinction may not be important. These same analysts recognize that IMF support can lead to moral hazard by providing the liquidity that allows national governments to provide their own expansive coverage.[37] True we cannot be absolutely confident that, absent IMF support, bank creditors in

---

31. Christiansen (2001) summarizes the literature on moral hazard and international financial crises.

32. International Financial Institution Advisory Commission (2000).

33. Eichengreen (2000, p. 15).

34. Krueger (1998, p. 2014).

35. For examples, see Professor Nouriel Roubini's renowned website, particularly under "Debate on IMF" and "World Bank Reform." See www.stern.nyu.edu/globalmacro [September 4, 2003].

36. Dell'Ariccia, Godde, and Zettelmeyer (2001, p. 2).

37. Jeanne and Zettelmeyer (2001) and Mussa (2002) discuss these points.

countries where IMF funding is made available would have taken losses. But those creditors at potential risk of loss have made the link. As one observer notes, "The fact that the strategy of investing in Russian debt securities in 1997–1998 was referred to as the 'moral hazard play' suggests that the international community's repeated resort to financial rescue packages influenced investor behavior."[38]

Expansion of Bank Powers

Some countries that allow banks to engage in a wide range of activities have witnessed an increase in mergers between banks and other financial firms.[39] The United States had rules that restricted the scope of banking activities. Financial modernization legislation passed in 1999 removed many of the previous restrictions. And increased scope of actions for banking organizations can spread the safety net. Governments might protect some creditors of a failing insurance firm affiliated with a TBTF bank in order to ensure that the failure of the insurance firm does not spill over and imperil the bank. Because of the potential increase in the number of uninsured creditors protected by the government, a number of prominent economists argue that expanding bank powers, by, for example, allowing nonbank firms to affiliate with banks, prior to undertaking reforms limiting TBTF-like coverage for uninsured bank creditors is putting the "cart before the horse."[40] Reviews of cross-industry transactions, such as the merger of Citicorp and Travelers, show an increase in shareholder wealth that is consistent with an increase in TBTF coverage.[41]

Why FDICIA Is No Fix

We have argued that TBTF is a costly problem that is getting worse. Our view may strike some knowledgeable observers as anachronistic, particularly because we have not yet referenced the reforms in FDICIA that were designed to make TBTF a thing of the past. A number of prominent observers believe that FDICIA reduces the probability of providing uninsured coverage at large banks to negligible levels.[42] It is not surprising, then,

38. Eichengreen (2000, p. 1).
39. Group of Ten (2001, p. 9).
40. Boyd (1999b); Boyd, Chang, and Smith (1998); Kareken (1983); Santomero and Eckles (2000).
41. Carrow and Kane (2002).
42. For generally favorable views, see the essays in Benston and Kaufman (1997) and Kaufman (1997b).

that advisers often direct countries looking to better manage bank risk-taking to the reforms found in FDICIA.[43]

There are aspects of FDICIA to compliment, and we discuss those aspects in our recommendations. Moreover, as noted in chapter 4, there is empirical evidence that some creditors of large banks moved from believing they had 100 percent protection to something less than that around the time FDICIA became law. Such a change in market perceptions may also help to explain why large banks hold more capital.[44]

However, in the long run, we do not think that FDICIA's core provisions to reduce TBTF coverage will do much to achieve the desired outcome or counteract the trends just described.[45] That is, we do not believe that FDICIA significantly reduces the likelihood that policymakers will provide coverage for uninsured creditors at TBTF banks. We provide an abbreviated version of our argument in this section and the full argument in appendix A.

FDICIA enacted many reforms. The core attempt to limit TBTF coverage comes from the new "least-cost" resolution process. On a routine basis, the FDIC must follow a resolution calculation that makes it much less likely that the uninsured will receive coverage. But FDICIA also creates an exception to this rule. The FDIC can protect the uninsured after a multiple-approval process. The secretary of the Treasury, after consulting with the president, must find that the lowest-cost resolution would "have serious adverse effects on economic conditions or financial stability" and that the provision of extraordinary coverage would "avoid or mitigate such adverse effects." Two-thirds of the governors of the Federal Reserve System and two-thirds of the directors of the FDIC must approve the extraordinary coverage. Coverage for the uninsured also triggers what amounts to a special tax on large banks and an investigation of the decision.

There has been no test of FDICIA's reforms because no large bank has failed since its passage. We therefore choose to evaluate its likely effectiveness by comparing its requirements to those of previous regimes, identifying what has changed, and determining if the change is likely to make TBTF protection less likely. In our view, the main difference between the ability of policymakers to protect uninsured creditors at large complex banks in the pre- and post-FDICIA world is the public involvement of the Federal Reserve and the Treasury. Establishing a cost test and allowing

43. Kaufman (1997a, p. 41).
44. Flannery and Rangan (2002).
45. Peek and Wilcox (2003) make a related point, noting that the subsidy provided by government support to bank stakeholders fell in the early 1990s, only to rise later.

exceptions based on the systemic risk criteria described in FDICIA are not new. We do not believe a more formal, more visible role for the Federal Reserve and the Treasury will contribute to a significant change in the incentives that policymakers face when confronted with the bailout decision.

We come to this conclusion based on the historical record. It appears that the Federal Reserve, Treasury, and the FDIC consulted with each other in previous bailouts of large banks. Although no formal votes were taken before FDICIA, the bailouts that resulted were subject to almost immediate public scrutiny, some of which was quite hostile and directed by Congress. In short, consultations among senior policymakers followed by public exposure did not dampen bailouts in the past (nor did previous investigations of such bailouts). Finally, we do not find a tax on large banks to recoup the costs of bailout credible. Why would policymakers be willing to tax large banks, and thus reduce their financial strength, immediately after bailing out a large bank presumably to limit the chance that its failure would impair the financial condition of these same large banks?[46] In total, we see the core attempt to circumscribe TBTF protection as having limited potential to achieve its goal.

Before turning to our reforms, we examine how well our analysis does in explaining cases where large financial firms did not receive bailouts. This examination tests our conclusions in this chapter. It also helps to determine if our recommendations are aimed at the right problem.

46. The FDIC has also argued that this tax is potentially unfair, which suggests that the tax lacks credibility. Rob Blackwell, "FDIC Plots Big-Bank Bailout Alternatives," *American Banker,* August 10, 2000.

7

Testing Our Thesis:
The Cases of Not Too Big to Fail

A convincing explanation for what motivates bailouts of creditors at TBTF institutions should also clarify cases where uninsured creditors at large financial firms do not receive government protection. Fear of systemic risk would not offer a convincing explanation for TBTF bailouts if there were numerous counterexamples where policymakers allowed creditors to lose their shirts even in the face of instability. Some analysts viewed the government's decision not to protect creditors of Enron—a significant participant in several capital markets—as evidence of a change in policy toward the creditors of large financial firms.[1] The risk to creditors increased following Enron's collapse, it is alleged, because "the size of a company that is 'too big to fail' has suddenly become larger."[2] Decisions not to bail out the uninsured creditors of Drexel Burnham Lambert and Barings Securities might also suggest a greater tolerance for financial instability among policymakers than we have implied.[3]

1. Enron was a diversified firm active in marketing and delivering commodities and financial services, energy and facilities management, and energy production and transmission. It filed for bankruptcy in December 2001. Senior managers at Enron appeared to have engaged in complex financial transactions to hide the true condition of the firm.

2. Steve Liesman, "The Outlook," *Wall Street Journal,* January 21, 2002, p. A1. Similar thoughts are found in Jim Juback, "Let's Hope Global Crossing Dies Quietly," MSN Money, 2002, at moneycentral.msn.com/content/p18244.asp [May 20, 2003].

3. Drexel, a subsidiary of Drexel Burnham Lambert Group, created the modern junk bond market, and its failure was associated with its settlement of felony insider trading charges with

We believe that the factors already identified as motivating TBTF bailouts also help to explain why creditors of these firms did not receive special protection. Government protection was not forthcoming, at first blush, for two reasons. First, and most important, the failure of the firms was not generally viewed as posing significant systemic risk. Second, the institutional features that facilitate TBTF bailouts were not present.

Our review of these cases of no bailout is simplified. We do not mean to suggest that distinctions between financial firms that receive bailouts and those that do not are black and white. Some of the specific factors that we think make bailouts more likely, such as considerable complexity of the financial firm's structure and operations, were also present in cases of no bailout. And it is not simply a matter of letting the firms fail; the actions of supervisors made spillovers less likely and therefore gave them additional comfort in imposing losses on creditors. As such, policymakers who want to manage the TBTF problem better should continue the current practice of looking to these cases for instruction.

Systemic Risk

Policymakers made examination of potential systemic risk a core aspect of their analysis in many of the prominent cases where bailouts were not provided. It appears that they found the threat of such risk too small or too easily managed to justify a bailout. In the case of Barings, the executive director of the Bank of England noted, "There was just the possibility that the collapse of Barings would have carried right through the financial system with horrific effects. However, as we looked through the events and the markets, we could not persuade ourselves that there was a real enough risk to justify our seeking to apply public funds in support of the institution. . . . I don't think it can be said too often that the risk of serious systemic disturbance was the key consideration for us."[4] Particularly important in the calculus of the Bank of England were the limited bilateral exposure of firms to Barings and the idiosyncratic cause of Barings' demise. These factors suggested to policymakers that its failure would not spill over to other firms.[5]

---

the U.S. government and weakness in the junk bond market. Barings, a subsidiary of Barings PLC, was a securities firm whose failure was associated with massive losses incurred by a so-called rogue trader. We oversimplify our discussion by referring to the failure of subsidiaries. The holding companies of these entities, along with some subsidiaries, also declared bankruptcy or otherwise ceased to exist as independent entities following these debacles.

4. Quinn (1995).

5. Hoggarth and Soussa (2001); Persaud (2002).

The Federal Reserve also asserted that measures of systemic risk explain its decision to reject extraordinary protection for the creditors of Drexel (and explain its decision to provide such protection in other cases). This point is made clearly in an exchange between Congressman Jack Brooks, then chairman of the House Judiciary Committee, and Alan Greenspan, chairman of the Board of Governors of the Federal Reserve System, in the context of a discussion of too big to fail and Drexel.

> *Chairman Brooks:* If the investment house in question had been Merrill Lynch or Smith Barney instead of Drexel Burnham, would that have changed the Federal Reserve's decision to stand aside and allow bankruptcy to continue?

> *Chairman Greenspan:* If the conditions were the same financially in all respects, our actions would have been the same. Our actions were based solely on our considerations of the nature of the impact of that firm and its financial unraveling on the overall financial system. That's our key concern, and in many respects it really is our sole fundamental concern, and it would not have changed irrespective of the nature of the institution that was involved.[6]

Finally, influential observers have made similar claims regarding the absence of systemic risk in the case of Enron. Standard and Poor's noted shortly after Enron's bankruptcy filing, "It does not appear to have the kind of systematic impact that would give it too big to fail status. While some of the exposures may be material, they do not appear, at least on the basis of initial reports, to be life threatening to any institution."[7] Federal Reserve officials made comments to that same effect.[8]

These cases also indicate that policymakers examine the more specific factors we identify as important in deciding if and when to bail out uninsured creditors.[9] The firms not receiving bailouts had simpler corporate structures, a smaller presence in derivative markets, and a smaller scale relative to institutions that received bailouts. Even if their activities and structure were complex, these firms had a relatively small presence in

6. U.S. House of Representatives (1990, p. 106).

7. Platts Global Energy (2001).

8. Sophia Barker, "Fed Reassures on Enron Fall," *Telegraph*, December 6, 2001. More generally, see Greg Ip and Jathon Sapsord, "Bailout Is Unlikely If Enron Goes Under, As U.S. Thinks Impact Would Be Limited," *Wall Street Journal*, November 29, 2001.

9. Herring (2003).

traditional, commercial bank–like activities, an important point for policy-makers who view banks as unique or special sources of systemic risk. In sum, the activities and organizational structure of these firms raised red flags for policymakers, but the firms were simply not far enough along the continuum to tip the scales to a bailout.

To make this point more concrete, one could contrast cases such as Barings and Drexel, where concerns about systemic risk were small or manageable, with the failure of Long-Term Capital Management (LTCM), another very prominent nonbank financial firm, in the 1990s.[10] In the LTCM case, public authorities were convinced that liquidation would lead to spillovers that were undesired and, for the most part, avoidable through the collective action of government and creditors.[11] These spillovers would have arisen, it is argued, because of a number of the issues we have already identified as encouraging TBTF bailouts, such as the massive overall scale of LTCM's activity, the significant activity of LTCM in derivative markets, the similarity of exposures between LTCM and other large financial firms, and the large, direct exposures of banks to LTCM.[12] The response by the Federal Reserve System to LTCM would not fall under our definition of a TBTF bailout. Nonetheless, the Fed's close involvement in this case further supports our claim that fear of financial market instability drives government response to the failure of financial firms.

Institutional Factors

A deposit insurance system can increase the likelihood of TBTF bailouts by providing a source of funds that policymakers can access quickly to protect even the uninsured creditors of banks, a point we discuss in chapter 8 in greater detail. The absence of government-insured deposits, therefore, implies less likelihood of bailouts. While firms such as Drexel or Enron might have carried out some bank-like activities and offered products that could substitute, for example, for bank loans, these firms did not have bank charters and were not resolved by the deposit insurer. Observers have pointed to such institutional differences to explain why the creditors of these prominent failed firms did not receive government protection: "The

---

10. For such a comparison, see Richard Waters, "Meriwether: Emperor Stripped Bare," *Financial Times*, September 25, 1998.

11. Greenspan (1998b).

12. Edwards (1999) discusses many of these factors.

availability of deposit insurance funds may well lead to the treatment of a bank failure as a systemic risk problem because of the easy availability of funds when no systemic risk exists. One wonders if the Barings Bank failure would have been treated as a systemic risk problem had it happened to a U.S. bank where regulators have easy access to 'free' funds to solve any problem. How would the Drexel Burnham and Lambert insolvency have been handled if it had been a bank?"[13]

The chairman of the Securities and Exchange Commission (SEC) at the time that Drexel was resolved also noted the importance of these institutional features in preventing TBTF bailouts.[14] For example, in explaining to Congress his position on too big to fail in relation to the Drexel case, the SEC chairman highlighted his agency's inability to provide funds to the firms it supervises. Instead, the SEC pressures failing firms to achieve compliance with capital rules or forces them to liquidate.

A second institutional factor that could have played a role in cases where federal support was not forthcoming is the view of the policymaker responsible for the bailout decision. In the case of Drexel, the chairman of the SEC, speaking for himself, avowed strong opposition to special government protection for uninsured creditors of failed financial firms. We discuss the potential importance of this factor in chapter 8, where we recommend that elected officials appoint conservative policymakers to positions that have influence over the decision to bail out creditors.

Finally, the ethos of an institution can potentially reach beyond the views of any single appointed leader and influence bailout decisions. For example, central banks sometimes are believed to attach a higher cost to financial market instability than agencies that do not view management of instability as a primary charge. Deposit insurers or bank regulators may develop a culture largely supportive of bailouts, viewing them as the reasonable first response to preventing instability. Such institutional differences, rather than the predilection of a single leader, may help to explain bailout decisions.[15]

Gray Areas

We have simplified our story in several ways that may make it appear as if the decision to avoid bailing out certain firms while supporting creditors of

13. Kovacevich (1996).
14. Breeden (1990, p. 146).
15. Mayer (1997).

others is straightforward. This is not the case. Some participants in the no-bailout decisions we have reviewed apparently had serious enough concerns about the potential losses to which policymakers exposed creditors, and the related spillover effects, that they only reluctantly allowed uninsured creditors to take their hits.[16] We are also generalizing from a very few cases. Factors specific to these cases that we have not discussed—such as the perception that Drexel or Barings "had it coming" due to poor management, weak internal control, and economic conditions at the time—could have played a meaningful role in the bailout decision.

Moreover, other points certainly take away from the cases beyond our emphasis on what motivates bailouts. Although the activities and organizational attributes that we think make bailouts more likely were not overwhelming in cases like that of Barings, they still were present and posed real challenges to policymakers. As a result, retrospectives of the no-bailout cases provide some of the lessons learned that inform our recommendations.[17] Some of these cases, for example, suggest the need for better systems to coordinate the sharing of information across supervisory regimes (within and across countries) and to address problems raised by financial firms facing a wide array of bankruptcy regimes, two issues we review in more detail in the next chapter.

The fact that policymakers allowed these firms to go down without extraordinary protection for uninsured creditors does not imply a laissez-faire approach to their resolution. Indeed, supervisory agencies took a number of actions that reduced the threat of systemic risk and made bailouts less necessary. The Bank of England, for example, established special processes to settle transactions for Barings when counterparties of the firm were reluctant to use standard methods, such as paying into accounts Barings held at correspondents.[18] Likewise, a host of supervisory agencies took actions to ensure an orderly liquidation of Drexel's assets.[19]

Policymakers have learned and will continue to learn from cases where creditors did not receive government bailouts. Nonetheless, our main point still holds. Our abbreviated review of cases where firms did not receive bailouts suggests that we have identified the right factors as motivating bailouts. This conclusion also suggests that our recommendations aimed at these motivational factors are, at a minimum, pointed in the right direction. We now turn to the recommendations.

16. See, for example, Breeden (1997, p. 84).
17. For examples, see Board of Banking Supervision (1995).
18. Quinn (1995).
19. Breeden (1990).

Options

In this second part, we describe and recommend options for credibly reducing expectations of TBTF coverage. We begin by making the case that policymakers can, in fact, make a credible commitment to impose losses on creditors of TBTF banks (chapter 8). We rely on the historical experience of monetary policy where policymakers accomplished what some viewed as an impossible task: establishing a credible commitment to low inflation. Based on this monetary policy experience, we make our first recommendation: Policymakers who will give serious consideration to the moral hazard costs of bailouts should be appointed to the positions that grant and reject TBTF coverage.

We then move on to discuss the legal and policy foundation that countries should have in place when trying to reduce TBTF expectations (chapter 9). In addition to basic reforms—such as establishing and enforcing property rights—we recommend that government create budgets recognizing the potential liabilities created when bailouts of TBTF creditors are likely. These reforms could help to address the personal motivations that might lead to bailouts.

After establishing the foundation, we make recommendations that address too big to fail more directly. Credible commitments to not bail out creditors require policies that reduce policymakers' incentives to provide bailouts in the first place. We argue in part 1 that policymakers' primary motivation for providing bailouts is to prevent the failure of one bank from spilling over and causing the failure of other banks. In chapters 10, 11, and 12, we recommend policies that reduce the fear of, and potential for, spillover failures. Chapter 10 reviews options for reducing the uncertainty associated with a large bank failure. Chapter 11 analyzes options for reducing the losses that large bank creditors suffer at failure. Chapter 12 discusses reforms that make it less likely that payment systems would propagate the failure of one bank to another.

In chapter 13, we discuss alternative options for addressing too big to fail. Although there is some merit to these various options, we ultimately find them lacking. We think that policymakers, therefore, should put a lower priority on pursuing them. The options in chapter 13 receive a more complete discussion in appendixes A through D. The conclusion (chapter 14) summarizes our main points in a couple of pages.

8

Can the Problem Be Addressed?

We have argued that policymakers can only reduce TBTF expectations by credibly reducing their incentive to bail out uninsured
creditors at large banks. Other observers view the TBTF problem as more
intractable. For example, former vice chairman of the Federal Reserve, Alan
Blinder, recently argued, "Everyone knows that there are institutions that
are so large and interlinked with others that it is out of the question to let
them fail."[1] The representatives of small banks in the United States have
long argued that too big to fail is difficult to fix, and when a recent
appointee to the Board of Governors of the Federal Reserve System argued
that no bank should be too big to fail, a publication on central banks noted,
"Perhaps fortunately, nobody in the markets actually believes that doctrine,
but political correctness never did have much to do with the real world, did
it?"[2] Our conversations with domestic policymakers and with multilateral
lending organizations suggest that this skeptical view is not unusual.

Our specific reform proposals and their justifications serve as the primary response to such claims. But before discussing them, we respond
more generally by pointing to other examples where policymakers in the

---

1. Rob Blackwell, "'Too Big to Fail' Deniers Have a Tough Audience," *American Banker*,
June 4, 2001.
2. Guenther (2001); Central Bank Newsmakers, "Bernanke and Kohn Accept," August 9,
2002 (www.centralbanking.co.uk/newsmakers/news09082002.htm [January 2003]).

United States and elsewhere accomplished what was previously viewed as impossible. While there are other examples, such as the elimination of so-called economic regulation, the most powerful and relevant example for our purposes comes from monetary policy.[3]

In this chapter, we briefly describe how the Federal Reserve established a credible low-inflation monetary policy following the high-inflation period of 1975 to 1981. The point of this discussion is to demonstrate that policymakers can gain credibility if they behave in a time-consistent manner. Based on the monetary policy example, we argue that appointment of conservative policymakers "constitutionally" opposed to TBTF intervention combined with explicit announcements, or possibly legislation signaling a regime change, can help to put market participants on notice that their probability of loss in the event of the failure of a large bank has increased. We also discuss the policy of constructive ambiguity and find it wanting as a method for addressing too big to fail.

Monetary Policy Credibility

It is hard to imagine public pronouncements of central bankers that do not mention their strong desire for a low-inflation environment. Indeed, discussions about monetary policy in 2003 have focused on deflation. We often forget that, less than a generation ago, the conventional wisdom maintained that double-digit inflation was a permanent feature of U.S. economic performance. A few examples of this conviction perhaps will suffice. Economist Irving Friedman of First Boston Corporation indicated in an interview with Dow Jones News Service–*Wall Street Journal* in October 1980 that "the forces causing inflation have ceased to be temporary. What's changed, he contends, is 'the basic societal definition of what a human being is entitled to,' creating 'a fundamental, long-term gap between what people want and what economies can produce.'" Similarly, former Federal Reserve Bank of Minneapolis president Mark Willes, at the time chief financial officer of General Mills, said to Dow Jones a year later: "The probability is still reasonably high that inflation will either stay high or rise a little bit over the foreseeable future." Finally, in its February 1982 report to Congress on monetary policy and the economy, the Federal Reserve stated, "The behavior of financial markets and other evidence strongly suggest the

---

3. Derthick and Quirk (1985) discuss deregulation.

continued existence of considerable skepticism that progress in reducing inflation will be maintained."[4]

Underpinning these opinions was the view that the Federal Reserve was either unwilling or unable to take the steps necessary to restore price stability. Reflective of this environment, inflation at the consumer level ran 10 percent a year over the period 1977–81 and proceeded at a 9 percent pace at the wholesale level over a comparable period. During these years, interest rates reached nearly 14 percent on ten-year treasury bonds, more than 16 percent on a typical A-rated corporate bond, and more than 15 percent on thirty-year fixed-rate mortgages.

Paul Volcker, who became chairman of the Fed in 1979, set out to reduce inflation and to lower expectations of future inflation through the only means available, namely restrictive monetary policy. But the Volcker Fed did not conduct monetary policy in the typical way. In a sharp break with tradition, and in an effort to overcome inertia and an institutional reluctance to raise interest rates rapidly, Volcker adopted a monetarist approach that emphasized modest growth targets for the monetary aggregates. The policy change was announced on a Saturday, following an unscheduled, face-to-face meeting of the Federal Reserve's Federal Open Market Committee. It was, of course, well known that Volcker was not a monetarist, so the fact that he initiated this step illustrated the gravity of the situation and delivered a much-needed dose of shock therapy. Moreover, Volcker and his colleagues remained steadfast as interest rates escalated and business activity deteriorated.

The importance of the move to a monetarist policy cannot be overestimated. This step represented a sharp break with the past and signaled to financial market participants and others that the Federal Reserve had at last become serious about reducing inflation. Furthermore, in addition to the unambiguous signal inherent in the change, targeting the monetary aggregates provided a direct means of moving from statements to action and also embodied a ready way for government officials, the media, and the public to monitor policy.

The Federal Reserve was unusually clear about its intentions. Thus, in its February 1980 report to Congress, the Federal Reserve asserted, "Monetary policy clearly has a major role to play in the restoration of price stability. Regardless of the source of the initial impetus, inflation can be sustained over the long run only if the resulting higher level of dollar expenditures is

4. Board of Governors of the Federal Reserve System (1982, p. 41).

accommodated through monetary expansion. The Federal Reserve is determined not to provide that sustenance but will adhere instead to a course, in 1980 and beyond, aimed at wringing the inflation out of the economy over time."[5] And similarly, in its report of July 1980, the Federal Reserve stated, "A primary and continuing goal of monetary policy must be to curb the accelerating inflationary cycle."[6]

What made this objective so challenging was its short-run costs and the pressure to reverse course that it engendered. In particular, the United States endured a serious recession in 1980–82, with unemployment nationwide climbing to nearly 11 percent of the labor force at its peak and with minority unemployment considerably higher. The economy contracted nearly 9 percent in real terms over the seven quarters ending with the third quarter of 1982. At the same time, inflation dropped below 4 percent by 1982 and stayed there for several years, so there was little doubt that rapid progress was being made.

Paul Volcker's leadership in arresting inflation was essential. Volcker had the courage and the independence of mind to tackle a problem that had been undermining U.S. economic performance, recognizing that, for a time, policy was likely to exacerbate rather than ameliorate deterioration in business activity. It should be recalled that President Carter's appointment of Volcker as Fed chairman stemmed from a sense of desperation rather than from a strong personal preference. In Volcker, the administration recognized it was getting a man unlikely to bow to political considerations. But, as time passed, Volcker did a masterful job of building and maintaining a reasonable degree of public support for a highly restrictive and painful policy. This step, too, was essential, for without public support policy cannot be sustained in a democracy.

In any event, growth in real economic activity resumed in late 1982 and continued until mid-1990, when the Gulf War recession began. And inflation continued to move lower on average through much of the 1980s and through the 1990s as well. Throughout these two decades, monetary policymakers continued to emphasize, in word and deed, their ongoing commitment to a stable, low-inflation environment.

A typical example is reported in the minutes of the August 16, 1994, meeting of the Federal Open Market Committee. The minutes read, in part, "In the Committee's discussion of policy for the intermeeting period

5. Board of Governors of the Federal Reserve System (1980a, p. 30).
6. Board of Governors of the Federal Reserve System (1980b, p. 49).

ahead, the members agreed that a prompt further tightening move was needed to provide greater assurance that inflationary pressures in the economy would remain subdued. The members recognized that the Committee's earlier policy actions were exerting some restraining effects and that further lagged effects from those actions could be expected. Even so, the underlying strength in demand and narrow margins of slack in the economy pointed to a considerable risk of further inflation pressures in the absence of additional policy tightening." Accordingly, policy was adjusted further, the fifth tightening move of 1994. These actions were taken with Alan Greenspan at the helm of the Federal Reserve and demonstrate the underlying continuity that characterized U.S. monetary policy from 1979 into the succeeding century.

There seems little doubt that, over time, the congruence between policy statements and actions succeeded in convincing private sector decision-makers that low inflation was in fact a policy commitment on which they could rely. In turn, as their credibility grew, policymakers found it increasingly easy to maintain low inflation. The virtuous circle we alluded to in chapter 2 had been established.

Credibility assisted monetary policy in at least two ways. As credibility increased, market participants became considerably less concerned than formerly about transitory accelerations in the growth of money supply or other precursors of inflation, and thus inflationary expectations generally became quiescent. Second, and related to this, the short-run relation between growth and inflation became more favorable. Thus the economy was able to grow rapidly for a sustained period and to achieve higher levels of resource utilization with persistently modest inflation, a result largely unanticipated and virtually inexplicable without the diminution of inflation expectations.

Although today we take low inflation for granted, the environment was vastly different less than a generation ago. Monetary policy may not have accomplished the impossible, but it did, to the surprise of many astute observers, restore price stability through the combination of courageous and effective leadership and a dramatic change in policy regimes that embodied and demonstrated a new and deep-seated commitment. Appointment of conservative policymakers—in the sense that they will push for lower inflation than might the average person—is now a staple suggestion of both analysts and elected officials.[7]

7. Ireland (2002); Rogoff (1985).

TBTF Credibility

We and others find much to learn from the monetary policy experience when it comes to designing and maintaining a credible policy to limit TBTF bailouts.[8] Most important, policymakers can establish credibility even when they face a history of actions that undermine the goal. And, in that vein, personalities matter in establishing credibility and overcoming the pressure to bail out creditors. This pressure was nicely captured by the former research director at the Chicago Federal Reserve Bank: "I frequently recommended to certain policymakers that they should take no action. They wondered why they hired me. I always recommended no change. Their point was perhaps well taken, because when you are in these situations, you are expected to take actions to solve problems. If you do not act, you appear not to be doing your job."[9] Despite good intentions, when confronted with a potential crisis at a large bank, policymakers usually take an attitude of "not on my watch" or "not in my district," leaving credibility in shambles.

Based on these lessons, we offer two ways to establish credibility for actions that limit TBTF protection. First, appoint "conservative" bank regulators—that is, policymakers who have demonstrated a predilection for giving serious consideration to the costs of TBTF bailouts and an ability to reject bailouts where appropriate. Although this might seem a straightforward recommendation, it is likely to prove difficult to implement. Such a policymaker must possess traits beyond a preference for free market solutions to be successful—otherwise, most academic economists would make good candidates. Moreover, it is not sufficient, as some argue, simply to direct the policymaker to act "conservatively."[10] The policymaker has to believe these views in order to be effective in the face of fire.

Given prevailing TBTF precedents, a policymaker selected to rein in too big to fail needs to have a good deal of "intestinal fortitude" to ward off pressures for assistance. In this regard, it would be helpful if the policymaker had extensive hands-on experience in the financial markets, for this would add to the credibility of the argument that extralegal protection is unnecessary to preserve financial stability. The ability to persuade others, both in government and among the general public, that it is reasonable to refrain from TBTF coverage is another valuable attribute.

8. See Goodfriend and Lacker (1999) for a similar approach and conclusion.
9. Hunter (1999).
10. Blinder (1997).

Finally, it would also be desirable if the policymaker had some prior experience in dealing with financial disruptions. This is, again, partially a matter of personal credibility, but it is also the case, we think, that such experience helps the policymaker form a judgment about the degree of protection required to maintain stability. Although we hope and expect that the conservative policymaker will be skeptical about the need for extraordinary protection, we also recognize that, on some occasions, our preferred appointee will rightly find such protection to be justified. A healthy skepticism about bailouts, not a refusal to contemplate them in dire conditions, defines the conservative policymaker.

One of the roles such a policymaker should play is to build support for policies that put uninsured creditors and others similarly positioned at genuine risk of loss. In this vein, a second suggestion to raise the bar for too big to fail is to signal a major regime change, as the Federal Reserve did when it embraced monetarism to combat inflation. The optimal form of this commitment is not obvious, but, in light of the discussion of the Federal Deposit Insurance Corporation Improvement Act of 1991 (FDICIA) in the previous chapter, the policymaker could announce plans to reform the legislation to make TBTF bailouts less likely. The reforms could follow some of the ones we suggest, although the key is putting the uninsured on notice by establishing an easily monitored commitment. The public thus could judge adherence to the new regime.

Appointment of conservative policymakers is unlikely to be sufficient taken alone, and indeed our whole approach emphasizes that a plethora of policy changes will be required to limit significantly the proclivity for TBTF coverage. Nevertheless, installation of conservative policymakers may serve to limit the requests for TBTF assistance, since it will be known in advance that such requests may well be denied. Further, such policymakers may be particularly effective in resisting attempts to expand government assistance to cases where TBTF considerations should not even arise. In this vein, it is comforting to see recent signs that elected officials consider policymakers' views on too big to fail when deciding on their appointments. Both the current vice chairman of the Federal Reserve System and the chairman of the Federal Deposit Insurance Corporation were asked specifically to comment on the view that too big to fail is intractable during their confirmation hearings.[11] The long-serving chairman of the Federal Reserve System, Alan

---

11. Ferguson and others (2001). Rob Blackwell and Michele Heller, "Sarbanes to Take on 'Too Big to Fail,'" *American Banker*, June 18, 2001, p. 1.

Greenspan, is also well known for preferring limited use of government resources to bail out creditors.

Constructive Ambiguity

Instead of appointing conservative policymakers and taking explicit action to demonstrate commitment, some think the best we can do is to follow a policy of "constructive ambiguity." This term refers to general statements by policymakers that the government will not routinely bail out creditors of large banks, with little attempt to explain the specific conditions that would make such bailouts unlikely. The aim is to throw doubt rather than to clarify why creditors should view themselves at risk of loss. As the reported originator of the term puts it, "While the doctrine of 'constructive ambiguity' as to whether, when, and how central banks will resort to extraordinary actions in the face of financial disturbances is intellectually unappealing, it serves the very useful purposes of mitigating moral hazard problems while preserving a desirable degree of policy flexibility."[12]

Rather than viewing constructive ambiguity as the only viable alternative to TBTF coverage, we view it as having significant shortcomings and do not recommend it. There is a set of constructive actions that can and should be taken to reduce too big to fail and the resource misallocations accompanying it. And there are additional reasons not to follow the path of constructive ambiguity.

From one perspective, constructive ambiguity is an unnecessarily costly policy if policymakers rarely will address a large bank's failure through bailout. If policymakers do not take concrete steps to convince policymakers of their anti-TBTF bailout position, they may unwittingly give creditors more confidence of receiving a bailout than is deserved. That is, policymakers opposed to TBTF bailouts should clearly say so and take actions consistent with such statements. Such communication and behavior could even shield policymakers from ex post criticism of their actions and make the virtuous cycle more likely.

From another perspective, one might argue that ambiguity is better than an explicit extension of the safety net in that it will produce more market discipline, at least initially. But this honeymoon period will come to an end or at least be greatly attenuated once a bailout occurs. Driving a strategy of ambiguity, in our experience, is a desire to keep the door open as wide as

---

12. Corrigan (2001). See Freixas (1999) for a model justifying constructive ambiguity.

possible for future bailouts, a point not lost on creditors. Assuming that policymakers do not act randomly, the delivery of TBTF coverage will effectively eliminate much of the ambiguity, and market participants will come to learn who is covered and under what circumstances. Moreover, with ambiguity, bailouts effectively trick those who believed the government would adhere to its commitment, a result some consider inequitable.[13]

These steps, although helpful, will not in and of themselves deal effectively with too big to fail. A broader array of tools is required, especially tools that address the incentives driving policymakers to TBTF coverage. The next several chapters delve into these matters in detail.

13. Lamm (2001).

9

Creating the Necessary Foundation

Basic institutional and legal arrangements appear to play an important role in a country's economic performance. Countries that have, for example, legal systems that protect property rights have better-developed financial intermediation and higher levels of growth than those that do not. As we discuss with regard to deposit insurance, there may also be a link between legal and institutional factors and banking crises, although this remains subject to disagreement.[1]

We believe that the same basic foundation is necessary for effective management of too big to fail. We doubt that policymakers can credibly commit to limit TBTF protection when property rights are weak or not enforced and corruption is rampant. Without the rule of law, explicit and implicit government guarantees may be the only way to draw funds into the banking system. Such guarantees may also facilitate corrupt practices, such as providing state support and resources to a favored elite.

This basic foundation is necessary, but not sufficient, to effectively manage too big to fail. More advanced institutions and laws need to play a role in TBTF management. Examples of this second layer include rules governing bankruptcy of commercial firms, privatization of state-owned enterprises, and effective accounting standards. Without rules governing the

1. For examples, see Levine (1999); Levine, Loayza, and Beck (2000).

orderly resolution of weak commercial firms, such as a bankruptcy code, governments may end up encouraging banks to keep weak firms afloat. In the long run, support for insolvent firms could deplete the capital of banks and require bailouts.[2] Establishment and enforcement of antitrust statutes could also indirectly manage concerns about TBTF expectations.[3]

The value and virtues of these elements of the infrastructure largely speak for themselves, and so we do not dwell on them. Instead we focus on two other aspects of a foundation for improving management of too big to fail: deposit insurance and government budgeting for contingencies.

The available evidence suggests that a limited deposit insurance program could reduce TBTF protection in countries with the foundation just described. However, explicit deposit insurance might actually increase the likelihood of expansive coverage in countries with less well-developed legal and institutional arrangements.

The importance of improved budgeting became clear after the unexpected collapse of several Asian Tigers in the late 1990s. In these cases, the red flags associated with previous financial crises were not evident. Inflation, for example, was low. Perhaps more important, government budgets appeared to be in fiscal balance.[4] Only in the aftermath of the crisis did it become clear that the reported accounting balances of countries' fiscal budgets were misleading. Specifically, the willingness of countries to provide TBTF coverage led governments to assume contingent claims and potentially large future costs.[5] Government budgets did not disclose these potential costs.

Incomplete budgetary disclosure and accounting, in our view, reduce policymakers' incentives to recognize the size of potential losses and enact reforms to limit expectations of TBTF coverage. The old cliché that "you can't manage what you don't measure" rings true in this case. As a result, we believe that budgetary accounting and reporting reforms should be one focus of reforms to better manage too big to fail. Recognizing the potential challenges of and resistance to enacting profound changes in budgetary practices in a short period of time, we provide a range of recommendations for improved budgeting that allow for a phased-in approach appropriate for the sophistication of a country's specific circumstances.

2. Robert E. Litan ("Bankruptcy Bailout Could Fix Asia's Woes," *Newsday*, March 4, 1998) stresses the importance of establishing bankruptcy codes.

3. Vives (2001).

4. Krugman (1998).

5. Claessens and Klingebiel (2002).

Deposit Insurance Programs

Too big to fail is an extension of a country's formal and informal deposit insurance system.[6] The frequency and degree to which policymakers violate restrictions on deposit insurance coverage, or any other government insurance program for that matter, color creditors' expectations of TBTF protection. Both the decision on whether to have deposit insurance and the specific structure of the insurance program affect TBTF management.

The TBTF-related argument against explicit deposit insurance focuses on the moral hazard it creates. Some countries, notably Japan, have at some point established deposit insurance regimes that cover all deposits, essentially formalizing a good part of a TBTF policy. But even a more limited deposit insurance program can make TBTF protection more likely to the degree it encourages excessive risk-taking or suggests a high level of concern about bank failures to creditors. Deposit insurance also provides a handy fiscal mechanism the government can use to protect creditors of large banks, thereby facilitating coverage of the uninsured.

Staff of the International Monetary Fund (IMF), in contrast, recommend that countries establish guaranteed deposit insurance programs with clear caps on coverage.[7] They believe that countries with legal limits on protection for bank creditors face less moral hazard, presumably because limits reduce the likelihood of providing excessive support.[8] Setting a limit on coverage, from this perspective, could signal a new policy commitment to less TBTF support.

Analysts have evaluated these arguments by examining experience across a number of countries with formal and informal deposit insurance systems. Results are mixed, although a growing consensus suggests that country-specific factors and history should guide policymakers' decisions.[9] For example, countries with both a strong legal and institutional foundation and

6. Moss (2002) discusses government guarantees on deposits in the context of government bearing of risk more generally.
7. Garcia (1999).
8. Milhaupt (1999) makes a similar point.
9. For examples of this literature, see Cull (1998); Bartholdy, Boyle, and Stover (2001); Demirgüç-Kunt and Detragiache (1997, 2000); Demirgüç-Kunt and Kane (2002); Gropp and Vesala (2001); Laeven (2002b). For an alternative view, see Eichengreen and Arteta (2000); Giannetti (2002). Institutional factors, such as deposit insurance, have little role in other models that try—not always successfully—to predict financial crisis, such as Bell and Pain (2000); Borio and Lowe (2002); Bussiere and Fratzscher (2002); Goldstein, Kaminsky, and Reinhart (2000).

a history of providing implicit coverage could more likely benefit from establishing a formal system that creates barriers against expansive coverage. In other cases, establishing a deposit insurance system might actually make bank system instability and related bailouts more likely.

The details of a deposit insurance program, and not just whether it exists, could also affect expectations of TBTF coverage. Having modest deposit insurance coverage—again assuming that deposit insurance should exist in the first place—could also facilitate limited expectations of TBTF coverage. As a result, we and several multilateral organizations favor insurance programs that restrict coverage by, for example, carefully defining which liabilities are covered, extending coverage only to small depositors at a small number of institutions, limiting deposit coverage to a small amount, and requiring coinsurance (for example, all depositors bear at least some loss when a bank fails).[10] In our view, such an approach is associated with a lower chance of banking crisis, less risk-taking, and therefore a lower chance of TBTF coverage.[11]

Perhaps most important, even a deposit insurance system that fits a country's circumstances and is well designed will not, by itself, help to effectively manage expectations of TBTF protection. For example, changes in deposit insurance in the European Union that led to an overall reduction in bank risk-taking did not change the risk-taking proclivities of the very largest banks that control the vast majority of banking assets.[12] Additional reforms are required.

Budgeting and Policymaker Incentives

The processes and rules governing the allocation of government expenditures provide important incentives for many policymakers. We refer to these sets of rules and activities as the budget process. When it functions at its best, the budget process fulfills a market-like role, inducing policymakers to set a cap on their total spending (that is, the budget constraint), identify their preferences, and then choose spending allocations that maximize utility. The price of government programs is reported to policymakers from the budgetary accounting system. As in the market system, the price guides decisions regarding the allocation of resources.

10. Evanoff (2001); Financial Stability Forum (2001a); Garcia (2000).
11. Demirgüç-Kunt and Detragiache (2000); Demirgüç-Kunt and Huizinga (2000).
12. Gropp and Vesala (2001).

mkt,
fail

The market fails when prices do not reflect the full range of costs associated with the consumption of a good or service; the price of a good or service can be too low or too high when the market fails. The budget can generate faulty prices as well when the accounting scheme does not accurately reflect the amount of resources that a given program will consume. Policymakers will allocate too many resources to a program whose real costs are understated in the same way that consumers will consume too much of a product whose price understates the real resources used in its production. Faulty prices in both cases lead to a mismatch between preferences and outcomes. The broader question of whether policymakers' decisions are consistent with their constituents' preferences remains open to debate.[13]

Clearly, one can take the analogy between budgeting and markets too far. For example, governments with the power of taxation do not face budget constraints in the same way that households and firms do. That said, the vast majority of governments face real constraints on their ability to raise funds simply because of the limited resources in their countries. Excessive spending matters to policymakers, for example, because it affects bond ratings and, potentially, the regime's political viability. In numerous countries, ranging from the United States to Sweden, voters have replaced the party in power with one advocating a slower rate of growth in spending.

If getting prices right plays a meaningful role in ensuring the proper level of government programs, then the current state of budgeting with regard to insurance contingencies helps to explain excessive coverage for the uninsured. The expected future costs from explicit and implicit government guarantees for bank creditors typically do not show up in the budget. We first discuss the deficiencies of the current budgetary treatment and then discuss reforms we think could help to correct the situation.

Deficiencies with Current Budgeting for Too Big to Fail

Most government budgets cannot recognize contingent liabilities because they are on a cash basis. The revenues of government insurance programs are recognized when cash flows in from sources such as premiums. However, the cost of the government insurance program is recognized only when a cash outflow occurs to pay off an insurance claim. A cash system could accurately reflect the financial condition of the government program

13. See Levitt (1996) for one discussion of the issue.

if the inflows and outflows of cash occur around the same time. However, the costs and outflows of an insurance program can occur at a much later date than the inflows. As a result, a cash system produces a perverse bottom line for explicit and implicit insurance programs. For example, a deposit insurance program that charges a nominal premium and does not suffer from many costly bank failures shows a profit under a cash system, even if during this same period banks make decisions that will produce enormous losses in the future.

Faulty recognition in the cash-based system leads to excessive amounts of government contingent liabilities. The oversupply will be larger as the gap between the budget costs of a program and the true economic costs increases. This gap is large for the TBTF policy because it can lead to large budget outflows, but the costs of these policies typically are reported as zero in the budget. Excessive supply of TBTF coverage would manifest itself in a number of ways, including an absence of limits on coverage, few attempts to rein in expectations of coverage, and a paucity of reforms to limit spillovers from large bank failures, to cite just a few examples. All of these signs of excessive coverage are evident today.

Budget experts have long recognized that cash-based accounting for contingent liabilities provides poor incentives for policymakers. The *Handbook of Government Budgeting*, for example, notes, "Cash accounting, which provides no budgetary signal of the need for or incentives to adopt loss-control measures, bears significant responsibility for the absence of federal efforts to align the self-interest of the insured with the need to control losses."[14] Because insurance programs appear to have no cost, policymakers naturally let the programs run themselves. Yet active management of an insurance program's exposures is crucial to limit the potential for catastrophic losses.

By sending the wrong signal, weak budgeting increases total costs to taxpayers. In a cash-based system, the act of closing and resolving a failed institution produces charges against the budget. Policymakers seeking to avoid the costs of insurance policies have a strong incentive to pressure supervisors to keep failing institutions open. In the United States, for example, Congress refused to provide funding that would have hastened the closure of insolvent thrifts. Supervisors, therefore, kept insolvent institutions open, which was costly. Closing thrifts when they became insolvent

14. Phaup and Torregrosa (1999, p. 707). Schick (2002) also discusses weaknesses with budgeting for fiscal costs.

(that is, when tangible net worth fell below zero) could have saved taxpay-ers as much as $66 billion in 1990 dollars.[15]

To provide policymakers with incentives to actively manage too big to fail, the budgetary system should reflect higher costs when expected TBTF coverage and losses increase. Expected losses to the government could rise if the condition of large banks deteriorates and if policymaker actions make coverage of the uninsured at large banks more likely. The budgetary system should also provide budgetary savings when future costs fall. Actions to reduce estimated TBTF exposure should provide tangible benefits.

Budgetary Fixes: Addressing the Arguments against Accrual Budgeting

If cash-based budgeting systems lead to a number of the problems we have outlined, the solutions should come from accounting that recognizes changes in long-term costs at the time the action producing the cost occurs. Such budgetary systems are said to be on an accrual basis. In this section, we provide details on how an accrual system for contingent liabil-ities might work and then discuss why policymakers have resisted the move to accrual budgeting (see box 9-1).

There has been resistance in moving to accrual budgeting, which is both explainable and manageable. The resistance comes from policymakers who benefit from budgetary procedures that obscure their actions and who do not want costs reflected accurately. On the one hand, it is these policy-makers whose proverbial ox is gored by the reform, and we recognize that there is no easy sell of our reform to them. On the other, policymakers who participate in the cover-up may have their careers cut short, while those who support reforms that reduce costs may prosper.

Some of the resistance could also reflect policymakers' natural resistance to having a potentially dramatic increase in the cost of government policy during their terms. An increase in cost from an accounting shift may strike policymakers as unfair if the higher costs reflect policy decisions made by a different set of policymakers from an earlier period. To address this con-cern, analysts could design the new accrual system to hold policymakers

15. U.S. Congressional Budget Office (1991b). To make matters worse, Congress later overturned the method by which supervisors kept institutions afloat. This decision was chal-lenged by acquirers of failed institutions who, in some cases, have won compensation for the congressional breach of contracts. Bierman, Fraser, and Zardkoohi (1999) and Feldman (1996) discuss these legal cases.

harmless when costs that have accrued over the years are finally recognized. Only future costs would affect current budgetary totals and decisions.

Finally, there are those who have more substantive concerns with accrual-type budgeting. We briefly raise and reject some of their objections to it. One general concern is that budgetary rules and accounting do not change policymakers' behavior. Empirical evidence supports the notion that budget rules and institutional policies do influence outcomes.[16] More specific evidence on accrual accounting and related reforms is limited but positive. The Credit Reform Act of 1990 shifted from cash accounting for government credit programs to an accrual regime. Budget analysts report that virtually all policy changes to credit programs since the reform have reduced expected losses, although data for comparisons are sketchy.[17]

A second objection to an accrual system focuses on premature cost recognition. An accrual system would have the government record costs that it may not ultimately bear because the costs are not legal responsibilities of the government or because the government can take action in the future to prevent them from becoming a reality. Recognition of the contingent costs in official government accounts, some argue, could even create the expectation that the government will continue to absorb costs for which it is not strictly liable.

In our view, an objection based on premature cost recognition is tantamount to arguing that government can credibly commit to a no-TBTF policy by feigning ignorance or perhaps by engaging in a strategy of constructive ambiguity. We wish that addressing potential TBTF exposure were so easy, but neither of these tactics has worked in practice, and we therefore reject them. Requiring policymakers to recognize the cost of future TBTF coverage, in our view, could make creditors believe that policymakers will take action to avoid the budgetary pain.

A third concern is that accrual accounting requires analysts to make estimates of the size of the government's contingent liability, particularly its implicit liability, that amount to educated guesses. Precise determinations of the probability that a large bank will fail or that creditors of the bank will receive TBTF coverage are very difficult to make. But all government budgets include an estimate of contingent liabilities. Some budgetary systems just make that estimate less transparent. In a cash-based budget, for

16. Hahm and others (1992); Poterba (1997). Jagger and Hull (1997) review how changes in budgetary practices changed policy.

17. Phaup and Torregrosa (1999).

Box 9-1. *An Example of Accrual Budgeting*

Budget analysts have developed a number of methods for recording contingent liabilities on an accrual basis. We summarize one specific proposal to show that accrual budgeting reform can be designed and implemented and to contrast more clearly the incentives of an accrual system with those of a cash-based system. With a meaningful accrual accounting system, the costs of deposit insurance in 1992 would have been significantly different than reported with the cash-based system ($50 billion versus $80 billion).

The specific proposal summarized was offered by the administration of George H. W. Bush in the fiscal year 1993 federal budget for deposit insurance and other federal insurance programs.[1] The key to the Bush reform proposal was the creation of an on-budget program account that recorded accrued costs (see figure 9-1 for a highly stylized flow chart of the proposal). For deposit insurance, the program account would record "the amount by which the resolution costs for insolvent firms increases between the beginning of the year and the date of their closure or, for those that remain open, the end of the year." The methodology used to estimate this increase in costs was based on fairly basic financial and statistical simulations. The resolution costs were calculated on a net basis (that is, cost to the government minus expected collections).

Costs that had accrued prior to the budgetary change were accounted for in a liquidating account. Again, this account was on budget. Both accounts would make payments to an off-budget financing account. Because of its off-budget status, payments to the financing account would trigger recognition of budget outlays for the program. The off-budget financing account would record the cash flows associated with the insurance program, including the collection of premiums, the payment of claims, and the investment of assets. As a result, this accrual system would generate the annual cash flow information that some analysts find helpful. If needed, the financing account could also borrow working capital funds to pay claims that it would repay with cash inflows. Removing such cash transactions from the budget would eliminate short-term fluctuations that amount to a wash (for example, large outflows in one year to pay off creditors followed by large inflows the next year as assets are sold).

1. U.S. Office of Management and Budget (1992, pp. 273–76).

Figure 9-1. *Simplified Schematic of Accrual Accounting for Deposit Guarantees, 1992*

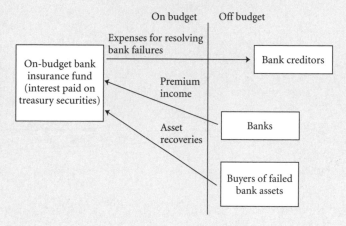

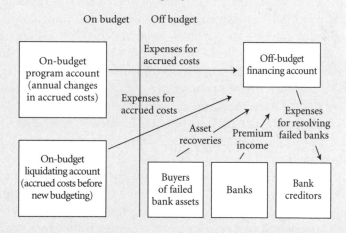

Source: Based on 1993 U.S. federal budget.

Figure 9-2. *Measures of Banking System Health, 1978–2002*

Percent of banking system assets

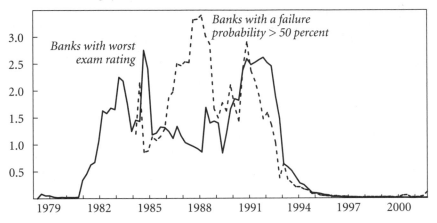

Source: Authors' calculations based on Federal Reserve exam and surveillance data.

example, the estimated cost of contingent liabilities is implicitly zero because no figure for such contingencies is recorded. Given the historical cost of TBTF bailouts, we do not believe that a standing estimate of zero is correct. Advancements in calculating the costs of the government's financial contingencies also make it harder for governments to justify their refusal to estimate the potential budgetary costs of too big to fail.[18]

A fourth concern is the potential increase in volatility in budgetary figures. Estimates of the cost of government contingencies over a long period of time captured in an accrual budget can fluctuate a great deal in the short run. Even if these measures are accurate, some analysts argue that policymakers should not have to respond frequently to changes in estimates. Cash flows, in their view, smooth out the fluctuations in a manner that allows policymakers to effectively address long-run exposure.

In contrast, we find the volatility of estimates that result from a sound estimating procedure to be important information that policymakers should consider when debating the potential exposure they assume. We might very well expect government exposure from guarantees of bank liabilities to be volatile. After all, banking conditions tend to deteriorate in a staggered, sudden fashion rather than smoothly over time. Figure 9-2 plots the percentage of banking system assets in the United States held by banks

18. These techniques are discussed in Brixi and Schick (2002).

that have received the worst safety and soundness ratings from examiners (that is, CAMEL 5). It reports a similar statistic for the banks with a probability of failure that exceeds 50 percent, as calculated by a failure prediction model used by the Federal Reserve. These plots reveal the sudden changes that can occur in the condition of the banking system. These changes are assumed to affect the exposure of the government to the failure of a large bank. Smoothing out this volatility prevents policymakers from understanding that insuring bank liabilities has consequences for short-term economic and fiscal stability.

Variations in Budgeting

Policymakers can apply accrual budgetary treatment to the contingent liabilities of potential bank bailouts in many ways. The budgetary system a country chooses should support its major objective. Some types of accrual budgeting systems may, for example, be better suited for encouraging reforms to banking policy.[19] More generally, countries do not have to move to a budgetary system that records the estimated future costs of TBTF bailouts as current costs if that step is too great a leap. Developed countries with a substantial capacity for budgeting could follow the example described earlier and use the estimates of future losses for government contingencies to trigger budgetary outlays in the current period. Countries with less analytical capacity to devote to budgeting could increase disclosures of the potential costs of too big to fail, followed by efforts to better measure the costs and, finally, by increased inclusion of these estimates in budgetary bottom lines.

The disclosures could include a range of estimates for the cost of a TBTF policy, measures of the uncertainty of the forecasts, and the key assumptions and sensitivities used to generate the forecasts. Distributing this information on a wide scale could pressure policymakers to limit future exposure before failures occur, a tactic that has been successful with some government insurance programs in the United States.[20] The World Bank has also provided useful analytical tools and training for countries choosing to follow these iterative steps.[21] As World Bank staff argue, "For international institutions, such as the World Bank and IMF, it is time to (a) extend the scope of

19. U.S. Congressional Budget Office (1991a); U.S. General Accounting Office (1997a).
20. Lockhart (1996). In contrast, see ERISA Industry Committee (1997).
21. Polackova (1998a); Brixi and Mody (2002). For an example of World Bank training, see www1.worldbank.org/wbiep/decentralization/courses/china%2006.12.00/china.htm [September 8, 2003].

their fiscal, policy, and institutional analysis beyond the budget and debt; (b) require countries to disclose information about their contingent government risks; and (c) assist countries to reform their analytical, policy, and institutional public finance frameworks to address all major fiscal risks."[22] Unfortunately, we do not believe that the multilateral institutions of either developing or developed countries have done enough to meet the three objectives.

22. Polackova (1998b, p. 25).

10

Reducing Policymakers' Uncertainty

After recognizing that they can credibly manage TBTF expectations and establishing a foundation to begin to address them, policymakers must take additional steps to reduce their incentives to bail out creditors. Specifically, they should reduce the chance that one bank's failure will lead to the failure of other banks and increase their confidence in their ability to deal with the fallout from large bank failures. Such spillovers and uncertainty are the primary motivation for bailouts of uninsured creditors at large banks. We begin our discussion of such reforms in this chapter and continue it in the next two.[1]

In this chapter, we review policies and procedures that would reduce policymakers' uncertainty about the consequences of the failure of a systemically important bank. Several factors make policymakers highly uncertain about potential spillover effects from the failure of a large bank and therefore likely to resort to creditor bailouts. Reforms that reduce such uncertainty include the following: increased supervisory planning for, and simulation of, a large bank failure; targeted efforts that reduce the likelihood and cost of failure for banks dominating payment markets; legal and

---

1. These reforms have several characteristics that influence our discussion of them. The reforms are numerous and often highly technical. In addition, a number of specialized policy and industry groups have analyzed them. As a result, we focus on just a few examples of reform and often refer to existing analysis of them.

regulatory adjustments that clarify the treatment of bank creditors at failure; and more rapid provision of liquidity to uninsured creditors.

Scenario Planning

Policymakers could reduce the uncertainty that they face when a large bank fails by knowing the potential exposures other banks have to the failing institution in advance and practicing their response to such failures. Furthermore, policymakers could put creditors at greater risk by letting them know that such stress testing and contingency planning are occurring. We now flesh out these arguments.

Supervisors and banks have long stressed the importance of business resumption and contingency planning, defined as "the process of identifying critical information systems and business functions and developing plans to enable those systems and functions to be resumed in the event of a disruption. The process includes testing the recovery plans to ensure they are effective."[2] The "Y2K" problem moved such planning from theory to practice and reinforced the need to identify events that could disrupt business and to develop methods for quickly resuming it.[3]

The high level of importance placed on the resumption of business has been accompanied by an emphasis on stress testing, defined as "the examination of the potential effects on a firm's financial condition of a set of specified changes in risk factors, corresponding to exceptional but plausible events."[4] Stress tests have become a standard risk management technique, influencing the type and size of exposures that financial institutions will bear.[5]

Contingency planning and stress testing typically are not lumped together. However, in both cases, bank managers make decisions about how they structure their operations and the risks they will assume based on these scenarios. Likewise, stress testing and contingency planning influence supervisory assessments of the risk-taking of individual banks. Supervisors judged banks that did not have clear contingency plans in the face of Y2K as unsafe and unsound. Supervisors also consider stress tests in evaluating the riskiness of a single bank (and, as we discuss, the risks posed to an entire banking system).[6]

2. Board of Governors of the Federal Reserve System (1997, p. 3).
3. Board of Governors of the Federal Reserve System (2000b, pp. 2–3).
4. Committee on the Global Financial System (2000, p. 1).
5. Committee on the Global Financial System (2001).
6. Board of Governors of the Federal Reserve System (1999b) discusses supervisory reviews of stress tests.

Because stress testing and scenario planning can reduce supervisors' uncertainty about the riskiness of banks and banking sectors, they should play a role in the management of too big to fail. Information gleaned from the simulations of large bank failure should help policymakers to minimize coverage provided to uninsured creditors without creating excessive financial instability. Simulations also should help supervisors to take steps now to make such resolutions less likely in the first place.

Supervisory Stress Testing

Supervisors should first determine if and how the failure of one large, systemically important bank could spill over to other banks and capital markets. To make the task manageable, analysts should study a small number of institutions—say, the three to five largest institutions in a country. Supervisors would first determine how a specific event—say, a stock market crash, a large shift in interest rates, or the reduction of liquidity in short-term funding markets—would affect the solvency of these institutions. Supervisors could potentially rely on existing results from specific banks for this initial screen. If these scenarios indicate a low chance of insolvency for any of the institutions under review, policymakers could have more confidence in responding to such events without bailouts.

Some initial scenarios could show one of the large institutions in the study group becoming insolvent or nearing insolvency. This result would lead to a second stage of testing: examining how the failure of one institution would affect the solvency of the two to four other institutions in the cohort. This amounts to checking out how much one bank in the cohort owes the others at a point in time—say, at the end of a business day—a task that would require a review of data from the institution and its payment processors. Over time, the review of cross-firm exposures could better account for the variation of such exposures during the day and at different points in the year.

Although the process might start off as a one-time evaluation of a small number of scenarios at a very small number of banks, we envision this exercise ultimately carried out across many scenarios and a larger range of institutions (for example, the population of large complex banking organizations). Such a significant collection of data and analysis would be costly. It could prove particularly difficult for institutions to report comprehensively on their exposure to another institution across the full range of their activities. We are sure it will take considerable time and experience to move to more comprehensive reporting, and even then the results may fall short of the ideal.

But having a public authority require such costly analysis seems justified. Individual institutions have incentives to explore their exposures to failing firms rather than to understand how their failure could affect others. The government has the incentive and the powers to measure, monitor, and mitigate potential spillovers because the taxpayer might otherwise absorb the spillover costs. Unlike the analysis for a private firm, the government would focus on spillovers and cross-institution exposure. Even imperfect information on these potential exposures would advance the knowledge and ability of policymakers to make informed decisions. Moreover, other countries report that similar data collection efforts have improved their ability to gauge the actual rather than merely the hypothesized potential for spillovers.[7]

Supervisory Contingency Planning

Whereas the steps just discussed are similar to stress testing, the next set of activities we propose is a supervisory version of contingency planning. Supervisors should develop detailed plans for addressing the failure of a large bank, test those procedures in simulations, and revise the procedures to account for test results. Supervisors should repeat the cycle regularly, given the rapidly changing operations of the largest banks. As part of the process, supervisors must identify the documents and data they will need to determine a bank's solvency and the exposures it would present to other banks at the time of failure. Such an effort should include a review of the form the data must take for supervisors to access it and the specific variables that supervisors expect the institution to have available. It may also cover issues such as the ability of supervisors to use the banks' proprietary models to value portfolios. Ultimately, supervisors must identify the gaps between what institutions can provide and what supervisors require. *We view it as of the highest priority for supervisors to eliminate such gaps.*

Given that the objective of scenario planning is to reduce coverage of the uninsured, policymakers should pay particular attention to simulating the use of a wide range of resolution options, a task made somewhat easier by the substantial literature—often practitioner focused—on bank resolution.[8] Indeed, this literature emphasizes the need for supervisors to consider resolution options (ranging from liquidation to a shift of failed bank

---

7. Blavarg and Nimander (2002). McAndrews and Wasilyew (1995) describe a highly stylized simulation for the United States.

8. For examples, see Basel Committee on Banking Supervision (2002a); Bovenzi (2002); Santomero and Hoffman (1998); U.S. Office of the Comptroller of the Currency (2001).

assets to temporary state-owned or "bridge" banks) before a large bank fails in order to respond effectively and hence not forbear. The literature also suggests that the appropriate method of resolution will depend on the case and specifics at hand.[9] The potential need to tailor the resolution bolsters the case for intensive practice and simulation, for only with such experience will those responsible for resolving a large bank feel comfortable modifying their approach and minimizing the coverage of uninsured creditors.

We think it sufficient for our purposes to establish the general goals of the planning effort and to direct supervisors to the guidelines for similar activities, such as contingency planning, that they provide to banks.[10] Supervisors should also reflect on the best-practice guidance that they and other study groups have authored. For example, a number of reports in recent years have identified the analysis in which banks should engage prior to becoming counterparties. Given that the government effectively becomes a counterparty when it offers creditors protection, this guidance should indicate the information and data that policymakers should have prior to a crisis.[11]

Our read of history as well as recent trends supports the value of scenario planning. Although federal government officials in the United States argued that contingency planning was of significant practical value, they admitted to being caught flat-footed by the timing of the run on Continental Illinois, despite what they viewed as extensive monitoring of the situation.[12] Scenario planning of the type we describe has also been the norm for central bankers in areas where they have had success, such as the what-if analysis used in the setting of monetary policy.[13] Finally, there has been a growing movement to use scenario planning to assess the vulnerability of a country to financial crisis. Stress testing is a key component of this more general approach, called macro prudential analysis.[14]

Making Scenario Planning Public

Almost as important as the planning itself is the disclosure of scenario planning to bank creditors. If policymakers only communicate the existence of scenario planning to a select group of insiders, they pass up a valuable

9. Federal Deposit Insurance Corporation (1998).
10. For one example, see Federal Financial Institutions Examination Council (1998).
11. Basel Committee on Banking Supervision (1999a); Counterparty Risk Management Policy Group (1999).
12. U.S. General Accounting Office (1997b).
13. Ferguson (2002c, p. 7).
14. For examples, see Blaschke and others (2001); Bank for International Settlements (2001).

opportunity to provide their views on moral hazard, commit themselves to imposing losses, and alter the expectations of creditors.[15] Unfortunately, whatever scenario planning supervisors and the deposit insurer have had under way has not been disclosed to supervisors in general, let alone to the public. Because heightened publicity about scenario planning would not "name names" and therefore would not encourage instability, we see little downside in making these efforts known more widely, and, in fact, we think there is considerable upside.[16]

This suggestion for greater transparency in scenario planning also reflects lessons we take away from the experience of monetary policy. During the period in which the U.S. central bank established and maintained greater credibility with regard to price stability, it also made its analysis and objectives more transparent. The greater transparency may have helped the Federal Reserve to establish its credibility. In a similar vein, going public with the steps that make coverage of the uninsured less likely could establish credibility in reducing TBTF coverage.

Clarifying Legal and Regulatory Positions

A lack of certainty with regard to the legal and regulatory standing of bank creditors—many of which are banks themselves—makes bailouts more likely. Uncertainty makes bank creditors skittish about the losses they might suffer if a bank fails. As a result, they could run to retrieve their funds or be unwilling to provide new funds, making it more likely that a large bank will suffer a sudden loss of liquidity or net worth. Policymakers fear rapid failure and related spillovers, making them more likely to offer support for uninsured creditors in such circumstances. Uncertainty also could lead creditors to suffer larger-than-expected losses. For example, creditors may find themselves unable to exercise their right to liquidate the collateral the failed bank pledged to them. High losses could also prompt bailouts.

We highlight a few examples of reforms that could reduce these unnecessary or unexpected losses.[17] One important initiative seeks to reduce

15. Kane (2001b) reviews the relationship between moral hazard and the absence of government contingency planning for financial crises.

16. Eisenbeis and Wall (2002) make a similar suggestion. They also examine challenges in implementing FDICIA, a topic discussed in appendix A.

17. See Contact Group on the Legal and Institutional Underpinnings of the International Financial System (2002) and the World Bank Insolvency Initiative (www4.worldbank.org/legal/insolvency_ini.html [December 2001]) for a discussion of many of these issues. For past and current efforts that touch on these issues, see Group of Thirty (2000).

variability in the documentation of financial contracts, specifically those for derivative products. Such variability increases the time needed to resolve the claims on a failed bank and can inadvertently prevent creditors from exercising their rights.[18]

Ensuring that creditors can enforce the terms of standard financial contracts should also reduce potential instability. In the United States, for example, many financial institutions and regulatory agencies support reforms to enforce so-called early termination and closeout netting provisions.[19] Closeout refers to the ability of a bank creditor under a financial market contract to terminate the contract on default. Netting allows the creditor to act on the total amount it is owed by (or owes to) the failed bank under all relevant financial contracts. Closeout provisions allow creditors of a large bank to avoid the lengthy bankruptcy process.[20] Netting reduces losses by preventing "cherry picking" (that is, when the bank liquidator validates financial contracts in which the failed bank made a profit, while nullifying those in which the failed bank had a loss).

Many observers believe that closeout netting could reduce the risk of spillover failures by reducing the losses creditors suffer, allowing the bank to reestablish quickly its hedging strategies, and fostering the continuation of payments. In contrast, some analysts argue that closeout netting could actually encourage instability—by leading many counterparties to unwind positions and then scramble to reestablish hedges. On balance, these concerns would not seem compelling enough to reject the reform. The need of counterparties to reestablish positions after a large bank fails would exist even if closeout netting did not.[21]

The degree to which creditors under derivative contracts in the United States benefit from closeout netting remains unclear.[22] Similar legal uncertainty may exist in some countries with regard to the use of collateral and the ability of a bank liquidator to nullify "irrevocable" payments to

18. The Bond Market Association, the International Swaps and Derivatives Association, and Global Documentation Steering Committee have played roles in addressing these concerns.

19. These reforms are briefly described in Ireland (1999).

20. The International Financial Risk Institute offers a clear definition of closeout netting: "Closeout netting is an arrangement to settle all contracted but not yet due liabilities to and claims on an institution by one single payment, immediately upon the occurrence of one of a list of defined events such as the appointment of a liquidator to that institution." See risk.ifci.ch/134740.htm [December 2001] for a discussion.

21. Bliss (2002) discusses these concerns.

22. President's Working Group on Financial Markets (1999).

creditors.[23] Certainly, some countries and even entire regions, such as the European Union, have tried to increase legal certainty in order to reduce the risk of spillovers. But we chose to discuss closeout netting because, even with what appears to be strong political support, obtaining final enactment of reforms has been challenging.

Although legal uncertainty can create the potential for spillovers in a single country, many analysts have noted that considerable uncertainty exists with the legal and regulatory treatment of creditors of large and complex multinational banks (the ones most frequently viewed as too big to fail).[24] As in the domestic case, creditors of an internationally active bank may have reason to worry that legal or regulatory systems will deny them access to or wipe out their assets. This could lead to runs, paralysis, or creditors suffering large losses. These reactions can lead to spillover failures and bailouts.

Some of the legal or regulatory uncertainty arises from a basic conflict. The shutting down of a large multinational bank occurs on a country-by-country basis where it operates or on a business-by-business basis. However, the multinational bank is managed on a more unified basis. For example, authorities in a country may try to resolve a failed multinational bank in order to maximize the return for creditors in their country (that is, ring fencing).[25] Such a parochial approach can deprive other creditors of funds, impose unexpected losses, and greatly complicate the ability of the home supervisor to maximize the returns to creditors.

Policymakers have several options for reducing uncertainty surrounding the failure of a large multinational bank.[26] First, they could harmonize laws and practices across countries, an effort that the United Nations, for example, has supported.[27] This approach seems most likely to be effective if the rules in question are quite narrowly tailored and affect a small number of banks and countries. Alternatively, harmonization may work with countries moving to common legal frameworks more generally. The European Union, for example, was able to develop the European Directive on the Reorganization and Winding up of Credit Institutions.

23. Harding (2002).
24. For examples, see Basel Committee on Banking Supervision (1992); Group of Thirty (1997, 1998).
25. Marino and Bennett (1999) discuss ring fencing in the United States.
26. Mayes, Halme, and Liuksila (2001) and Mayes and Liuksila (2003) offer a detailed plan for resolving large complex banks, while minimizing special protection for uninsured creditors.
27. Jordan and Majnoni (2002) discuss the issues raised in harmonization efforts.

Rather than trying to harmonize rules, a second approach would have individual countries clarify a priori how they approach the failure of a multinational. Although countries may choose not to maximize returns to creditors, this approach would at least minimize surprises. A third and final approach would focus on supervisory coordination and communication across countries. Less-than-ideal informal coordination and communication have led to unnecessary costs and uncertainty for creditors following recent multinational failures (for example, BCCI). In response to such concerns, multinational supervisory bodies have generated lists of "essential elements of a statement of cooperation between banking supervisors."[28] The goal of such cooperation, in our view, is to have supervisors try to maximize the returns to creditors overall, as opposed to creditors in their own country, which greater sharing of information, appointment of a lead resolving authority, and the like would make more likely. Because they may help to counter pressure that a supervisor faces to maximize returns to home-country creditors, more formal agreements among supervisors, such as a treaty on the treatment of a failed multinational bank, may better facilitate cooperation.

As in the domestic arena, some observers believe there has been inadequate progress to date in effectively addressing uncertainties associated with multinational insolvency.[29] The question is how to motivate implementation of the recommendations. We raise a couple of options to encourage discussion, recognizing that additional analysis would be required to better identify the net effects of these reforms. Capital regulation offers one model. Such regulation has provided favorable capital treatment for banks operating in countries that could legally take advantage of netting. This appears to have encouraged passage of the requisite legal codes. When countries or important interests in a country gain a tangible benefit from reducing systemic risk, they pursue such reforms more aggressively. Policymakers could implement this approach by, for example, limiting market access for banks whose home country has not adopted widely accepted legal and regulatory rules.[30]

Targeted Reforms for Dominant Payment Providers

Two banks offer the full set of services for major market participants that allow transactions involving U.S. Treasury securities to settle (that is, that

28. Basel Committee on Banking Supervision (2001a).
29. Hüpkes (2002).
30. Group of Thirty (1998).

have the proper exchange of cash for securities): the Bank of New York and J. P. Morgan Chase.[31] Banks that dominate such payment transactions—and they exist outside of the Treasury market—pose a particular challenge for policymakers seeking to reduce expectations of TBTF coverage. Even if the failure of these banks, which we call dominant payment providers, did not impose a substantial direct financial loss on counterparties, their inability to provide crucial services to commercial firms, other banks, and other capital market participants could lead to spillovers. Without these firms, capital market trades could not occur, payments between firms would be disrupted, and commercial and financial firms might not be able to determine the amount and type of financial assets they own. The disruption of service could come following an operational event, such as the terrorist attacks of September 11; a voluntary decision by a dominant provider to exit certain payment business; or a failure.[32]

Although dominant payment providers have a profit motive to ensure that they provide regular service, it may prove insufficient. The decisions of dominant payment providers affect all the other firms and consumers who benefit from robust trading of securities and processing of payments. The inability of a single critical bank in one of these payment networks to offer its services can grind the entire system to a halt. However, the dominant providers would not factor such systemic costs into their decisions. What makes the most sense from the view of the dominant payment provider—such as leaving the payment business altogether—may not make sense for and may impose significant costs on society.

Policymakers therefore have reason to make it less likely that dominant payment providers will fail and more likely that markets can effectively respond to one firm's reduction in service. That is, because of their critical role in payments, society should have a lower tolerance for breaks in service provision from dominant players.[33] Such policy interventions will give policymakers greater confidence in rejecting bailouts.

We find the current changes under discussion in the United States with regard to dominant payment providers sensible and worth enacting, so we briefly summarize them.[34] One policy direction under review focuses on

31. Board of Governors of the Federal Reserve System and U.S. Securities and Exchange Commission (2002).

32. See Fleming and Garbade (2002) for the effect of the September 11 attacks on operations of the Treasury market.

33. Ferguson (2002a, 2002b).

34. This summary is based primarily on the Board of Governors of the Federal Reserve

the standards that supervisors apply when reviewing the ability of dominant payment providers to recover (that is, complete transactions disrupted by a break in service) and resume the provision of services. Reflecting the notion that some banks should be held to a higher standard, supervisors have suggested in draft guidance that an emerging objective of the industry is for banks and other financial firms that "play significant roles in critical financial markets ... [to] set a recovery time target of no later than four hours after the event [that leads to the break in service]." So-called core clearing and settlement organizations should resume no later than two hours after the event. The final guidance reflects these general goals but does not express them as requirements.[35]

A second potential policy direction would try to reduce the dependence of the payment system on dominant providers, but policymakers rightly seem to have discounted this option. Encouraging new entrants into the market might not be effective because switching from an established payment provider to a new entrant is likely to be very costly. Switching from one established provider to another after one fails may not be feasible in today's regime because the data on the client's current financial status could be lost during a disruption in service. And if government entrants acquired a large market share, innovation and efficiency could suffer.

A third option is to shift from private provision of some key payment services to provision by "utilities" that have an explicit objective of keeping the network operating. This option recognizes that supervisory standards do not address all the major sources of service disruption, particularly the voluntary exit of firms from the market. The utility option, depending on its structure, could potentially respond to concerns by creating a payment provider with a limited mission, small range of activities, and ownership by firms that use its services. Because the utility did not happen into the provision of payments, it would not exit the market voluntarily. In addition, the utility would not be threatened by losses in unrelated activities under some proposals. Ownership by its users would encourage innovation and cost-efficiency.

System and U.S. Securities and Exchange Commission (2002); Board of Governors of the Federal Reserve System and others (2002); Board of Governors of the Federal Reserve System, U.S. Office of the Comptroller of the Currency, and U.S. Securities and Exchange Commission (2002, 2003); Federal Reserve Bank of New York (2002).

35. Board of Governors of the Federal Reserve System, U.S. Office of the Comptroller of the Currency, and U.S. Securities and Exchange Commission (2003).

Finally, a hybrid option combines features of higher supervisory standards, less dependence on monopolists, and a utility. It envisions dominant payment providers having real-time backup of their activities. A third-party, utility-like firm would control the backup and make accessing it low cost for firms. A lack of service delivery by one dominant player should not bring down payment systems under this setup.

We support all options still in play, while recognizing that they have important weaknesses. Supervisory standards must be designed and implemented with great care. By raising costs for dominant payment providers, supervisory standards could make an exit from service provision more likely. Industry participants, including both Bank of New York and J. P. Morgan Chase, had serious reservations about certain types of utilities, arguing that they would reduce innovation and face significant operational constraints (for example, the need to raise funds to operate). However, they and regulators seem at least somewhat open to the hybrid option, suggesting a path for near-term reform.[36]

Expediting Payments to Creditors

When a bank fails, uninsured creditors may still be entitled to funds based on the return from the sale of bank assets. Although it varies across countries, uninsured creditors can lose access to the funds owed them for years at a time. To avoid this cost, creditors may try to get their money at any sign of trouble at a bank, producing a run and encouraging excessive protection. Creditors deprived of funds rightly due them would pressure governments for bailouts.

Recognizing the link between creditors' access to their funds and bailouts, several analysts have reemphasized the rapid return of funds to creditors.[37] The immediate provision of cash should reduce the chance of a run, lead to less pressure for bailouts, and get banks back into operation in a reasonable period of time. These results would increase policymaker confidence in imposing losses on the uninsured. In fact, this same logic led the Federal Deposit Insurance Corporation (FDIC), as far back as the early 1980s, to view the advancement of funds to uninsured creditors, based on the liquidation value of the failed bank's assets, as a tool for preventing

36. Board of Governors of the Federal Reserve System (2002b); Bank of New York (2002); J. P. Morgan Chase (2002).
37. Kaufman and Seelig (2002).

more extensive coverage of the uninsured. The FDIC experimented with this method and found it workable but dropped it when confronted with Continental Illinois.[38]

True, some conditions outside the control of government make immediate provision of funds difficult. Fraud, difficult-to-value assets, or weak record keeping may make it difficult to determine how much creditors are owed. In many cases, however, governments can take action to provide liquidity to creditors. Basic supervision and regulation can help to ensure that banks keep proper records. Governments can also protect against advancing too much money to a creditor by making conservative payments. The FDIC paid roughly $300 million in advance dividends to uninsured creditors from 1992 to 1994, with an ultimate overpayment of close to zero. The FDIC argued that this process gave "uninsured depositors an opportunity to realize an earlier return on the uninsured portion of their deposits without eliminating the incentive for large depositors to exercise market discipline."[39]

The government can also pass laws making advance payments possible. The Federal Deposit Insurance Corporation Improvement Act of 1991, for example, authorized the FDIC to make final settlement payments to uninsured creditors equal to the average recovery experience. Such an advance payment option could have allayed policymakers' concerns following the failure of Continental Illinois. The average recovery rate was something on the order of 90 percent, meaning that creditors would suffer a loss, but not one so large as to wipe out their own capital.[40]

It may prove difficult for some countries to acquire the human capital and funds to pay uninsured creditors rapidly. Nonetheless, it seems worthwhile for countries to head in this direction. It is unsettling that only a few countries besides the United States have a legal system supported by the operational components necessary to remit funds quickly following a bank failure.[41]

38. Davison (1997); Isaac (1997).
39. Federal Deposit Insurance Corporation (1998, p. 249).
40. Litan and Rauch (1997, pp. 98–99).
41. See Kaufman (2002) for a history of the issue in the United States.

11

Limiting Creditor Losses

nother general method for addressing spillovers and increasing policymaker confidence is to limit creditor losses directly or to allocate
losses such that market discipline increases without an excessive increase in
instability. We discuss four examples of this approach. First, the direct
approach to reducing losses would have supervisors close institutions while
they are still solvent. A related option would require banks in a weak position to increase the financial cushion that reduces the chance that liability
holders will suffer losses. A third option would allow for some ex ante protection to otherwise uninsured creditors of banks to reduce the threat of
spillovers while allowing for sufficient losses to motivate better pricing of
bank liabilities (that is, coinsurance). A final option would allow for select
coverage of the nominally uninsured, while, in general, making it more
likely that creditors will suffer losses, and also would rely on the timing of
failure to determine coverage of the uninsured.

Limiting Losses by Shutting Down Insolvent Banks

A theme of this chapter is that the likelihood that policymakers will bail out
uninsured creditors at large banks is dependent in part on the losses that
creditors are expected to suffer on bank failure. If creditors would suffer
substantial losses—potentially leading to their own failure—policymakers

naturally would expect more significant spillovers and thus would have greater reason to provide protection. The most direct method of reducing the chance of bailouts, therefore, is to reduce the expected losses of creditors. The most direct method of reducing expected losses is to close banks expected to fail while they have sufficient assets to repay creditors in full. In short, governments need a system for closing weak but solvent banks.

Because of the difficulty of identifying weak banks and the length of time required to address those weaknesses, a traditional safety and soundness regime is unlikely to shut down banks while they still have capital. An alternative approach with greater conceptual appeal would require supervisors to take prespecified actions against banks, such as limiting dividends or restricting growth, based on observable characteristics of the banks. The observable characteristics are used to set triggers. As the observable characteristics of the bank deteriorate, additional triggers would be set off, and penalties and limitations on bank actions would become more severe. Under this alternative, a bank that does not improve its performance in a clearly defined manner will be closed while it has positive capital.

This alternative approach has been called "structured early intervention and resolution."[1] Staff of the International Monetary Fund call it a "key component of an efficient and competitive banking system."[2] The United States implemented the archetype of this approach under the title of prompt corrective action (PCA), which the Federal Deposit Insurance Corporation Improvement Act of 1991 (FDICIA) put into effect. We find these reforms attractive on a conceptual basis, while recognizing that they have (mostly fixable) flaws in their existing implementation.

One concern with early closure regimes is credibility. Some observers find it difficult to believe that policymakers will, in fact, shut down the dominant bank in a country even if it has positive capital because, for example, banking systems could be concentrated and bankers could have strong ties to political leaders.[3] The credibility of an early closure regime might be particularly challenged when a bank becomes insolvent in a short period of time. The triggers would not have given supervisors time to respond to the change in condition, and the capital position of the bank may be difficult to determine.

1. See Benston and Kaufman (1994b) for a history of the proposal and Shadow Financial Regulatory Committee (1989) for an early version.
2. Garcia (2000, p. 7).
3. Caprio (1997).

Implementation would be challenging even if policymakers were willing to close down banks with positive capital, regardless of size. To get the most out of these regimes, policymakers must set effective triggers. To be effective, the triggers must be (1) largely outside the manipulation of banks, (2) reflective of the current risk profile of the institution, (3) feasible to calculate routinely and observe, and (4) set to close banks likely to fail while allowing those likely to survive to stay open. And although it may appear obvious, to be effective, the early closure regime must take real steps to remove the discretion of supervisors.

The triggers of prompt corrective action would not meet these standards. FDICIA requires the use of a leverage limit and a risk-based capital requirement and sets the minimum allowable amount of tangible equity to assets. But it allows supervisors to determine how to define these triggers and to establish others. Supervisors set PCA triggers based on book value capital ratios. The book value of capital is the difference between the value of assets and liabilities as determined by banks, often on the basis of historical information. Critics have long complained that book value capital ratios provide "rear window" information on bank risk-taking. Declines in this ratio reflect losses incurred in the past, and a bank that does not fully recognize its losses in a timely fashion could report high levels of book capital and still be insolvent on failure. Book value will be a particularly inappropriate trigger for the largest, most complex banks. A book valuation of assets assumes the context of a going concern (that is, a bank that will stay in business in its current form). As discussed, supervisors may face real difficulties in transferring the assets of a large or complex bank at once. If assets are sold piecemeal, outside of the going concern, losses could be quite high.

The limited empirical research on prompt corrective action is consistent with these concerns. This work finds that banks with high probabilities of failure during the pre-FDICIA period would not have been considered undercapitalized under FDICIA rules.[4] The U.S. Government Accounting Office sums up the problem, finding that PCA provisions "may not fully address one significant weakness that existed in the 1980s as noted by GAO [U.S. Government Accounting Office] and others—i.e., the failure of regulators to take strong forceful enforcement action early enough to prevent or

4. Jones and King (1995); Peek and Rosengren (1997). However, Aggarwal and Jacques (2001) find that prompt corrective action leads to an increase in bank capital without an increase in risk-taking.

minimize losses to the deposit insurance funds. . . . Most troubled institutions experience problems in other areas, such as asset quality and management, long before their capital becomes adversely affected."[5] And, in fact, according to the failed bank cost analysis of the Federal Deposit Insurance Corporation (FDIC), the loss ratio for failed banks has not fallen since FDICIA. Indeed, the last several years have been characterized by extremely costly bank failures, with loss ratios far above average levels, leading some to question the effectiveness of prompt corrective action.[6]

Recognizing these limits does not negate the benefits that even an imperfectly implemented system of early closure could yield. A less-than-optimal system, for example, could still signal creditors that policymakers seek to reduce losses from bank failure so that they can impose costs on the uninsured. If such a signal changes behavior, it will encourage the type of market discipline that can reduce bank risk-taking. Moreover, an imperfect reform can still reduce the chances for TBTF coverage if it improves current conditions. Finally, reform is a multiple-step process. The creation of an infrastructure to limit losses is a constructive first step in the process of improving management of too big to fail. Once a system of trigger-based supervision is established, it may be easier to institute additional reforms.

Several reforms that would address the weakness associated with prompt corrective action's use of book value triggers have been offered. Supervisors could set the book value capital ratios at very high levels so that even banks with lots of book value capital are subject to strict regulation and supervision and potential closure.[7] We would not support this step. Setting capital ratios at very high levels would simply lead to the closure of banks that have sufficient capital. Indeed, supervision could always eliminate bank failures by eliminating bank risk-taking, but the cost of such a regime is too high.

Instead, we would base triggers on market valuation of assets and liabilities. There are three points to make about this suggestion. First, market assessments, as opposed to book measures, are attractive because they incorporate the future prospects of the asset or the firm. We discuss the importance of incorporating market-based measures of risk into prompt corrective action, and more generally into supervisory systems, in appendix

5. U.S. General Accounting Office (1996, pp. 4–5).

6. Rob Blackwell, "Latest Crop of Failures Brings Steeper Costs," *American Banker,* July 8, 2002, p. 1; Rob Blackwell, "Does Superior Prove S&L Reform a Flop?" *American Banker,* August 20, 2001, p. 1.

7. Benston and Kaufman (1994a, p. 109).

D. Second, this suggestion is hardly novel. The original plans in the United States for the early closure system were based on market measures of bank net worth. Finally, the fact that substituting a better, already identified trigger makes prompt corrective action more effective suggests that current problems are not systemic but rather are related to specific choices made by policymakers.

Rapid Recapitalization

Prompt corrective action addresses policymakers' concerns about spillovers by distributing to creditors the assets of a failed bank, while these assets still exceed the bank's liabilities. Another method for assuaging policymakers' concern is to ensure that banks in weakening condition can quickly increase their net worth such that assets continue to exceed liabilities. Timely recapitalization would limit the potential for creditors to suffer losses or for insolvency to spill over to other firms and markets. To make rapid recapitalization a viable option, one analyst has proposed a financial instrument that would automatically increase a big bank's capital position when it approaches insolvency.[8] That is, the instrument is issued as debt but would convert to equity capital.

This proposal remains in its incipient stage and ultimately may not prove viable. For example, by allowing large banks to avoid resolution, the recapitalization might actually make matters worse. Nonetheless, we find the direction of this proposal worthy of additional study.

Coinsurance

We began the book by outlining the reasons for imposing losses on creditors, while rejecting proposals to eliminate TBTF coverage by fiat. Refusal ever to bail out the uninsured is not credible because such a policy may not hold up in the face of excessive instability. The goal is to give creditors enough market discipline to address the moral hazard problem without removing the potential benefits of offering government support. Insurers have long faced a similar dilemma. They address it in part through coinsurance.[9] Under a coinsurance scheme, the insured has to bear some of the loss rather than have the insurer pick up 100 percent of it.

8. Flannery (2002).
9. Dionne and Harrington (1991, p. 2).

Policymakers can impose coinsurance when bailing out uninsured creditors. For example, the government could give itself the right to provide
coverage to the uninsured under extraordinary circumstances up to a
capped amount (say, 75 percent of their funds). There are, however, a
number of ways for policymakers to implement a coinsurance policy.[10] The
main variations arise from different methods for calculating the coinsurance rate and determining the range of creditors covered.

We have heard three objections to coinsurance. First, it is not practical
enough to be implemented. We have already noted that coinsurance is an
integral part of private sector insurance contracts. About fifteen countries
incorporate coinsurance into deposit protection schemes (nearly three-
quarters of countries with coinsurance are European).[11] The directive
requiring that countries in the European Union provide a deposit insurance
scheme also allows a role for coinsurance.[12] In the U.S. context, the American Banker's Association proposed a coinsurance plan specifically to eliminate 100 percent coverage of some uninsured creditors at TBTF banks.

Second, some argue that providing explicit caps for uninsured coverage
would make the moral hazard problem worse by extending the safety net.[13]
However, our proposal would not force the government to provide extraordinary coverage. It is unclear why capping coverage could make bailouts
more likely.

Third, and more substantive, setting the coinsurance rate to achieve a
better balance between moral hazard and instability will prove challenging.[14] By providing some coverage for large bank creditors, this policy
should reduce the threat that a creditor will suffer such large losses that
they too will fail. This objective certainly requires a balancing act, and we
should not pretend that we know the optimal coinsurance rate that shields
against spillovers but addresses moral hazard.

However, policymakers in other countries seem to have been able to
achieve the right balance in practice in setting the coinsurance rate. The
only empirical evidence on the issue, as noted, indicates that the inclusion

10. See Feldman and Rolnick (1998) for more details.
11. Authors' calculations based on the World Bank's Deposit Insurance Database, available at www.worldbank.org/research/interest/confs/upcoming/deposit_insurance/data.htm
[September 5, 2003].
12. Cartwright and Campbell (1999); European Parliament and Council of the European
Union (1994).
13. Jones (2001).
14. Hanc (1999).

of coinsurance features in deposit insurance reduces the potential for financial system instability. Coinsurance also appears to control the attempts of creditors to shift the risk of loss from them to the government without discouraging flows of deposits into banking systems.[15] Moreover, the trade-off between too much moral hazard and too much financial system instability exists whether or not policymakers formally implement a coinsurance regime. Right now we think the balance has shifted to too much coverage.

Losses and the Timing of Failure

A fourth option for limiting and reallocating losses is based on the timing of failures. It allows for protection of uninsured depositors at some large banks, while limiting or refusing coverage at others. The difference in coverage would depend on when the bank failed. One such proposal was made nearly thirty years ago. The author summarized his plan:

> One compromise is to announce that when a large bank begins to fail it will be allowed to go under, but that once it has failed no other large bank will be allowed to fail for a period of, say, two years. Such an announcement would prevent the failure of one bank from starting runs on other large banks and would thereby safeguard the money stock. At the same time, it would not remove the incentive to safe management since no large bank would want to be the first one that fails. To be sure, once the first large bank has failed, all other large banks would feel safe. But, since their safety net would be there only for two years, while a reputation for riskiness could easily last beyond two years, they would not be likely to abuse this protection.[16]

A more recent plan follows this model but removes the two-year window and accords the policymaker more discretion.[17] The key to both plans is that, because creditors do not know if their institution will fail first, they have an incentive to exert market discipline. At the same time, the chance to bail out creditors once spillovers occur gives policymakers more comfort in allowing the first to go down.

15. Among other issues, Hovakimian, Kane, and Laeven (2003) discuss coinsurance and risk-shifting, and Huizinga and Nicodeme (2002) examine the effect of coinsurance on deposit flows.
16. Mayer (1975, p. 607).
17. Mishkin (1999); Mishkin and Strahan (1999).

There are downsides to this option as well. In theory, one might imagine bank creditors trying to prop up their institution so that it does not fail first. To the degree that creditors could overcome significant coordination issues and carry off a rescue, we think it unlikely they would roll the dice, allow the bank to fail, and hope for a bailout (recall that only systemic failures would get such protection). This reform also might not be credible in the case where the failure of the first bank could, in and of itself, impose a substantial cost on the economy. For this very reason, we suggest multiple reforms to managing the TBTF problem. Although this reform may not give policymakers comfort under some conditions, perhaps other reforms—such as those targeted at dominant payment providers—would.

12

Restricting Payment System Spillovers

We now turn to our final method for addressing spillovers, the return of payment systems. Spillovers may result when a large bank fails and cannot make good on promised payments of cash or delivery of other items of value such as a security. Without the cash or security, the bank expecting receipt of the payment could become insolvent or have its operations severely disrupted. Policymakers may step in to limit the spillover damage by bailing out the creditors of the initial bank that failed and potentially even the creditors of banks affected via spillovers.

Some payment systems—defined as the mechanisms, including the institutions, people, rules, and technologies, that make the exchange of payment possible—can lead a bank to have a significant exposure to the failure of another bank (that is, make them a creditor of the failing bank).[1] This potential has been well known to policymakers and banks for some time. A number of payment system reforms have been suggested and implemented to reduce the threat of spillover.

In this chapter, we summarize some of the more significant payment system reforms undertaken to date. Although the reforms are quite complex in implementation, they are fairly straightforward in concept. One

---

1. This definition of payment systems is from New York Federal Reserve's Payments Glossary at www.newyorkfed.org/banking/payment_glossary.html# [October 23, 2003].

type of reform seeks to eliminate or significantly limit the amount that banks owe each other through the payment system. A second type of reform establishes methods by which a bank owed funds by a failing institution can offset losses (for example, by seizing collateral).

Some of these reforms have only recently been implemented, suggesting an important role for policymakers in ensuring that the reforms are brought to fruition and in monitoring them after implementation. This summary also suggests that policymakers have successfully reduced the threat of spillovers that had previously concerned them. As such, they should internalize this accomplishment in their decisionmaking.

Finally, we discuss some additional steps that policymakers should take as well as some trade-offs implicit in these reforms. For example, the payment reforms that reduce credit extensions in payments between banks typically shift the risk of loss from a failing bank to the central bank. That is, the central bank becomes the counterparty to the failing bank, a step that also raises concerns about moral hazard. We discuss the efforts by central banks to minimize the potential for government support of payment systems to increase risk-taking. However, we first review how the operations of payment systems contribute to the potential for a spillover failure.

How Payment Systems Make Spillovers Possible

When two banks are involved in a payment, one may end up owing the other huge amounts of money. Credit extension results because of delays in settling payments and not necessarily from a desire to extend credit. Implicit credit extensions can occur, for example, in the process of exchanging securities for cash and in foreign exchange transactions. A bank may give cash to the bank selling the securities but not receive the securities for hours or days. The bank buying the securities could suffer a potentially massive loss if the selling bank fails after it receives the cash but before it has transmitted the securities.

Likewise, in a foreign exchange transaction, one bank may complete its end of the transaction (for example, transmit dollars) before it receives the other currency from the second bank. In the most famous case, bank supervisors closed a German bank involved in foreign exchange trading at the end of the day in Germany, after payments had been made in Germany. However, the German bank had not yet finalized the sending of funds to institutions outside of Germany, and its failure led to the stoppage of those payments. While the various time zones present in many foreign exchange trades receive attention, the ultimate source of the exposure in foreign exchange trading is that the two legs of the transaction are not made final at the same time, a problem that can arise in a single time zone. Similar payment exposures between large banks can arise when a bank makes a payment on behalf of a client or when it makes a very short-term loan.

In these cases, the actual time during which one bank is exposed to another's failure is quite small, measured in several days at maximum. But the size of the exposure is enormous. Global, daily interbank exposures for foreign exchange transactions are more than $1 trillion; securities exposures—also measured through daily turnover—are smaller but still staggering (for example, roughly $200 billion in the U.S. Treasury market).[2] A relatively small number of banks appear responsible for a large percentage of these payments. So the sums owed by large banks could be extremely large. Eliminating the small time period of exposure would reduce the ability of one bank's failure to bring down the other.

Banks surely have an incentive to measure and manage such large exposures, and bank-led initiatives, as we describe, have made progress toward these goals. However, as we have noted in other areas, banks would not take into account the costs that their failure may have on other institutions and society. As such, their efforts to manage payment system exposures may prove insufficient, justifying a role for government in reducing such expenses (as well as in payments in the first place).

By linking the hypothetical large exposures created in payment systems to the potential for systemic risk and TBTF protection, we admittedly follow convention. Others suggest that the problem has been overstated or at least has not been described with the appropriate nuances. For example, some have noted that certain risks in the payment system are not inherent but arise from actions of central banks and supervisors.[3] Others have found that important sources of liquidity and payments operate well during a crisis and do not create sufficient exposures to make spillovers a real threat.[4] Although we may not follow their reasoning, we agree that the exposure associated with payment systems may not be as prominent a threat as it once was. We discuss the reforms that helped to achieve that outcome next.

2. Hills and Rule (1999, p. 106); Kahn and Roberds (2001, p. 192).
3. Eisenbeis (1997).
4. Furfine (1999, 2002) focuses on the Fed Funds market, noting the limits of his analysis for policymakers.

Summarizing the Why and How of Payment System Reforms

Policymakers and bankers realize that moving to more of a real-time basis for payments reduces (1) the exposure created through the payment system, (2) the threat of spillovers, and (3) the potential for a financial crisis. That is, eliminating or significantly reducing the time period when one bank has exchanged cash or securities but has not yet received the funds or securities in return could make spillovers less likely. We naturally stress the attendant benefit of reducing the rationale for TBTF coverage. Policymakers have less reason to protect uninsured creditors if spillover failures are unlikely. Others in the Federal Reserve System and academia have also argued, at least implicitly, that reducing the exposures created in payment systems is the key step in putting uninsured creditors at risk of loss.[5]

There are other methods for reducing the exposures created in payment systems besides moving to real-time payments. Payment system operators could cap the total credit that one firm implicitly grants another. Another method for limiting exposure is to reduce the number of payments made between banks through netting. We earlier noted the case where banks make a single payment to each other based on the bottom line of their various transactions rather than making payments for each transaction. An even more comprehensive form of netting across many institutions can take place in markets where a central organization tallies a firm's bottom line across many trades and counterparties. Firms owed money in total from other participants receive one payment from the central body, while firms that owe money need only make a single payment to the central body.

Instead of limiting loss in the first place, banks could decide to offset losses after the sending bank fails. This approach typically is implemented through collateral requirements, making it critical for such arrangements to have proper legal backing. Finally, banks participating in the payment system could decide to share at least some of the loss from the failure of a counterparty. Spreading the risk along the lines of an insurance policy could reduce the threat of spillovers.

Significant progress has been made in the last decade or so in reducing payment system–related exposures through the methods just described. We note several of these successful efforts with our usual caveat about selectivity.

---

5. Flannery (1999); Hoenig (1996, 1997); Todd and Thomson (1990).

—Typically countries in the G-10 and European Union, as of the early 2000s, use a real-time system for processing large-value payments (technically these systems are called real-time gross settlement, meaning that individual payments between two institutions are settled and made final in real time). Although these systems reduce exposures between banks and make spillovers less likely, they do so by shifting exposure to government, which raises issues we discuss at the end of this chapter. Where a large-value payment system does not operate in real time (for example, the Clearing House Interbank Payments System [CHIPS] in the United States), authorities have instituted reforms that experts believe significantly reduce payment exposures.[6] Many payment systems also have made greater use of collateralization and caps.

—Important steps have been taken to reduce the payment exposure in foreign exchange trades. Increased use of netting in foreign exchange transactions has helped, as will the CLS Bank, which began operation in September 2002. The CLS Bank allows the settlement of the two ends of the foreign exchange transaction to occur at the same time, a process called payment versus payment. Initial assessments suggest that the CLS Bank could reduce exposure for foreign exchange settlement.[7] Rather than having credit exposures for a day or more, the CLS Bank could reduce the time of exposure to something closer to an hour.

—There have been both renewed attention to exposures arising from the settlement of securities trades and effective responses to previously identified concerns.[8] There appears to have been movement, for example, to delivery versus payment systems since 1989, when the establishment of such systems was strongly recommended.[9] Delivery versus payment—an analog to the more real-time systems described for foreign exchange trading—means that banks no longer have to irrevocably commit cash before they receive securities.

However, additional reforms of securities transactions continue to receive serious consideration and recommendation (beyond establishing the proper legal environment already mentioned). Reducing the time to

6. McAndrews and Trundle (2001).

7. Galati (2002); Kahn and Roberds (2001) argue that the CLS Bank could lead to improvements but note that important concerns with foreign exchange settlement will remain.

8. Committee on Payment and Settlement Systems and Technical Committee of the International Organization of Securities Commissions (2001).

9. Group of Thirty (1989).

confirm the details of a security trade could prove beneficial. Moreover, staff with the Bank of England argue that delivery versus payment systems that do not have real-time settlement, which describes a number of such payment systems, fail to address important concerns regarding systemic risk.[10] Some securities markets, such as derivatives markets, could potentially benefit from making additional use of centralized organizations that provide netting, risk management, liquidity, and others services. Other markets that have such central bodies could address risk more robustly.[11]

Conclusions about Too Big to Fail, Payment System Reform, and Policymakers' Priorities

Based on our understanding of payment system reforms, we come to several conclusions about how they should affect the approach to the TBTF problem. First, the reforms have addressed at least some of the major potential causes of spillovers. In particular, through the activities of central banks, policymakers have paid constructive attention to payment system exposures, providing tangible examples that such efforts can be successful. Policymakers can, and should continue to, address such issues.

The success of policymakers to date supports our second conclusion: Policymakers must monitor recently implemented reforms and apply pressure where additional reforms are needed. Specifically, reforms that have recently gone into effect, such as the development of CLS Bank and reforms at CHIPS, deserve extensive surveillance. A number of reforms directed to securities settlement need action.

Perhaps most important, it is clearly time for policymakers to internalize some of their victories. The reforms we have summarized should affect the approach to bailouts. Although it is always true that new developments in banking activities, such as greater complexity, raise new means by which spillovers occur, policymakers should have greater confidence today that the concerns that might have motivated bailouts five or ten years ago have been at least partly addressed. Policymakers are aware of reforms specific to their country and perhaps even the overall trend across a specific type of payment system (for example, large value). But we are not sure if most policymakers fully comprehend the changes made across the wide array of payment systems.

10. Hills and Rule (1999, p. 109).
11. Euro Clearing Standing Committee of the Central Banks of the Group of Ten Countries (1998); Knott and Mills (2002). Hills and others (1999) also discuss clearinghouses.

Additional Reforms and Trade-offs

Although the accomplishments are significant, there are clearly limits to the reforms. By definition, these reforms aim to reduce exposures created in the process of making a payment. Even with optimal payment systems, one bank could find itself with significant direct exposures to another bank's failure through, for example, a large long-term loan. A similar type of exposure would arise if a bank (called the respondent) holds a significant amount of money in the accounts of another bank (called the correspondent) that provides it with services.

A number of options are available to address direct exposures and make coverage for the uninsured less pressing. Putting creditors at risk of loss and simply disclosing these large exposures is one alternative. A more interventionist approach would involve limiting the amount of funds that one bank can lend another. Many supervisors enforce so-called single-borrower limits, and the Federal Deposit Insurance Corporation Improvement Act of 1991 required that the Board of Governors limit interbank exposure of correspondents and respondents. The Board of Governors issued Regulation F, which limits the amount of deposit exposure a bank can have to a correspondent that is not adequately capitalized. The limit of exposure to the weaker bank is equal to 25 percent of the respondent's capital, although the measure of capital could be made more market based or the limit could be applied more broadly.[12]

We have not discussed additional important trade-offs in reducing exposures created in the payment system. There is, for example, a cost to requiring collateral. And having collateral seized en masse could put downward pressure on the value of similar assets held by banks.

A more general and important trade-off has even greater implications for TBTF coverage, largely because the method by which it has been addressed could encourage excessive bank risk-taking. The reforms we have discussed reduce the risk that one bank will lose principal on a transaction. Unfortunately, they also increase liquidity risk, defined as the chance that a counterparty (or participant in a settlement system) will not settle an obligation for full value when due.[13] The failure to complete the transaction has to do with one bank having too little cash on hand, as opposed to being

---

12. Litan and Rauch (1997, p. 99).
13. Committee on Payment and Settlement Systems (2001).

insolvent.[14] The implicit granting of credit in payment system transactions helps to ensure that sufficient funding is available to allow transactions to move forward. Requiring banks to settle their transactions in real time increases the challenge a bank has in managing its funding and could lead to more failed transactions (the failure to complete trades can also result in what is known as replacement cost risk).

An increase in the number of failed transactions raises systemic issues. Banks depend on incoming funds or securities to complete their own outgoing transactions. If the expected funds or securities do not show up, then other banks could fail to provide expected payments and so on. The move to real-time payments could occasionally gum up payment activity, leading to payment system gridlock. Yet a desire to ensure against breakdowns in the payment system is what motivated policymakers to reduce credit-related payment exposures in the first place.

To avoid the increase in systemic risk, policymakers could rely on banks to meet the challenge of real-time payments.[15] Much more typically, policymakers simply shift intraday credit provision from private parties to central banks. In a number of central bank wholesale payment systems, a payment from one bank to another becomes final even if the paying bank does not have sufficient funds in its account to make the payment in real time. Intraday credit from the central bank makes many payments possible.

This outcome may be preferred because the central bank may be in a better position than private firms to provide the socially desirable amount of intraday credit.[16] Moreover, having the central bank bear the payment system–related loss from the failure of a large bank directly addresses spillover concerns. At the same time, central bank assumption of payment exposures raises the same moral hazard concerns we have emphasized throughout this book. Through its intraday credit program, the government assumes loss that otherwise would accrue to private creditors. This could alter the behavior of the protected creditors, leading to behavior on their part—such as pricing that is too low—that increases risk-taking. The acceptance of credit risk in wholesale payments by central banks thus could magnify rather than eliminate the TBTF problem.

14. For models of the payment system that incorporate such trade-offs, see Kahn, McAndrews, and Roberds (1999); Kahn and Roberds (1999); Rochet and Tirole (1996a).
15. Payments Risk Committee (2000) describes some private market participants' responses to concerns about payments and liquidity management.
16. Zhou (2000).

Whether the benefits of central bank intraday credit (for example, reduction in payment system exposure in private markets) outweighs its costs (for example, increase in moral hazard) depends on how central banks manage their credit exposures. Central banks—and we focus on the Federal Reserve from here on out—clearly are aware of the potential for moral hazard. To address that potential, the Fed has taken steps to reduce its exposure and better manage bank risk-taking in the payment system.[17]

By some measures, these steps—which include imposing a cap on intraday credit, explicitly pricing such credit, and developing systems to monitor and respond to increasing risk exposures—have led to a reduction in risk-taking. Total daylight credit, for example, has fallen. Moreover, some banks seem concerned that Federal Reserve credit management has led to a shortage of short-term liquidity. Such complaints imply some success in managing moral hazard.

At the same time, total intraday credit extended by the Federal Reserve not related to securities transactions has not fallen. In any case, the Federal Reserve continues to explore additional reforms to reduce its exposure even further. For example, other central banks require full collateralization of payments processed with the state guarantee, a practice that does not exist in the United States.

In our view, current Federal Reserve policy and consideration of additional reforms seem to be in the ballpark, although there is some room for improvement. In particular, changes in Federal Reserve policy that would encourage greater collateralization are options worth exploring in more detail. For example, the Federal Reserve continues to explore a credit pricing strategy in which collateralized exposures pay a lower price than an unsecured position.[18] More important perhaps than specific proposals is frequent Federal Reserve review of its policy on risk in the payment system. These high-priority reviews signal a desire to monitor moral hazard and offer a chance to alter policy if the balance between competing forces gets seriously out of balance. Such fairly regular checks by the central bank seem a superior tool for addressing potential moral hazard than irregular and often nonexistent reviews of implicit TBTF policies.

17. Coleman (2002).
18. Board of Governors of the Federal Reserve System (2002a).

13

Alternatives for Managing Too Big to Fail

We recognize that the policies and reforms recommended in the preceding chapters do not constitute all the options. There are other alternatives for policymakers seeking to diminish expectations of TBTF coverage. We briefly summarize the alternatives in this chapter and provide more extensive discussions of them in appendixes.

The first alternative responds to the concern, described in chapter 5, that personal motivations may lead policymakers to bail out creditors. Reforms of this type would raise the costs to policymakers of bailing out uninsured creditors (see appendix B). The second alternative relies on supervision and regulation (S&R) of banks. S&R could make bailouts less likely by reducing the risks taken by banks and the subsequent losses that the failure of a bank imposes on creditors (see appendix C). The third alternative seeks to reduce bank risk-taking by increasing the market forces or "discipline" that banks face (see appendix D).

Policymakers should put a lower priority on these alternatives as a means of managing expectations of TBTF. We already have offered recommendations to address personal motivations, and we feel that additional reforms to address this issue go too far and have significant weaknesses. We do not think the second alternative of S&R would reduce bank risk-taking or creditor losses enough to make it the dominant tool for suppressing bailouts of large bank creditors. While we support the third option of increasing market discipline, we think strategies to achieve that goal are best followed after, or in support of, our recommendations to put creditors at greater risk of loss, making them more sensitive to the risk-taking of banks.

Penalizing Policymakers

Imposing costs on policymakers inclined to provide bailouts could alter their personal calculus so that the benefits of creditor protection do not outweigh its costs. We focus on two ways of imposing costs on policymakers. Elected officials could impose financial penalties on policymakers, or the agencies they head, in response to undesired behavior. This option would require writing a contract specifying the types of behavior meriting penalties and rewards. For example, policymakers who do not close banks while they are still solvent could forfeit their jobs. Or, to discourage protection for the uninsured, all or some of the payment for TBTF bailouts could come out of the budget of the agency that approves it.

The second major tool for imposing costs is publicity and disclosure. If policymakers know that their involvement with the bailout of uninsured creditors will receive a high level of review, they might be less willing to provide one. There are many ways to structure disclosures to generate public heat on policymakers. Elected officials can require mandatory audits of bailouts after a large bank failure or sworn statements from policymakers explaining their actions. The Federal Deposit Insurance Corporation Improvement Act of 1991 (FDICIA) brought a number of these options into force.

We think these reforms do not deserve much attention for several reasons: We already have reviewed reforms that address personal motivations, this motivation is of secondary importance relative to concerns about spillovers, and these policies have several specific drawbacks. For example, elected officials may not follow through on the contract—to the degree it can be written effectively in the first place—and impose a financial penalty on a policymaker. The policymaker's decision to bail out creditors may violate the contract, but, at the time of the bailout, it may generate support from elected officials and the public. Because of similar near-term support for bailouts, additional publicity may not prove sufficiently harsh to generate a change in behavior.

Supervision and Regulation

Countries already supervise and regulate banks in order to reduce bank risk-taking. As part of the S&R regime, for example, countries require banks to hold a certain amount of capital and examine them for compliance with standards of safety and soundness. If banks take less risk because of S&R, creditors of failed banks should suffer fewer losses. As a result, S&R already offers a method for reducing the potential for spillover failures and TBTF bailouts.

There is good reason for supervising and regulating banks. S&R minimizes the relatively high costs that individual creditors face in analyzing risk-taking by banks. It also creates a counterweight to the weakened market discipline that explicit and implicit government guarantees produce. Moreover, empirical evidence suggests that S&R can identify some risks taken by banks that private creditors have not registered and can encourage banks to take steps to reduce such risk-taking.

While S&R is a necessary component of the foundation to address excessive bank risk-taking and TBTF expectations, it should not be the only or even the primary response to the problem. S&R, even though it is effective, has limitations. For example, supervisors face legal constraints on their actions and limited resources. Legal limits on supervisory responses are consistent with the demands of a democratic society but reduce the speed of an S&R regime in responding to solvency concerns at a large bank.

Moreover, the responses from supervisors and regulators to bank risk-taking tend be fairly blunt. Again, this limitation reflects an underlying philosophy that many observers would support. For example, most observers would not want supervisors in market economies making all of the business decisions for banks. But it also means that supervisors would find it difficult to encourage banks to take the "right" amount of risk. Finally, policymakers must consider the fact that S&R has proven insufficient in preventing banking crises where too big to fail is present. These observations do not suggest that S&R is fatally flawed, but they do highlight the limitations of this policy tool, suggesting that it must be accompanied by other reforms in the management of too big to fail.

Increasing Market Discipline

A credible no-bailout policy puts creditors at greater risk of loss and leads to more market discipline. Some observers and policymakers believe that policymakers can enact policies right now that would enhance market discipline, lead to more optimal bank risk-taking, and thus make TBTF bailouts less likely. Specifically, they believe that additional public disclosures of risk-taking by banks would lead to more informed creditors and better discipline. They note correctly that banks might need at least a little government nudge to disclose their risks more fully.

Other observers call for a more structured way of putting creditors at risk of loss. More specifically, they would require banks to have a subordinated notes and debt (SND) plan because the holders of SND would have little recourse to bank assets if the bank fails and would suffer large losses in a resolution (unless the government protects them). They thus have an incentive to impose additional discipline on banks.

Both types of policies have merit. However, we view them as complements to the preferred reforms we have already discussed. Putting creditors at risk of loss in the ways we have suggested in previous chapters may generate more cost-effective disclosure and more comprehensive use of such information by creditors than mandates in the current period. A creditor viewing herself at a relatively low risk of loss, after all, does not have much incentive to make good use of information generated by mandatory disclosures.

SND plans could also benefit from creditors who are more convinced that their investment is at risk of loss. We think the general reforms discussed in chapters 9 through 11 provide more effective methods for putting SND creditors at real risk of loss than efforts to that end in the SND plan itself. Certainly, policymakers need not wait until all the reforms we recommend have been in place before acting on disclosure and SND. Indeed, an SND pilot project begun in the short run might make sense. That said, policymakers will maximize direct discipline on banks by closely coordinating the rollout of these alternatives with the higher-priority reforms we recommend.

Market discipline could also play a role in TBTF management if incorporated into supervisory assessments of, and responses to, bank risk-taking (that is, indirect market discipline). The information in market signals could help supervisors to gauge more effectively the risk-taking of banks and make supervisory actions more responsive to risk-taking. Here, too, we think such signals would be of the greatest value after our other reforms have moved forward. However, our experience suggests that it takes some time for supervisors to make effective use of market data. Policymakers might emphasize greater indirect discipline in the current period to account for the time lag before supervisors address the concerns with market data and make effective use of it in the supervisory process.

Another venue for indirect discipline is the setting of deposit insurance premiums based on the risk-taking of banks. Risk-based premiums could better align the prices that banks face with the risks they take and therefore help to manage bank risk-taking, particularly after establishing credible TBTF policies. In a similar vein, we see potential for using market data to trigger supervisory actions in a future early closure regime.

We have emphasized the future with regard to the third alternative in order to provide policymakers with the time to put creditors at credible risk of loss. Reforms to increase market discipline will also benefit from technological trends making banks more transparent to creditors. For example, a greater percentage of bank loans have attributes of securities that traders price in financial markets. Greater transparency should allow creditors, who have been given an incentive to care, to better understand the risk-taking of banks and incorporate those assessments into their decisions. Because of these technological advances, we also think it more realistic to value the assets of banks based on the market's assessment of them in the future. Market value accounting should, in turn, improve the ability of creditors and supervisors to evaluate banks.

14

Summary:
Talking Points on Too Big to Fail

We began the volume with a summary of our arguments and an identification of our target audience, namely policymakers; their staff; and other professionals seeking to influence policy. We hope that these professionals convey our main points to their bosses and clients and that the bosses and clients internalize our story. At the risk of trivializing the process, convincing higher-ups these days requires short oral briefings, PowerPoint presentations, or summary memos. To help with those communications and recognizing that a reader probably does not want or need a traditional summary at this point, we list some talking points on too big to fail.

Three Bottom Lines

First, the TBTF problem has not been solved, is getting worse, and leads, on balance, to wasted resources.

Second, although expectations of bailouts by uninsured creditors at large banks cannot be eliminated, they can be reduced and better managed through a credible commitment to impose losses. Policymakers can establish credible commitments by addressing and reducing the motivation for bailouts.

Third, although other reforms could help to establish a credible commitment, policymakers should give highest priority to reforms limiting the chance that one bank's failure will threaten the solvency of other banks.

We now provide supporting points for these conclusions.

The Problem

—Even though they are not entitled to government protection, uninsured creditors of a large or systemically important bank believe they will be shielded from at least part of the loss in the event of bank failure.

—Anticipation of government protection warps the amount and pricing of funding that creditors provide a TBTF bank, which, in turn, leads banks to take excessive risk and make poor use of financial capital. The costs of poor resource use resulting from TBTF guarantees appear to be quite high. We believe these costs exceed the benefits of TBTF coverage in most cases, but even those who weigh the costs and benefits differently should be able to support many of our reforms.

—Expectations of TBTF coverage have likely grown and become more strongly held because more banks are now "large" and because a smaller group of banks controls a greater share of banking assets and provides key banking services. In addition, banks have become increasingly complex, making it more difficult for policymakers to predict the fallout from bank failure and to refuse to provide subsequent coverage to uninsured creditors.

—Reforms over the last decade aiming to limit TBTF protection, including those adopted in the United States, are unlikely to be effective in the long run (although they have yet to be tested and may have made a dent in TBTF expectations).

Commitment as the Solution

—In order to change the expectations of bailouts, policymakers must convince uninsured creditors that they will bear losses when large banks fail; changes in policy toward the uninsured must involve a credible commitment.

—A credible commitment to impose losses must be built on reforms directly reducing the incentives that lead policymakers to bail out uninsured creditors.

—Reforms that forbid coverage for the uninsured are not credible because they do not address underlying motivations and are easily circumvented.

—Policymakers have considerable experience in establishing credible commitments in the setting of monetary policy. The experience of monetary policy over the last two decades demonstrates the feasibility of reducing long-held expectations, such as those likely held by uninsured creditors of large banks.

Specific Motivations and Reforms

—The most important motivation for bailouts is to prevent the failure of one bank from threatening other banks, the financial sector, and overall economic performance. To reduce that motivation, we recommend that policymakers in developed countries take three general steps: enact policies and procedures that would reduce their uncertainty about the potential for spillovers; implement policies that directly limit creditor losses or allocate losses such that market discipline increases without an excessive increase in instability; and consider or follow up on payment system reforms that reduce the threat of spillovers.

—Reforms that reduce policymaker uncertainty include the following: increase supervisory planning for, and simulation of, a large bank failure; undertake targeted efforts that reduce the likelihood and cost of failure for banks dominating payment markets; make legal and regulatory adjustments that clarify the treatment of bank creditors at failure; and provide liquidity more rapidly to uninsured creditors.

—Reforms that could address concerns of excessive creditor loss include the following: close institutions before they can impose large losses; require banks in a weak position to increase the financial cushion to absorb losses; impose rules that require creditors to absorb at least some loss when their bank fails (for example, requiring coinsurance); and allow for select coverage of the nominally uninsured while, in general, making it more likely that creditors will suffer losses.

—Although payment system reforms are quite complex in implementation, they are fairly straightforward in concept. One type of reform would eliminate or significantly limit the amount that banks owe each other through the payment system. A second type of reform would establish methods by which a bank owed funds by a failing institution could offset losses (for example, by seizing collateral).

FDICIA: An Incomplete Fix

C laims that the Federal Deposit Insurance Corporation Improvement
Act of 1991 (FDICIA) largely solved the TBTF problem in the United
States often appear as fact even in articles where too big to fail is mentioned
tangentially. Consider a recent Federal Reserve article on the performance
of small banks:

> The competitiveness of the largest banks would also be improved if
> depositors believe that the government will treat these banks as "too
> big to fail." . . . However, the Federal Deposit Insurance Corporation
> Act of 1991 substantially circumscribed the ability of regulators to
> use too-big-to-fail by requiring that the Federal Deposit Insurance
> Corporation (FDIC) [to] pursue the resolution method that mini-
> mizes the cost to its insurance fund. In addition, exceptions to the
> "least cost" method are allowed only with the approval of at least
> two-thirds of both the Federal Reserve Board and FDIC board of
> directors and the approval of the Secretary of the Treasury in consul-
> tation with the President.[1]

FDICIA enacted various types of reforms, many of which improved
supervision and regulation (S&R) and other facets of banking policy. That

---

1. Bassett and Brady (2001, p. 720).

said, we do not think FDICIA will significantly reduce the chance that some TBTF coverage will be provided when large banks fail. We come to this conclusion by comparing the legal regime governing TBTF bailouts and the decisionmaking process that led to bailouts in the periods before and after FDICIA. Many aspects of the general legal regime and the decisionmaking process did not change, and the changes that did occur seem unlikely to limit the granting of some TBTF protection.

We are also skeptical about limitations that FDICIA put on the ability of the Federal Reserve to lend via the discount window. These reforms were intended to reduce the ability of the Fed to prop up banks through such credit extensions. Such loans were viewed as allowing banks to dig themselves a deeper hole, which made TBTF coverage more likely. However, as was the case with the reforms linked directly to too big to fail, these changes do not appear to have made the undesired outcome less likely. (We discuss other changes implemented by FDICIA, such as early closure of banks, throughout the book.)

The Least-Cost Test and TBTF Exemption

A number of analysts assert that FDICIA's least-cost-test reforms, along with a special procedure for providing government support to uninsured creditors, mean that TBTF bailouts will occur "rarely, if at all."[2] Ideally, we would judge FDICIA's effectiveness through empirical tests. As noted in chapter 4, the two event studies of FDICIA's effect on too big to fail produce mixed results. There is evidence, noted in chapters 4 and 6, that FDICIA led uninsured creditors to believe that they would not receive 100 percent protection if a TBTF bank went under. At the same time, the most closely related empirical examination finds that, post-FDICIA, banks were still shifting their risk of failure onto the government. Although this work is not limited to the largest institutions and is influenced by the very weak pricing of deposit insurance, it suggests that government guarantees for bank creditors continue to encourage bank risk-taking even after FDICIA.[3] More fundamentally, FDICIA's reforms have not been tested by the failure of a large bank.

The absence of experience with large bank failures under FDICIA and limited and conflicting empirical evidence require us to take a more deductive approach to evaluating FDICIA. Those who believe that FDICIA

2. Benston and Kaufman (1997, p. 150).
3. Hovakimian and Kane (2000).

corrected many of the problems from the prior regime argue, at least implicitly, that it materially improved the regulatory and legal incentives facing policymakers and banks. Therefore, we compare the pre- and post-FDICIA regimes to judge the adequacy of the TBTF regime created by FDICIA. The repeated praise for the major components of FDICIA implies that prior to its passage (1) supervisors did not have to seek special dispensation from standard resolution practices and cost tests when providing TBTF-like protection, (2) supervisors did not consult with one another and the administration in power, and (3) these decisions were not subject to intense public scrutiny. We believe these conditions do not hold and exaggerate the difference between the pre- and post-FDICIA regimes. We now describe the pre- and post-FDICIA regimes in more detail.

The Pre-FDICIA Cost Tests and Exceptions

The FDIC historically resolved failing banks through the purchase and assumption (P&A) method.[4] Under this method of resolution in the pre-FDICIA world, the failed bank was acquired by another institution, which assumed all the deposits (insured and uninsured) of the failed bank. The acquiring bank also typically purchased some of the assets of the failed bank. Reliance on P&As led the deposit insurer to cover all depositors. The FDIC covered more than 99 percent of all uninsured deposits from 1985 to 1991, a period in which roughly 1,200 commercial banks failed.[5]

Under a pre-FDICIA purchase and assumption, the FDIC also routinely covered nondeposit liability holders who were considered "general claimants," including sellers of Fed funds, holders of banker's acceptance, and the like.[6] In contrast, holders of equity and subordinated debt did not receive coverage under a typical P&A transaction. However, holders of subordinated debt issued by the bank may have received coverage when the FDIC used a resolution method called "open bank assistance." Under this method, which is not currently in use, the FDIC provided financial assistance to a bank still in operation. During the banking crisis—roughly 1985 to 1992—the FDIC used open bank assistance to manage failing banks that held about 10 percent of the assets of banks that failed or received assistance.[7] Thus, while the FDIC does not have easily accessible

---

4. Seidman (1991).

5. Glauber (1991, p. 105).

6. Private communication with Lynn Shibut of the Federal Deposit Insurance Corporation, February 2002.

7. Authors' calculations based on the Federal Deposit Insurance Corporation's Historical Statistics, available at www2.fdic.gov/hsob/ [September 9, 2003].

records indicating the precise level of coverage provided to uninsured creditors, it seems that many uninsured creditors had a reasonable chance of receiving government support.

One might wonder how the FDIC justified a regime that so clearly violated the distinction between insured and uninsured creditors. The rationale for extensive coverage, perhaps surprisingly, was cost. The FDIC argued that P&As were cheaper to the government than insured deposit payouts. In an insured deposit payout, the FDIC pays out insured depositors and sells or liquidates the rest of the institutions. In contrast, buyers in the P&A context pay a premium to acquire the entire deposit base as well as other aspects of the institution. The P&A allowed the FDIC to capture the institution's franchise value, which otherwise would be lost during liquidation.

The cost justification for protecting uninsured creditors, ironically, had its roots in attempts to limit excessive government protection for failed bank creditors.[8] During congressional hearings in 1951, Senator Fulbright challenged the FDIC's provision of 100 percent coverage for all depositors (a record that the FDIC touted in its 1950 annual report). Fulbright argued that such extensive coverage went beyond congressional intent and resulted from the absence of cost calculation. In response, the FDIC chairman agreed that the FDIC would choose a deposit payoff unless another option was cheaper, thereby creating a cost test to determine which method of resolution was chosen.

An exception to this cost test was related in several cases to concerns about systemic risk. Although most banks that failed during the banking crisis (roughly 1985 to 1992) were quite small, those banks with more than $1 billion in assets at failure held about 50 percent of the assets of banks that failed during this period.[9] The very largest failed banks—associated with MCorp, First Republic Bank, Bank of New England, and First National Bank and Trust—held most of the assets of the large failed banks (see table A-1 for measures of the size of failed banks). The FDIC believed the failure of these institutions posed a risk of spillovers, leading it to invoke the "essentiality" clause, which offered an escape from the comparison to the insured deposit payout.[10] The essentiality clause, like the cost test, had its roots in the 1950s. In 1950 the FDIC requested the ability to provide funding to banks

8. Federal Deposit Insurance Corporation (1984, pp. 86–87) discusses the history of the cost test.

9. Authors' calculations based on the Federal Deposit Insurance Corporation's Historical Statistics, available at www2.fdic.gov/hsob/ [September 9, 2003].

10. Federal Deposit Insurance Corporation (1984, pp. 94–95).

Table A-1. *Failed and Assisted Banks by Asset Size and Treatment of Uninsured Depositors, 1986–2000*

Year	Failed banks where uninsured depositors were protected			Failed banks where uninsured depositors were not protected		
	Average assets (millions of U.S. dollars)	Number of failed banks	Percent of failed banks	Average assets (millions of U.S. dollars)	Number of failed banks	Percent of failed banks
1986	60	105	72	33	40	28
1987	45	152	75	48	51	25
1988	218	244	87	37	36	13
1989	167	175	85	75	32	16
1990	89	149	88	124	20	12
1991	659	106	83	75	21	17
1992	454	55	45	306	67	55
Median 1986–92	167	149	83	75	36	17
1993	35	6	15	95	35	85
1994	125	5	38	98	8	62
1995	0	0	0	124	6	100
1996	36	2	40	37	3	60
1997	26	1	100	0	0	0
1998	39	1	33	197	2	67
1999	47	3	43	310	4	57
2000	10	1	17	75	5	71

Source: Federal Deposit Insurance Corporation (various years).

to prevent their failure (essentially a lender-of-last-resort function). Congress provided this power in the FDI Act of 1950 but limited such assistance to cases where "in the opinion of the Board of Directors the continued operation of such bank is essential to provide adequate banking service in the community"—that is, where a finding of "essentiality" is made.

The essentiality clause was used four times in the early 1970s for small banks for which a buyer could not be found immediately and for other banks in fairly unique situations, such as those that were minority owned and served inner-city communities. In 1980, however, the FDIC found for the first time that the large size of an institution—First Pennsylvania Bank, with assets of $8 billion—justified a finding of essentiality.[11]

11. Federal Deposit Insurance Corporation (1984, pp. 94–95); Davison (1997, p. 248).

The Garn–St. Germain Act of 1982 formalized both the notion of a cost test and an exception to it (while also expanding the ability of the FDIC to assist failing banks). The act stated, "No assistance . . . shall be provided . . . in an amount in excess of that . . . necessary to save the cost of liquidation." A finding of essentiality would allow a resolution that did not pass the cost test. The essentiality finding was made formally by the board of the FDIC. Garn–St. Germain also coupled an exception to the cost test with concerns of systemic risk. The legislation allowed the FDIC to provide direct assistance to a failed bank if "severe financial conditions exist which threaten the stability of a significant number of insured banks or of insured banks possessing significant financial resources," as long as a finding of essentiality is made.[12]

FDICIA and the New Cost Test and Essentiality Doctrine

In passing FDICIA Congress took aim at the extensive protection offered by the FDIC to uninsured creditors at small and large banks. The reforms took a two-part approach. First, it changed the cost test. The FDIC had to ensure that the method of failure resolution was the least costly, not just less costly than an insured deposit payout. This change required the FDIC to consider the cost of transferring only insured deposits to an acquirer, an option that typically is cheapest because it avoids the loss of franchise value.

Second, FDICIA reaffirmed the essentiality doctrine with changes. The changes include the following: FDICIA requires (1) a determination by the secretary of the Treasury that the least-cost resolution would "have serious adverse effects on economic conditions or financial stability" and that extraordinary insurance coverage would "avoid or mitigate such adverse effects," (2) consultations between the secretary of the Treasury and the president, (3) written recommendation from two-thirds of the Board of Governors of the Federal Reserve System, (4) written recommendation from two-thirds of the FDIC's board of directors, and (5) a special assessment on banks to pay for the coverage based on their total tangible assets.

The main difference between the ability of policymakers to protect uninsured creditors at large complex banks in the pre- and post-FDICIA world is the public involvement of the Federal Reserve and the Treasury. Establishing a cost test and allowing exceptions to it during exceptional circumstances are not new.[13] Moreover, consideration of systemic risk when

12. U.S. Senate (1982, p. 3099).
13. Isaac (1997) discusses how the pre-FDICIA cost test facilitated the lack of a bailout in the failure of Penn Central. See U.S. Code (1991, p. 2275).

calling for an exception to the cost test was not novel to FDICIA. The key question is whether the difference amounts to much in substance. In fact, we do not believe a more formal, more visible role for the Federal Reserve and the Treasury will lead to a significant change in the incentives that policymakers face when confronted with the bailout decision.

Agency Involvement and Publicity

Before FDICIA, both the Federal Reserve and the Treasury appear to have been intimately involved in deciding when and whether to bail out the creditors of large banks. Consider a description of the bailout of Continental Illinois. According to the comptroller of the currency,

> We debated at some length how to handle the Continental situation. ... Participating in those debates were the directors of the FDIC, the Chairman of the Federal Reserve Board, and the Secretary of the Treasury. In our collective judgment, had Continental failed and been treated in a way in which depositors and creditors were not made whole, we could very well have seen a national, if not an international, financial crisis the dimensions of which were difficult to imagine. None of us wanted to find out.[14]

Comptroller C. Todd Conover was later asked, "Is it correct to say that the decisions made on what the Government would and would not do with respect to Continental Illinois and its holding company, those decisions were made by yourself, Mr. Volcker [chairman of the Board of Governors of the Federal Reserve System], Mr. Regan [secretary of the Treasury], and Mr. Isaac [chairman of the FDIC]?" The comptroller responded, "Yes, that is correct."[15]

According to the FDIC, significant involvement by the Treasury and the Federal Reserve was not restricted to Continental Illinois. In testifying to Congress about FDICIA-like reforms to limit too big to fail, the chairman of the FDIC noted, "The provisions that the Treasury has proposed will make very little difference. We gave you the four cases where we actually invoked that [essentiality] doctrine. In every case we have been encouraged to invoke it by the Federal Reserve, and at least the Treasury has not been willing to say that they would advise us not to invoke it. I am concerned

14. Inquiry into Continental Illinois Corp. and Continental Illinois National Bank (1984, pp. 287–88).

15. Inquiry into Continental Illinois Corp. and Continental Illinois National Bank (1984, p. 345).

that we look at reality in terms of what is really going on."[16] Chairman William Seidman later repeated the same even more strongly, claiming that he gave the Treasury power to veto the bailout of the Bank of New England.[17] His characterization was not disputed by Treasury and Federal Reserve officials with whom he testified.

While FDICIA creates a more public process, it seems unsupportable to believe that the chairman of the Federal Reserve, the chairman of the FDIC, or the secretary of the Treasury thought their involvement in the Continental Illinois case or in other large failures were secrets. Congressional hearings and spotlights on the role that supervisors play in bank failures have a long tradition, preceding the Great Depression, which Continental Illinois merely affirmed. This tradition has continued; one of the first routine business hearings held by the Senate Committee on Banking after the September 11 terrorist attacks investigated the costly failure of a thrift (Superior Bank).

Others have argued that the increased formality of the review of large bank resolutions is a significant change. For example, a prominent academic and former Federal Reserve official has argued, "An extremely important part of FDICIA that is often overlooked is that FDICIA requires a mandatory review of any bank failure that imposes costs on the FDIC. . . . These provisions of FDICIA are extremely important because they increase the incentives of regulators to prevent costly bank failures."[18] The General Accounting Office carries out these reviews (as does the inspector general of the FDIC). But these reviews are hardly new. General Accounting Office staff were assigned to the House Committee on Banking to investigate the failure of Continental Illinois, testified during the hearings on Continental Illinois, and prepared a report evaluating the bailout of Continental Illinois.[19] Again, Continental Illinois was not the genesis of this practice. Congress has a long history of using its staff to investigate bank failures. To cite one example, in 1976 the Committee on Government Operations held oversight hearings into the effectiveness of federal bank regulation, focusing on the failure of Franklin National Bank. In 1989 the General Accounting Office played a central role in providing information on the behavior of thrift supervisors.[20]

16. Seidman (1991, p. 13).
17. Seidman (1991, p. 19).
18. Mishkin (1997, p. 24).
19. Dugger (1984); U.S. General Accounting Office (1984b).
20. U.S. General Accounting Office (1989).

FDICIA surely will have some effect on the behavior of policymakers when they debate bailouts. However, the small change in incentives from the prior regime leads us to believe that the magnitude of changes in behavior will be small as well. In our view, this result is not surprising because, despite rhetoric to the contrary, FDICIA's reforms did little to change the treatment accorded creditors of the largest and most complex banks. Claims in the legislative history of FDICIA that Congress "strongly intends that the too-big-to-fail policy is hereby abolished" must be understood in a context where too big to fail had multiple meanings, including the policy of providing routine coverage to uninsured creditors at all but the smallest banks.[21] For example, the undersecretary of the Treasury at the time argued that "'too-big-to-fail' is part of the FDIC's current policy to routinely extend deposit insurance protection beyond the $100,000 limit to *uninsured* depositors. . . . In a very few of these situations, the failure to provide such protection would clearly have resulted in serious risk to the financial system. But, in most cases, the protection of uninsured depositors occurred in resolutions that did not involve systemic risk through the routine use of so-called 'purchase and assumption' transactions."[22]

We do not mean to imply that FDICIA is toothless. The change in the cost test led to a substantial difference in the resolution of smaller institutions, for example. Indeed, where FDICIA intended to make significant changes, it appears to have succeeded. The treatment of the uninsured at smaller institutions posing no systemic risk, for instance, has changed dramatically. As table A-1 indicates, FDIC protection of uninsured depositors has declined a great deal since FDICIA went into effect.

The Lender of Last Resort

Lending from the central bank can prop up large banks and their creditors. Some policymakers believe that discount window lending by the Fed played such a role during the banking crisis of the late 1980s and early 1990s in the United States. Such lending would effectively protect those creditors who should be taking losses. Moreover, by allowing a weak bank to stay open past the time it should have been closed, the discount window loans could have increased the losses the creditors ultimately would suffer.

---

21. U.S. House of Representatives (1991, p. 1917). For a skeptical view on the validity of legislative histories, see Kozinski (1998).
22. Glauber (1991, p. 103).

To prevent the spillovers from such losses, the government could be more likely to provide bailouts. In these ways, restrictions on Fed discount window lending could make too big to fail less likely.

FDICIA responded with two types of restrictions on Fed lending that we do not think will do much to change behavior. They will fail in our view, and in the views of other Federal Reserve officials, because (1) they do a poor job of identifying weak banks because they are based on very weak measures of risk, specifically book capital; (2) they impose very small penalties on the Federal Reserve for lending to a weak institution; and (3) the effect of increased publicity for Federal Reserve lending is unclear.[23]

We have argued that the most salient tests of FDICIA's effectiveness are pre- and post-FDICIA comparisons. A Federal Reserve Bank president carried out such a thought experiment where the subject was one of the largest failures in his district prior to FDICIA. He argued that the losses to the FDIC surely were higher due to discount window lending and concluded that nothing in FDICIA would have changed the outcome of this case, largely because the uninsured, unsecured creditors fled during the time when it was still permissible for the Fed to provide discount window loans without penalty.

23. This analysis of FDICIA and discount under lending relies on Broaddus (2000).

Penalizing Policymakers

To the extent that the personal motivations described in chapter 5 explain TBTF coverage, then modifying that behavior is a logical response. In short, we might consider specific steps to raise the costs to policymakers of bailing out uninsured creditors and thus to prevent bailouts from happening. Costs to policymakers could be increased through several means, including direct imposition of penalties on supervisors, such as fines or the loss of jobs, reductions in budgets or other financial repercussions for supervisory agencies or governments, negative publicity, and policy changes that develop anti-bailout coalitions. (Some of the reforms we discuss in the text, such as more accurate budgeting and appointment of conservative policymakers, also address personal motivation.)

We are sympathetic to the intent of these suggestions, but with some exceptions, we do not endorse them as part of the near-term agenda for better managing expectations of TBTF coverage. They do not address the major motivations for bailing out creditors at TBTF banks, and implementing them successfully would prove challenging.

Imposing Direct Costs on Supervisors

To address concerns about motivation and potential forbearance, bank supervisors and elected officials could commit to closing banks aggressively. To make the "no-forbearance pledge" credible, policymakers could impose direct costs on supervisors for undesired behavior. In one such approach, governments could define unacceptable behavior and attach penalties to it. Supervisors or their agencies could be subject to fines, restrictions on activities, or imprisonment if they engage in illegal behavior. This reform sounds extreme. However, it is commonplace in the private sector. For example, boards of directors and bank officers are subject to punishment if they issue misleading information about the condition of their institution.

Another method for imposing costs on policymakers has it roots in monetary policy. Some countries commit to low inflation through so-called central bank contracts.[1] Such contracts link evaluations of the central banker's performance to inflation targets. Exceeding targets constitutes poor performance punishable by, for example, reductions in pay or dismissal. Analysts have termed an arrangement along these lines in New Zealand as quite similar to an "optimal central bank contract."[2] The ability to hold policymakers personally accountable, particularly through dismissal, can be an important aspect of such contracts.[3]

Societies could address problems of forbearance and the like by writing explicit contracts with policymakers that punish such behavior. Specifically, contracts could be written to encourage (1) the dissemination of accurate information on the health of the banking system and the potential for covering uninsured creditors and (2) steps, such as rapid closure of insolvent institutions, that reduce the potential for covering the uninsured. Failure to close insolvent institutions promptly, or provision of coverage to the uninsured, could lead to the loss of salary or a job. In other versions of such reforms, public officials could sign employment contracts that hold them personally liable for some small but nontrivial portion of a bailout.[4]

The contracts should have certain attributes to ensure their effectiveness, and we summarize several that seem particularly important.[5] First, a material amount of the payment for performance (or assessment of liability) should come after the supervisor finishes her term. Deferred action reduces the incentive to push losses into the future.

Second, the contract should establish incentives for outsiders to conduct routine assessments of the banking system and the likelihood of

1. Persson and Tabellini (1993); Walsh (1995b).
2. Walsh (1995a).
3. Walsh (2002).
4. Kane (1997) raises this concept.
5. These attributes are based, in part, on the discussion in Kane (2002).

government bailouts. The government could, for example, link the supervisor's future compensation to an accounting statement prepared on assumption of the position. If the likelihood of bailouts is understated initially, for example, the supervisor will lose out as the true condition is revealed on her watch.

Third, measures of supervisory performance should include some assessments generated by parties outside of the supervisory process. For example, market participants or bank creditors can generate an assessment of bank health and the probabilities of bailouts that supervisors cannot manipulate. Such assessments, therefore, provide a valid check on supervisory behavior.

Fourth, the contract should carefully define and incorporate the preferences of society in its terms. The intent of the contract is to align the objectives of policymakers with those of society. If the contract does not capture the correct preferences, then, by definition, it does not provide supervisors with the proper incentives.

Imposing Costs on Supervisory Agencies

An alternative reform links the performance of the supervisory agency to penalties and rewards rather than to policymakers directly. For example, the supervisory agency would face penalties through a loss of budgetary resources, if subject to the appropriations process, or through other sanctions that would curtail its standing and authority if it engaged in undesirable behavior. Given that the leaders of such agencies normally care a great deal about reputation and about issues such as the size, scale, and turf of their responsibilities, such steps could prove effective. This alternative also has the likely advantage of appearing more reasonable. Observers may be loath to target individuals for punishment but may not have the same concerns with regard to impersonal bureaucracies.

Not only does this approach mirror actions in the private sector in some sense, but it also reflects the fate of the Federal Home Loan Bank board. The bank board failed miserably in supervising the savings and loan industry in the 1980s and was abolished following the thrift debacle. Although this form of organizational punishment was applied in the case of the bank board for supervisory failure rather than for TBTF indulgences, we suspect the terminations also sent a message about the costs of supervisory failure to other agencies.

Another way to raise the costs of policies that encourage too big to fail is to mandate the issuance of federal debt that pays holders a lump sum if a bailout of a large complex banking organization, say, occurs and pays nothing if bailouts are avoided over the life of the instrument.[6] The payment for the debt could come out of the budget of the deposit insurer, thus imposing financial pressure on the agency. The structure of such debt is not completely novel. Insurance firms have issued so-called catastrophic bonds that make payouts if a disaster occurs but pay nothing if it does not. Moreover, several U.S. financial institutions issued so-called goodwill certificates that paid investors some portion of payments the firms would receive if they won a series of legal decisions from the federal government.

In addition to levying a financial penalty, market pricing of this instrument would provide information about the likelihood of bailouts. A high nominal yield, and therefore a low bond price, would signal a relatively low probability of bailout. One could accomplish something similar by having private insurers assume some risk for payments to bank creditors. The pricing of private insurance would provide both a cost that would rise if policymakers behave poorly and a signal of riskiness to outsiders.

Imposing Higher Costs on Policymakers via Publicity and Disclosure

Another approach to raising the costs to decisionmakers of undesirable behavior relies on greater disclosure and publicity. Disclosure would provide interested parties and the public with information so as to enhance the accountability of policymakers. The press also would have a significant role in using the disclosures to expose subpar performance. If decisionmakers recognize that their actions will be reviewed immediately, they will be unable to pass the buck and will be less likely to take actions that bring such repercussions.

Increased disclosure can take several forms. Many of these reforms are well known, as they were incorporated into the Federal Deposit Insurance Corporation Improvement Act of 1991 (FDICIA):

—Require investigations of bailouts and bank closures to be released publicly. The investigation could address the public cost of the bailout, the need for the bailout, and beneficiaries of the bailout.

—Require policymakers to articulate the conditions under which they would provide bailouts. Policymakers, including those elected to office, could then be required to approve bailouts publicly, to explain the rationale

6. This suggestion is based on Wall (1997).

for their actions in general and the weight given to moral hazard consider-ations in particular, and to compare their ex ante statements to their actions.

—Require analysts to estimate and report on the expected costs of pro-tecting uninsured creditors of large banks. The estimates should be subject to audit and independent verification. Similar analysis could be conducted on the condition of the banking system and the efficiency with which supervisors close banks.

—Require analysts publicly to compare outside, presumably market-based, assessments of the condition of banks and of the government deposit insurer to supervisory assessments.

Encourage Third Parties to Impose Pressures on Policymakers

The options we have discussed so far impose costs directly on policymak-ers. Another option would impose the costs of bailouts on a small group of individuals or firms with the resources and skill to influence legislators. Currently, the cost to individual taxpayers from bailouts is small, while the benefits to the protected firm and its creditors are large. This distribution of costs and benefits gives taxpayers little reason to oppose bailouts and provides protected firms and creditors with significant reason to make sure such bailouts can occur.

Focusing bailout costs on a small group would motivate its members to identify the chance of a bailout and act to reduce it. This logic helps to explain FDICIA reforms that effectively require large banks to pay dispro-portionately for bailout coverage for the uninsured in the United States.[7] A similar plan to alter the costs and benefits of TBTF protection would allow taxpayers to bring lawsuits against policymakers, or their agencies, for vio-lations of their duties. With lawsuits, the benefits of stopping too big to fail increase appreciably for taxpayers.

Reservations

We have multiple reservations about approaches to discourage TBTF cov-erage that rely on increasing the costs to policymakers. These reservations include a lack of credibility, potentially adverse consequences for interme-diation and economic activity, and the failure to come to grips with key incentives underpinning too big to fail. In some cases, these reservations

7. Benston and Kaufman (1997, p. 150).

are widely shared, reflecting concerns that have become fodder for text-books.[8] Because we believe that other reforms discussed in this book have either more strengths or fewer weaknesses, we generally would not make the reforms discussed in this appendix a priority.

Lack of Credibility

These reforms rely on a commitment to impose costs on policymakers in the future based on actions specified in the current period. In trying to solve a one-time consistency problem, these reforms create another. When the time comes, will the policymaker who violated the commitment really have to take her lumps? If the policymaker has doubts about bearing future costs, she has less incentive to change her behavior.

Experience with central bank contracts suggests that strict enforcement of the contract may prove challenging. In New Zealand, home of the supposedly optimal central bank contract, the government changed the targets by which it judged the central banker after an election. Although it did not technically violate the contract, the New Zealand government twice passed on penalizing the head of the central bank after inflation exceeded the amounts specified in his contract. Such permissiveness is not necessarily consistent with the spirit of the literature on optimal contracting.[9]

The problem is more general than suggested by a discussion of central bank contracts. After accepting reforms discussed in this chapter, the supposed undesirable behavior may not strike policymakers who have to enforce the contract as being all that bad. Elected officials may agree that they do not want TBTF bailouts immediately after the expense of a failed institution but have less conviction several years later. As a result, the penalties may seem unfair at the time they go into effect.

As a specific example, consider a policy of mobilizing large banks to oppose bailouts by sticking them with the costs. Bailouts often come during troubled times, when policymakers seek to burnish the strength of the banking system rather than impose additional taxes on it. We think that policymakers with the steel to impose losses on banks would not have bailed out banks in the first place. If, in fact, policymakers felt comfortable imposing the bailout tax on banks, it seems more than likely to us that the tax would be levied at an insignificant level unlikely to generate the opposition of large banks to bailouts.

8. For example, our concerns about central bank contracts mirror those of Obstfeld and Rogoff (1996).
9. This discussion of New Zealand is based on Bernanke and others (1998).

Limitations in Contracting

Almost all of the reforms discussed in this appendix rely on contracts to link performance of policymakers to rewards and punishments. Explicit contracts work well if the nuances of the desired outcome are adequately represented, compliance can be verified at low cost, the terms do not need frequent updating, and the penalties for failure to perform are credible. In addition to our skepticism about credibility, we do not think that the other prerequisites for effective contracting apply in the case of many of these reforms.

A couple of examples make our point. It could prove quite challenging for the contract to reflect the subtle goals of government banking policy. Citizens may want supervisors to give some banks a fair or second chance to regain their health, while deeming others as needing swift punishment depending on the idiosyncratic situation of each institution.

More generally, ensuring compliance with the goals of the contract requires it to consider and address the contingencies and actions that supervisors might use to evade its dictates. We doubt such a comprehensive contract could be written. Would, for example, a contract preclude the ability of one government to bail out another? Such bailouts could benefit domestic banks with large loans to that country and circumvent the intent of the contract.

Effectiveness of Disclosure

Additional information on the condition of the banking system and on the performance of bank supervisors is a good thing, particularly if produced by parties not directly involved in the supervision. As a general matter, we support reforms that would provide such information, assuming it is not too costly to produce. The open question is how effective such disclosures will prove in reducing protection for the uninsured. In some cases, such as the budgeting of public resources, we think additional information will prove particularly effective.

However, the effectiveness of budgeting reform comes not from new data per se but rather from its institutional context. In the budgeting environment, the new information forces policymakers to give up other priorities if they want to allocate more resources to bank creditors. The disclosure reflects a real cost imposed on policymakers through lost opportunities. Likewise, we recommend greater use of outside assessments of banks and the government insurer in the context of setting insurance premiums or levying supervisory action. Again, in this context the new information is linked explicitly to specific actions that impose costs.

It is less obvious that information released with the intent of applying public or political pressure would have the same salutary effect. Warnings of large taxpayer exposures due to weakness in the banking system might generate considerable public concern and motivate decisionmakers to change their ways. Likewise, policymakers might be reluctant to support a creditor bailout if their involvement in such action is immediately disclosed. But numerous press accounts documenting costly, inefficient, and regressive government programs (for example, agricultural subsidies, trade tariffs, costly regulation) appear to have had limited effect. Perhaps the story of poorly implemented banking policies will grip the public's attention, but numerous counterexamples suggest that poor policies continue after exposure.

Why might disclosure and publicity fail to materially improve policy?

—Efficiency losses represent the bulk of the costs imposed by TBTF policies. Such losses are ephemeral to most taxpayers and are difficult to explain in a compelling manner to the average citizen.

—Fiscal costs from TBTF bailouts, while large in the aggregate, do not amount to a large figure per taxpayer. As such, rational taxpayers may not get up in arms about such protection.

—Calculations of the health of the banking system and the likelihood of TBTF bailouts are likely to be ambiguous. Thus, even if certain figures receive official sanction, we assume that interested parties will find seemingly reputable analysts to produce alternative estimates. Given that some genuine uncertainty about the calculations certainly exists, the public and press face a significant challenge in sorting through the debate.

A final point: Some assume that the public and press will applaud policies that impose losses on bank creditors, allow banks to fail, and even shutter banks that have positive capital. Surely, this assumption will prove correct in some cases. Yet we can easily imagine stories about creditors who unfairly lost life savings, about an overly aggressive government closing down healthy banks, and about policies that put financial stability at risk. Policymakers may receive as much bad press if they try to maximize benefits to society as they would if they try to maximize their own gains. This may help to explain why negative press on forbearance and bailouts has not proven sufficient to radically alter the potential for TBTF protection in many countries.

An Overall Assessment of the Reforms

We have raised a number of reservations about reforms that seek to reduce the likelihood of bailouts by making them costly to policymakers. But one can easily go too far in criticizing such proposals. Reforms need not pass the perfection standard but instead must have a reasonable chance of achieving a better benefit-cost outcome than current policy. The often tenuous connection between the performance of policymakers with regard to banking policy and the rewards and punishments they receive implies that some improvement is possible.

Even with flaws in the New Zealand central bank contract, this policy appears to have helped to restrain inflation. Likewise, some of the concerns about contracting could also apply to private sector firms that make use of sticks and carrots to motivate their leaders. Although they do not work in every case, linking performance with rewards and costs, increasing the amount of information available to outsiders, and holding leaders accountable for results appear to have benefited shareholders. Indeed, a move to hold supervisors explicitly responsible for desired outcomes seems sensible even if TBTF were not a significant problem.

But we cannot ask policymakers to focus on all possible reforms at the same time. We must suggest some priorities, especially since we are considering a wide range of reforms. Because of their real limitations and because most of the reforms discussed in this appendix would face significant difficulty in becoming law, we view them as of secondary importance. Perhaps the overriding reason for not endorsing them in the short run is that, as discussed in chapter 5, we view other forces as playing a larger role in leading to TBTF protection.

APPENDIX C

Supervision and Regulation

Virtually all countries have a regime in place to limit bank risk-taking: the supervision and regulation (S&R) of banks by government employees. A primary justification for S&R is to offset the excessive risk-taking induced, in part, by government guarantees. In many countries, S&R is the de facto policy to prevent costly bank failures and spillovers, thus limiting the incentive to bail out uninsured creditors.

The outstanding question is, however, whether S&R is robust enough to serve as the primary or exclusive tool for managing the TBTF problem. While S&R is one tool that can help to address the TBTF problem, we do not think it should be viewed as a complete response. We come to this conclusion based on some practical limitations of S&R and a blemished track record.[1]

Why Supervision?

We first briefly describe what we mean by supervision and regulation.[2] Bank regulation involves the issuance of rules that govern bank operations. The rules can vary a great deal in their specificity and formality (ranging

1. Wilmarth (2002) also raises a number of concerns about using S&R to address the TBTF problem.
2. Supervision and regulation are described in general in Mishkin (2001) and Federal Deposit Insurance Corporation (1997, pp. 463–75) and in great detail in Board of Governors of the Federal Reserve System (1994).

from examiner handbooks to incorporation in law). Typical regulations govern minimum capital levels, limitations on the type and amount of assets that banks may hold and the activities in which they can participate, and the creation and ongoing ownership of banks. Other types of regulations address concerns about competition and antitrust, consumer protection, and service to the community, but since these are tangential to safety and soundness, we do not address them.

Supervision involves, in part, a review of bank activities to ensure that they are in compliance with regulation. It also involves, more generally, the assessment of the riskiness of banks. Part of this assessment involves analysis of data from mandated financial reports as well as sources specific to any given bank. This off-site data analysis supplements the on-site supervisory reviews of loan quality, risk management, and other factors that take place on the physical premises of the bank. Based on their assessment, supervisors take steps to ensure that banks operate prudently. Many of these general supervisory and regulatory practices have been codified in listings of essential practices for bank supervisors.[3]

These types of supervisory and regulatory activities can play a positive role in managing bank risk-taking. As a result, we consider them important tools to wield against the TBTF problem. We now explain this view in more detail before discussing the limitations of S&R.

Economic Theory

As noted in chapter 5, a defining feature of banks is the opaque nature of their assets and the difficulty in analyzing their risk-taking.[4] Because it could be quite costly for depositors to evaluate the risk-taking of a bank, they may not price bank liabilities correctly. Depositors may charge too little for the use of their funds given the bank's true risk.

Banks may take on too much risk for another reason. We have already noted how the failure of one bank may affect the solvency of another. However, banks have no reason to factor this potential cost into their actions. The cost of spillovers is borne largely by society and not by the bank that failed. If banks fully considered the cost that failure could have on society as a whole, they would take on less risk. Finally, some argue that even if creditors could become fully informed at a relatively low cost, having many

3. Basel Committee on Banking Supervision (1997).
4. Although they note that disagreement remains as to the rationale for bank supervision and regulation, Dewatripont and Tirole (1994) focus on protection of small depositors as the primary motivating factor. For other reviews of the economics of bank regulation, see Bhattacharya, Boot, and Thakor (1998); Freixas and Santomero (2002).

small depositors carrying out similar analysis is wasteful. A central party could carry out the analysis more cost-effectively.

Several firms in the United States perform this centralized analysis, as do credit rating agencies. However, private markets may produce less than the desired amount of analysis because of the so-called free-rider problem. A bank creditor may decide not to purchase private analysis of bank risk-taking, hoping to acquire the information for free from others. For example, a creditor who did not buy the analysis could observe the behavior of creditors who did. Free riders reduce the demand for information below the amount society would prefer. Some analysts also doubt that the small depositor we describe could effectively act on this analysis even if it were produced and widely available.

S&R could address the excessive risk-taking of banks, the inadequate amount of public information on the risk-taking of banks, and the subsequent weak market discipline in several ways. S&R could, for example, prohibit banks from holding assets deemed particularly risky or require banks to reveal the true quality of loans. In the best case, supervisors would represent creditors, particularly small unsophisticated ones, and take the actions that these creditors would call for if they were fully informed.

There is a second rationale for S&R, namely explicit and implicit government guarantees. Federal Reserve Board chairman Greenspan has summarized the situation nicely:

> As a society we have made the choice to create a safety net for depository institutions, not only to protect the public's deposits but also to minimize the impact of adverse developments in financial markets on our economy. Although we have clearly been successful in doing so, the safety net has predictably created a moral hazard: the banks determine the level of risk-taking and receive the gains therefrom but do not bear the full cost of that risk; the remainder is borne by the government. Since the sovereign credit of the United States ultimately guarantees the stability of the banking system and the claims of insured depositors, bank creditors do not apply the same self-interest monitoring of banks to protect their own position as they would without discount window access and deposit insurance.... Put another way, the safety net requires that the government replace with law, regulation, and supervision much of the disciplinary role that the market plays for other businesses.[5]

5. Greenspan (1998a, p. 3).

A natural question is whether S&R, even if justified in theory, works in practice. The evidence is generally positive. There is a role for S&R in reducing risk-taking.

Practical Evidence

Several types of evidence suggest that supervision has practical value, particularly in revealing information to market participants that they may never uncover or would uncover only with a long time lag. As a recent analysis notes, "Supervisory exams have an important role in uncovering financial problems and ensuring that bank accounting statements reflect them." This effect of the supervisory exam can show up, for example, in an increase in the reserves banks hold against loans.[6]

Examinations of the "informational content" of assessments or ratings given to U.S. banking organizations by examiners—we discuss these ratings below—also find that supervisors uncover negative information on institutions that market participants otherwise would not have discovered for some time.[7] And, at least for a short time, supervisory assessments predict bank failures as well as or better than the financial ratios often cited in analysis by market participants.[8] Market participants appear to value the role of supervisors in uncovering problems, putting greater stock in accounting statements released after a bank exam.[9]

In addition to identifying risk, supervisors can address and reduce at least some of the risk-taking of banks. For example, formal enforcement actions in the United States lead banks to behave in ways, such as reducing the growth in their assets, consistent with a reduction in risk-taking. These same salutary effects of supervision hold for all banks deemed in trouble by supervisors and not only those subject to formal restrictions.[10] A comprehensive review of the empirical research on capital regulation suggests that capital rules put into place largely since the late 1980s have induced poorly capitalized banks to raise capital faster than they would have otherwise.[11] (This empirical review is, however, not all positive, and reviews of capital regulations from a more theoretical standpoint are also ambiguous as to their likely effectiveness.)[12]

6. Gunther and Moore (2002, p. 1) and citations within.
7. DeYoung and others (2001).
8. Cole and Gunther (1998).
9. Flannery and Houston (1999).
10. Federal Deposit Insurance Corporation (1997, pp. 421–62); Gilbert (1997); Peek (1997).
11. Jackson (1999).
12. Santos (2001).

Recent financial crises have also convinced many observers of the importance of supervision and regulation. Specifically, according to these observers, Asian economies that suffered financial crises in the 1990s, as well as countries in other regions, had weak supervisory and regulatory regimes. They imply that more rigorous supervision would have effectively limited risk-taking. For example, one analyst notes, "Emerging market countries, and particularly those in East Asia, are notorious for weak financial regulation and supervision. When financial liberalization yielded new opportunities to take on risk, these weak regulatory/supervisory systems could not limit the moral hazard created by the government safety net, and excessive risk-taking was the result."[13]

Counterexamples

Not all are convinced of S&R's utility. The current regime—where government already intervenes through guarantees—may not provide a good test of the effectiveness of supervision relative to creditors. These critics point to historical periods, which we discuss in chapter 5, where neither deposit insurance nor public regulation was necessary to ensure financial stability. A more recent case implying that traditional supervision and regulation are superfluous comes from New Zealand. Several years ago New Zealand adopted what would strike bank supervisors as an unregulated banking system, and the country does not have deposit insurance either. New Zealand relies primarily on disclosure by the banks and on director oversight to limit risk-taking appropriately.[14] So far this approach has worked well, but we do not think it offers much guidance.

Virtually all of the bank assets of New Zealand are owned by foreign institutions. Although foreign ownership was not nearly as prevalent when the reformed S&R system was being planned, the effect of such foreign ownership means that the bulk of government monitoring of these institutions has shifted to foreign supervisors. Others have come to the same conclusion: "New Zealand was free-riding on the supervision of banks carried out by other countries."[15] Presumably, if one or more of these banks were to get into financial difficulty, the main resolution of the bank would fall to the foreign authorities as well. Thus, from our vantage point, it is not clear

13. Mishkin (1999, p. 3). See also Garcia and Saal (1996); Mishkin (2002).
14. See Lang (1996) for a general discussion of New Zealand's supervisory system and Mayes, Halme, and Liuksila (2001) for links between such a system and TBTF reform.
15. Bank of England (1998, p. 46).

if the New Zealand authorities are counting on effective market discipline to promote safety and soundness or if they are betting on a TBTF policy on the part of the banks' home countries. It would be interesting to know how bank liabilities are priced in New Zealand and if creditors distinguish among institutions, but apparently such data have not been collected and are of little interest to the authorities.

Even if the case of New Zealand does not lead us to reject traditional supervision and regulation, we must acknowledge that supervisors and policymakers cannot point to a robust body of research to support claims that certain types of S&R are more effective than others. While S&R works in the "right direction" (for example, leads to less risk-taking), reviews of supervision and regulation do not indicate if it is cost-effective or if it leaves society facing too much or too little risk-taking in the banking system.

Limited evidence puts hurdles in front of arguments that supervision and regulation would effectively limit the risk-taking induced by TBTF guarantees. In fact, we have not yet discussed some of the limitations to S&R. These limitations caution against relying on S&R exclusively or in the main for managing TBTF.

Limitations of Bank Supervision and Regulation

We discuss several limitations of bank supervision and regulation that explain our reluctance to rely on it too heavily to limit expectations of TBTF protection. They include factors that reduce the speed of supervisory responses to bank risk-taking and challenges to supervisory determinations of how much risk banks should take. In addition, the supervisory track record in many countries has not always been exemplary.

Inability of Supervisors to Respond in a Timely Fashion

Although supervisors do respond to bank risk-taking, their response may take some time. Profit-maximizing banks will always be searching for products, services, and transactions that add to the bottom line. They have ample incentive to be creative and inventive. Because of the mispricing of their liabilities, some of this creativity will be the means by which banks assume too much risk.

In contrast, supervisors do not devote time to thinking of new ways to add to earnings and naturally face challenges in trying to determine which of the many possible means banks will use to take on too much risk. Perhaps in response to difficulty in forecasting future areas of risk-taking, supervisors seek to measure the current state of the supervised institution and rely largely on historical performance to generate that assessment. Consider the Federal Deposit Insurance Corporation's description of the summary measure that results from bank exams. These assessments are "based only on internal operations, measure only the current financial condition of a bank, and do not take into account regional or local economic developments that may pose future problems but that are not yet reflected in the bank's condition. . . . [These assessments] by design are not forward looking and do not systematically track long-term factors that may cause losses several years later. Thus, the picture they provide of a bank's condition is current rather than prospective."[16]

The retrospective and thus reactive nature of S&R may also reflect the reliance that supervisors appear to place on banks to identify problem areas (asset quality being one notable exception). Supervisors can be caught by surprise, as a result, if banks withhold information, do not highlight for supervisors those activities that pose significant risk, or underestimate the risks that they do take on. In many cases, it is only after a shock—a collapse of an economic sector or country to which the bank lent considerable money—that the true risk of the firm's strategy becomes clear to supervisors, bank managers, and directors.

These observations are not meant as criticisms because we can think of no realistic way that supervision could move beyond its current reactive stage. And it may not necessarily be a serious problem that supervisors trail banking practices. But if there is, say, a new product that proves to be riskier than anticipated and if supervisors are slow to recognize this fact, there may be adverse financial repercussions for the bank before corrective action can be taken.

Even if they identify risks in a timely fashion, supervisors will face at least some delay before they act. The delay in action reflects a legal or rule-based environment where supervisors prefer to act against an institution if they have a rule or regulation in place to justify their steps. While supervisors wait to enact rules, banks can continue to engage in undesirable behavior. And this delay can be long. Rules to address the capital treatment of asset sales took roughly seven years to finalize.[17] Delays in supervisory action also arise because most countries believe banks should receive due process and that supervisory judgment should face review. As a result,

16. Federal Deposit Insurance Corporation (1997, pp. 437–38).
17. U.S. Treasury Department, Federal Reserve System, and Federal Deposit Insurance Corporation (2001).

supervisors have to amass considerable evidence before they act, particularly if the bank officials and members of boards of directors disagree with a supervisory assessment.

Finally, our impression is that there are meaningful differences between the human capital of bank and supervisory staff. While supervisors do hire staff who can match the human capital deployed by banks, the numbers do not strike us as favorable. For example, the Office of the Comptroller of the Currency has highly skilled staff, generally with doctorates in economics or finance, who assist examiners in their analysis of the more complex instruments and activities of large banks. Informal inquiries suggest that the total staffing of this unit is on the order of twenty people. Although other competent analysts at the Office of the Comptroller of the Currency surely can discuss these issues with their counterparts at banks, the small size of the analytical group is at least suggestive that supervisors could find themselves, at times, outgunned.

Imprecision of the Supervisory or Regulatory Response

A second reason not to rely too heavily on a supervisory response to excessive risk-taking induced by TBTF support is the potentially imprecise responses of supervisors. Consider the exam rating, probably the most important output of the supervisory process. In the U.S. context, banks rated 4 or 5 are the weakest; banks rated 1 or 2 are considered in sound condition. These ratings are critical inputs in determining the supervisory response to a bank's activities. Banks rated 3 or greater face restrictions on their activities, while banks with better ratings tend to face few supervisory limitations.

A trigger for supervisory response that can only take five values inherently lacks fine precision (in reality, bank ratings tend to take on very few values; during the last several years of the 1990s, for example, virtually no bank holding company had a rating greater than 2). Moreover, despite the use of numbers, these ratings are not quantitative measures of risk. Rather than being labeled 1 through 5, they could have been given the titles A through E. And just like many grades, the difference between these ratings— particularly between those considered satisfactory (rating 2) and those considered unsatisfactory (rating 3)—is subjective. Yet one class of institutions tends to receive automatic restrictions, while the other does not. That is, despite the lack of precision, the difference in ratings matters greatly.

To be fair, supervisors use a variety of tools to respond to banking conditions, and their analytical output goes beyond the overall bank rating.

Typically, supervisory actions work through board of director's resolutions, memoranda of understanding between regulators and banks, cease-and-desist orders, and other legal actions. These orders may require staff changes, limits on growth or new activities, exits from existing businesses, and the like. These responses do allow for some targeting of actions against a bank. However, even these more subtle responses are not really suitable for guiding bank activities. They would not, for example, require an institution to grow (or contract) at a rate conditional on a complex set of factors that varies over time. Without such conditions, it is not clear whether the supervisory response will encourage banks to take on something approaching the appropriate amount of risk.

All of the factors we have discussed combine to make it difficult for a supervisor to determine how much risk banks and the banking system should assume. Would it be the risk of failing one out of a thousand times or one out of a million times? We certainly could come up with a simple rule for supervisors to follow, such as preventing all failures. Such a broad mandate, however, must be incorrect for a dynamic economy.

Our concern is neither new nor a broadside aimed at supervisors per se. Governments cannot readily accumulate and process the information needed to determine the overall extent and type of risks that financial intermediaries should take. The fundamental conundrum facing supervisors is relived every time economies move into or out of recession. During such periods, critics or elected officials accuse supervisors of being too easy or too tough. Such claims may be spurious. Although supervisors can identify when they are trying to reduce risk-taking in the banking system, it would be difficult to determine whether the amount of risk generated by a change in supervisory posture is the right amount.

A similar problem occurs with regulations. Researchers do not know if the typical capital regime, for example, leads to more risk-taking by banks, as some theory suggests, or less, as most supervisors assume. However, researchers do know that the blunt nature of most existing capital regimes leads banks to game the system so that they can hold less regulatory capital without reducing their actual risk-taking.[18]

An Imperfect Supervisory Track Record

Our final reason for not relying exclusively on S&R is its track record. Supervisors have struggled to prevent the conditions that make coverage

18. Jackson (1999).

for uninsured creditors of large banks more likely. Such limitations were apparent during the most recent banking crisis in the United States. Analysts point to similar experiences across a wide range of other countries, as do empirically based reviews of banking performance, banking crises, and supervision and regulation. The most comprehensive review to date finds "measures of supervisory power, resources, independence, loan classification stringency, provisioning stringency, etc., are not robustly linked with bank performance or stability. . . . These results do not support the strategies of many international agencies that focus on empowering official supervisory oversight of bank practices."[19]

Likewise, capital regulation is not closely linked with bank performance or stability. In contrast, supervisory actions that lead to more disclosure and increase the chance that private creditors will monitor banks are associated with a higher level of bank performance. This and related analysis suggest that countries seeking to address bank risk-taking foster a regulatory environment encouraging "multiple eyes" to oversee banks.[20]

Surely many extenuating circumstances surrounded recent banking crises. The banking debacles in the United States, in the view of some, resulted from the "perfect storm," a once-in-a-lifetime confluence of events that we do not expect to see again. In addition to deregulation, there were regional economic depressions, massive swings in interest rates, and a corruption of the supervisory process by elected officials. For many decades S&R appeared adequate to the task of limiting bank risk-taking.

However, these explanations for the poor performance of S&R are not satisfying. Government supervision is, by definition, part of the political process. It should be able to withstand political forces precisely when taxpayers need protection. If S&R withers in a politicized environment, it cannot be the main bulwark against TBTF protection. Likewise, a trying economic environment and heightened competition cannot excuse limitations in S&R's ability to address excessive risk-taking. During such periods society needs an effective constraint on banks.

The Effectiveness of Supervisory Reform

Some may find our description of supervision and regulation outdated. Over the last decade, supervisors have developed what they view as new

19. Barth, Caprio, and Levine (2002, p. 39). See also Caprio (1997).
20. Rossi (1999) provides an alternative view.

techniques that maintain their relevance, speed their actions, and provide for more precise responses. Rather than point-in-time reviews of specific bank activities, supervisors have a continuous presence at large organizations and focus on risk management systems. By encouraging systems that establish limits on risk-taking, monitor risk-taking, and report and respond to exceptions to the limits, supervisors believe they can better ensure that banks do not take on too much risk.

The move to so-called risk-focused exams should help, but we do not see it as sufficient justification for making S&R the main limit on the risk-taking of big banks.[21] In some ways, the switch to risk-focused exams reflects the limitations we have discussed. Supervisors must try to overcome staff and information limitations when trying to assess the true risks of the institutions they supervise. As a result, they typically rely on the risk management reporting systems of the institution in question to discuss the activities of the bank with management. As noted, a high degree of reliance on bank systems could make it hard to quickly capture breakdowns in risk management. And the restrictions we have discussed on the ability of supervisors to determine how much risk banks should assume also make it quite difficult for them to determine what constitutes an appropriate risk management system. Moreover, the risk-focused approach does not make it any easier to figure out where banks take excessive risk when they are profitable and appear to be safe and sound.

21. Ward (2002) is also skeptical of the new supervisory approach.

Increasing Market Discipline

E xisting market discipline for TBTF banks is insufficient; hence the reforms we suggest in this book. This judgment does not prevent us from believing that market forces—to some limited degree in their current form, but especially in the future—could play a role in managing the risk of large banks and the TBTF problem. Market discipline should have a more important role in managing bank risk-taking in the future, when governments implement the reforms we discuss, dampen expectations of TBTF protection, and improve the quality of market prices. Several of the technological trends that we argue have made too big to fail a greater threat also have the potential to reduce the opacity of bank assets. As a result, market participants should better understand bank risk-taking tomorrow than they do today.

We begin this appendix by summarizing the technological changes that might make banks easier to analyze. We then discuss the benefits of direct discipline in more detail, explain why supervisors' current reliance on disclosure to increase direct discipline is misplaced, and review more structured methods for increasing direct discipline. By leading to more optimal risk-taking by banks, increased market discipline should lead to fewer cases of, and justification for, TBTF bailouts. We think this desired outcome is most likely if policymakers view reforms to increase direct discipline as supporting, or following, our reforms for putting creditors at risk of loss.

We conclude by making the case for greater incorporation of market data into the supervisory process (indirect discipline). We discuss specific suggestions for how supervisors could make better use of market data in their assessments, in the pricing of deposit insurance, and in the setting of triggers that require supervisory action. By doing so, supervisors could improve their capacity to manage bank risk-taking and make the perceived need for TBTF protection less compelling. Again, we see some benefits from moving forward in the near term with greater use of market data by supervisors, while recognizing that the most significant returns should come after creditors view themselves as being at greater risk of loss.

How Changes in Technology Might Increase Bank Transparency

In chapter 6 we identify several trends related to changes in bank technology and operations that should widen and deepen creditors' expectations of TBTF protection. We argue that these trends could make TBTF coverage more likely by, for example, making supervisors less certain about how the failure of one institution might affect another. At the same time, these trends could make bank assets more transparent and allow for better risk management. We think these trends will make it less costly to analyze bank assets and allow for improved risk management. As a result, policymakers should have additional confidence in the future ability of creditors to assess the riskiness of banks and improve their subsequent decisions regarding pricing and quantity.

One trend that is increasing the transparency of banks is the growing portion of loans that have attributes of securities trading in financial markets:

—The volume of bank loans trading on markets after original issuance grew from $8 billion in 1991 to $118 billion in 2001 (and nearly $90 billion in loans were traded in the first three quarters of 2002).[1]

—The dollar volume of syndicated loans outstanding roughly doubled from 1993 to 2001, growing to about $750 billion.[2] These loans are for amounts of more than $20 million, are held by three or more organizations, and can trade over their life (see figure D-1).

1. Loan data from Loan Pricing Corporation, found at www.loanpricing.com [November 4, 2002]. Demsetz (1999) and Dahiya, Puri, and Saunders (2001) discuss loan sales.
2. Jones, Lang, and Nigro (2001) and Board of Governors of the Federal Reserve System, U.S. Office of the Comptroller of the Currency (OCC), and Federal Deposit Insurance Corporation (2002) discuss syndicated loans.

Figure D-1. *Growth in Syndicated and Traded Loans and Asset-Backed Securities, 1995–2001*

Billions of U.S. dollars   Billions of U.S. dollars

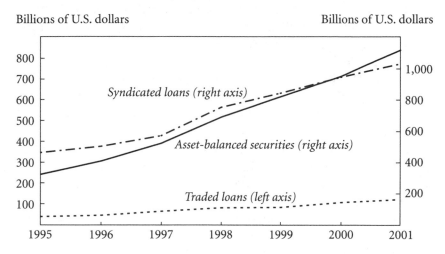

Sources: See www.loanpricing.com; OCC and FDIC (2002); www.bondmarkets.com/Research/absos.shtml.

—The market for securities backed by loans has grown substantially. Issuance of so-called collateralized debt obligations (CDOs)—securities whose payments depend on the performance of a pool of assets, including bank loans and bonds—went from roughly $8 billion at the end of 1998 to $500 billion at the end of 2001.[3]

—Issuance of loans in the so-called asset-backed securities market—securities backed by consumer loans or smaller business loans—has risen fourfold, from roughly $300 billion to $1.2 trillion between 1995 and 2002.

There are several reasons why having a loan assume attributes of a security increases transparency of the asset. For example, turning loans into securities—securitization—requires the loans to have a significant level of uniformity. It also requires the lender to provide loan-specific data so that investors can estimate their expected returns and monitor actual performance. Securitization therefore leads banks to structure loans so that they are easier to analyze.

3. John Glover, "Abbey National Shuns Junk in CDOs," *Bloomberg News*, September 23, 2002. See Board of Governors of the Federal Reserve System (1999a) for a description of these securities.

The benefits of the sale and trading of whole loans are more straight-forward. Such sales and trading generate prices—and other information, such as credit ratings—that reflect the expected performance of the loan. Particularly important, observers now have third-party measures of the riskiness of the assets that banks hold. For example, FitchRatings, like other major ratings firms, has a group dedicated to the analysis of CDOs and bank loans. The firm notes that this group "was formed in response to the increasing liquidity of the secondary loan and high-yield bond markets, the growing role of loan securitization in bank capital management, and increased institutional interest in loans as an investment."[4]

Ease in selling loans also facilitates risk management by allowing more investors to share the risk of the borrower. Whereas the banking sector may have assumed and kept most of the risk of lending to a given industry or region, these technologies now allow the risk to be deconcentrated. Not only can other financial institutions take on the risk of these borrowers, but so too can individuals. For example, a number of mutual funds, often called prime rate or loan participation, specialize in the holding of bank loans.[5] Advances in the development of financial instruments even allow banks to share the risks of their borrowers when they do not sell the loan (through a financial contract called a credit derivative).[6] Some policymak-ers have explicitly linked these developments to a reduction in spillover threat, noting that "if risk is properly dispersed, shocks to the overall eco-nomic system will be better absorbed and less likely to create cascading failures that could threaten financial stability."[7]

In addition to loans becoming more like securities, advances in comput-ing and financial technology have led to analytical tools that make the assets of banks easier for outsiders to comprehend. Many banks now assign a rat-ing or score to their loans that indicates the likelihood of default and some-times the loss given default. This advance reduces the need to have private information to understand the expected performance of loans held by banks, although this would require the bank to disclose such information.

We do not argue that these shifts will allow depositors to read the annual

4. FitchRatings CDOs/Bank Loans/Managed Funds (www.fitchibca.com/corporate/sec-tors/sector.cfm?sector_flag=4&marketsector=2 [December 2002]).

5. Sarah Bush, "Taking Stock of Bank-Loan Funds," *Morningstar.com Commentary,* Octo-ber 3, 2000; Theo Francis, "Bank-Loan Mutual Funds May Be Good Bet—Despite Corporate Debt Woes, They Provide Lower Volatility and Suffer Less When Rates Rise," *Wall Street Jour-nal,* May 24, 2002, p. C1.

6. Bomfim (2001) and Moser (1998) discuss these derivatives.

7. Greenspan (2002). In contrast, FitchRatings (2003) argues that credit derivatives could concentrate risk.

report of a large complex bank and understand the risks of the institution completely. They will not. And some of these trends could, in some cases, reinforce bank opacity. For example, when banks sell pools of loans, they sometimes hold on to a small piece of the pool that absorbs the initial losses the loans suffer. This piece—called a residual—is often very difficult to evaluate. Others have noted that the ability of banks to quickly change the types of assets they hold—which they could do more easily after loans take on security-like attributes, along with other factors—makes it difficult to evaluate their riskiness.[8] On balance, however, we view these trends as improving the ability of outsiders to value bank assets.

Furthermore, we doubt that all investors fully understand the risks of energy corporations, entertainment conglomerates, chemical producers, and food service providers, all of which have turned in performances that surprised their creditors. The assertion that banks are opaque relies, at least in part, on the argument that their assets, particularly their loans, pose significant challenges for outsiders to understand. Changes that make it easier for observers to evaluate their assets could make banks less opaque relative to other firms. If market participants can estimate more readily the risk-taking of banks and if risks are spread more effectively, then society should have greater confidence in creditors' ability to respond efficiently to changes in bank risk-taking. We now turn to consideration of the role of market forces in the direct discipline of banks as well as their ability to contribute indirectly through their influence on the bank supervisory process.

Increasing Direct Discipline

Direct discipline is simply another way to refer to the pricing and quantity decisions that creditors of banks make when they believe that their funds are at a risk of loss from bank failure. Although we believe that current direct discipline is less than ideal and could be improved by putting creditors at a more credible risk of loss, we need to stress that even in the current period we view market discipline as altering how much risk banks assume. The question is how to increase direct discipline.

While we believe that putting creditors at a greater risk of loss is the key, the public debate has focused largely on two other options: increasing mandatory disclosures and focusing market discipline through mandatory issuance of uninsured debt. Supporters of these alternatives believe they

8. Morgan (2002). However, using an alternative approach and data, Flannery, Kwan, and Nimalendran (forthcoming) find that banks are no more difficult for investors to analyze than other firms.

will lead banks to take on more appropriate amounts of risk by applying greater direct discipline. Because these are our ultimate goals in reducing TBTF expectations, we now consider the extent to which reforms along these lines are worth pursuing.

Disclosure

Bank supervisors have identified increased disclosure as a key policy objective. Indeed, sometimes when supervisors speak out in support of additional market discipline, they actually review plans to increase the amount of information that banks provide creditors. Although there may be good reason to have additional mandated disclosure in the future, we object to the priority given to this initiative by supervisors and would focus policymakers on putting creditors at a risk of loss.

Perhaps the most prominent examples of supervisory support for additional disclosures come from the various initiatives sponsored by the Basel Committee on Banking Supervision. The Basel committee has devoted considerable effort to tracking the disclosures that banks make, with the implication and sometimes direct conclusion that they need to do more.[9] The so-called third pillar of the proposed revision to existing international capital standards specifies the disclosures that banks will have to make under the new regime.[10] And there are other sources of supervisory calls for more disclosure.[11]

There are convincing reasons for supporting new, mandated disclosures. If left to their own devices, banks may disclose too little from society's point of view.[12] To give one example, the bank that decides to disclose information when competitors do not may end up punishing itself. Without a basis for peer comparison, market participants would have a hard time determining if reported exposures are typical or outliers. If no bank wants to go first, the disclosure might not occur.

At the same time, we find few of the typical objections to disclosure particularly compelling. For example, because banks already have to produce much of the information supervisors want to disclose, the cost of the disclosure per se is likely to be small. Supervisors also seem able to work out banks' concerns about the release of proprietary information.

9. Basel Committee on Banking Supervision (1999b, 2001b).
10. Basel Committee on Banking Supervision (2002b).
11. For examples, see Multidisciplinary Working Group on Enhanced Disclosure (2001); Board of Governors of the Federal Reserve System (2001a).
12. Board of Governors of the Federal Reserve System (2000a).

Nonetheless, we still have reservations about the current emphasis on disclosure as a way to increase direct discipline. We object to the priority that supervisors have given to disclosure to the veritable exclusion of other related reforms. Specifically, mandating additional disclosure without generating additional motivation for creditors to use the information in their pricing and quantity decisions might not lead to much more direct discipline.

Not only could reforms putting creditors at a greater risk of loss lead to better uses of disclosed information, but these reforms, in and of themselves, could lead to more disclosure. In a market with diminished conjectural government guarantees, we might see a much different demand for and supply of information about large banks than those currently prevailing. Moreover, the disclosures resulting from creditors being put at a risk of loss could be superior to mandated disclosures. For example, supervisors do not have an easy way to determine what creditors would find useful. The disclosure that supervisors mandate could miss the mark, particularly because disclosure mandates from supervisors tend to cover a wide range of banks engaged in many types of operations. Creditors, in contrast, have reason to prioritize and demand the information they find the most helpful. Likewise, banks have an incentive to respond to concerns about disclosure from markets in the most cost-efficient manner. We see mandatory disclosure as being supportive of, or a secondary objective to, putting creditors at a greater risk of loss.[13]

Structured Direct Discipline

A second critique of existing direct discipline concerns the ability of banks to avoid it. For example, banks can reduce the direct discipline they face by issuing additional insured liabilities. To better harness market forces, policymakers could force banks to issue uninsured debt on a regular basis. Well-known plans seek to implement this suggestion by requiring banks to issue a certain amount of uninsured subordinated notes and debt (SND).[14] SND plans take many forms, with several using SND as a trigger for closing banks.[15] For example, if a bank cannot issue SND below some rate, or if a majority of SND holders seek repayment, then the bank would be closed.

13. Cordella and Yeyati (1997) discuss the effect of disclosure on the stability of the banking system.

14. Flannery and Sorescu (1996).

15. Board of Governors of the Federal Reserve System and U.S Treasury Department (2001a, pp. 58–65).

We think the gist behind mandatory SND is sensible and should improve the quality of direct discipline even though we do not agree with all the details of the many plans. Nonetheless, and as is the case with disclosure, we think implementation of SND should be coordinated closely with the other reforms we advocate for reducing TBTF expectations. SND holders have been protected when banks have failed in the past, and thus they might expect to receive protection in the future. Policymakers should enact reforms to put SND holders at greater risk.

Certainly there are ways within a mandatory SND proposal to address TBTF concerns.[16] However, the government is probably better off putting creditors at risk through more general reforms. Broad-based reforms would affect a wider range of creditors and might signal a more credible commitment to impose losses. Thus, despite our support for the plans, we think it prudent for policymakers to implement them at the same time that they take concrete steps to put all uninsured creditors at a real risk of loss.

The Federal Reserve Board and U.S. Treasury Department did not support moving ahead with a mandatory SND program, in part because of concerns about the existing SND market.[17] They seemed particularly worried about requiring the issuance of SND because some aspects of SND plans—such as requiring banks and not holding companies to issue the securities—would run counter to current market practices and because some of the current costs of SND reflect factors unrelated to the fundamental safety and soundness of the issuing banks.[18] The SND market, for example, has had periods of considerable illiquidity, such as during the Russian debt crisis. Requiring banks to issue debt in such an environment could impose a stiff cost unrelated to bank risk-taking.

However, and again as is the case for disclosure, one should be careful about assuming that the current market will be a good guide to the future. For example, policymakers can design a mandatory SND proposal to yield greater or at least more routine issuance of SND than exists today. Current concerns about the cost of issuance might not apply in the market after such a significant regime change. While the Treasury and the Federal Reserve Board have called for more study to help resolve their concerns, others suggest that pilot tests are a better way to assess the concept.[19] With

16. See proposal in Lang and Robertson (2002).
17. Board of Governors of the Federal Reserve System and U.S Treasury Department (2001a).
18. Bigus and Prigge (2001) and Bliss (2001) also discuss concerns with SND plans.
19. Shadow Financial Regulatory Committee (2001).

the usual caveats about first putting creditors at a risk of loss, the more proactive stance is closer to our own.

Increasing Indirect Discipline

Banks face indirect market discipline when bank supervisors incorporate the risk assessments embedded in market prices into their decisions and actions. We believe that supervisors should take steps to increase such indirect discipline because it will improve their ability to manage bank risk-taking. With less risk-taking, the probability of failure of large banks and the cost of those failures should fall, making TBTF coverage less likely. In this concluding section, we discuss the timing of the task, explain methods for increasing indirect discipline, and conclude with suggestions for increasing indirect discipline in the future.

Why Increase Indirect Discipline Now?

In the preceding section we made the case for patience with regard to mandating new disclosure rules for banks. Why call on supervisors to incorporate market signals into their assessments now? Starting as soon as possible makes sense because it will take some time for supervisors to gain sufficient experience with market data to exploit its potential.

Incorporating market data into the supervisory process in the current period has raised concerns with at least some supervisors. For example, some supervisors find relatively little benefit from the use of market data because they already have access to inside information on banks. Increased use of market data also raises challenges because a supervisor can neither determine why a market signal goes up or down nor use the signal to support specific supervisory action, as is done with traditional supervisory data. These two concerns are closely related. Because a supervisor believes she cannot explain why a market measure changes (for example, too little capital or too much overseas exposure?), she cannot determine what supervisory response makes sense. Some supervisors may also consider calls to increase the use of market data in the supervisory process as outside the mainstream of current policy and thus not a priority for them. These are legitimate concerns, and we now discuss how we respond to them.

Responding to Concerns about Indirect Discipline

We see several tracks for increasing the use of market data by supervisors. The first is to note that policymakers responsible for supervisory agencies see merit in the use of market data by supervisors. Federal Reserve vice chairman Roger Ferguson summed up this view: "We as supervisors dealing with these large and complex institutions need as much help as we can possibly get. Our examiners are extremely good at what they do, but any good examiner recognizes that data should come from a variety of different sources, including the signals that come from the market. Therefore, market discipline can be an important adjunct to the supervisory process."[20] Such views could be bolstered by guidance from senior officials mandating the use of market data by supervisors.

A second tack is to appeal to the value of market data and respond directly to the concerns of supervisors. Our view, which we have discussed in much greater detail elsewhere, is that supervisors have self-interested reasons to review routinely a whole range of market data, including information from debt markets, probabilities of default generated from equity prices, measures of risk produced in the derivative market, and even changes in the types of funding banks use.[21] Such reviews would be particularly helpful for examiners of the largest, most complex banks, but they could also prove useful for banking organizations engaged in activities with which supervisors have limited experience (for example, Charles Schwab) or foreign banking organizations where information on activities may be limited. These benefits come at very low costs.

More specifically, market data could augment supervisors' assessments of the condition and risks of banking organizations. Supervisors already analyze a wide range of data, including standard financial ratios, measures specific to the business of the supervised institution, and results from on-site examinations. To this subtle analytical process, we simply suggest that supervisors add information on risk-taking teased out of market prices.[22] Market data deserve consideration because such information differs in important ways from the data—often accounting based—that supervisors typically review. In contrast to accounting-based data, market data come from sources with funds at risk, embody assessments of future performance, are outside the direct control of supervised entities, are generated on a continuous basis, and capture assessments of intangible aspects of a

20. Ferguson (2000, p. 32).

21. Feldman and Levonian (2001) and Stern (2001) provide this detailed discussion.

22. Gropp, Vesala, and Vulpes (2001) and Bongini, Laeven, and Majnoni (2002) provide evidence that looking at multiple indicators, including those from financial markets, would benefit supervisors.

firm (for example, quality of management). Market data add value to supervisory assessments precisely because they offer a vantage point, and thus information, that other sources do not. This logic also explains why market data can help supervisors to evaluate the credit quality of the firms that borrow from banks.

But what about the argument that supervisors already have all the information that could possibly be contained in market signals? Empirical research does not support that conclusion. For example, supervisors use a variety of statistical models to determine the financial condition of banks. Adding market data to such models improves their performance.[23] Such evidence is telling because the models used in this analysis are nearly identical to those employed by bank supervisors. More generally, the output from the models performs well relative to on-site bank exams. Supervisors would be better off relying on statistical models to identify problem banks rather than on ratings that are more than six months old.[24]

Once supervisors have come to a conclusion about the riskiness of a bank, market data could enhance their response by, for example, reducing the uncertainty that supervisors face. When market signals confirm supervisory judgment, we would expect supervisors to act more quickly and confidently. Even conflicting signals could reduce uncertainty because they provide supervisors with additional information to make their estimate of bank riskiness. Using both market and supervisory data would prove especially beneficial because, as already described, the respective assessments rely on different perspectives and calculations. As one noted bank economist argues, "If market information could reduce the uncertainty about a firm's condition . . . supervisors would probably respond sooner or more aggressively."[25] Supervisors do not need to link market data to specific bank ills to improve the quality of their actions.

Market data also should enhance supervisors' response by improving communication about, and support for, the response. Banks make considerable use of market data in their own operations. Market prices are generated by third parties outside the control of supervisors. Both attributes make it difficult for banks to refute findings based, in part, on market

23. See Curry, Elmer, and Fissel (2001); Gunther, Levonian, and Moore (2001); Krainer and López (2002). Berger, Davies, and Flannery (2000) and Evanoff and Wall (2001) also review the ability of market information to supplement supervisory assessments.

24. Cole and Gunther (1998).

25. Flannery (2001, p. 113).

data. If banks were less likely to challenge supervisors, we would expect faster resolution of identified problems. These attributes would also help to convince the public, in a legal proceeding, for example, that supervisors treat banks fairly when imposing discipline.

Market prices also make much finer distinctions in assessing risk than do supervisory measures. In the simplest example, market prices can take on a wider range of values. Signals based on market prices, such as an expected default probability of 20 percent, also have much more intuitive and precise meanings than a supervisory measure, such as a rating of 3. Because of its ability to help sort relative risks, market data should assist supervisors in allocating resources. Supervisors could, for example, use market data to rank order the riskiness of institutions, a task one cannot perform with supervisory ratings that fall into one or two categories. Those institutions posing the highest level of risk as judged by markets could receive the greatest attention from supervisors, thereby facilitating the appropriate allocation of resources.

Some of the arguments and evidence we point to may seem too removed from day-to-day supervision to convince supervisors of the need to make greater use of market data. As such, supporters of greater use of market data within supervisory agencies should consider gathering additional evidentiary support linked even more closely to supervisory processes. For example, case studies and analysis showing where market data would have been helpful to examiners and how often market data send the wrong signal might prove convincing. Supervisors may also be more receptive to simulations of existing supervisory processes, such as prompt corrective action, where the superior performance of market data relative to existing supervisory measures is demonstrated.[26]

Deposit Insurance Premiums

Setting deposit insurance premiums so that they vary with the risk-taking of banks should help to mitigate the moral hazard of explicit government guarantees. The insurer can compensate for the underpricing of risk by creditors by charging an insurance premium that reflects the bank's likelihood of failure. Under a risk-based premium system, the bank would pay more if it took on more risk. This would force the bank to incorporate the full cost of its risk-taking when deciding how much risk to take, reducing the amount of excessive risk-taking and the resulting TBTF protection.

26. Evanoff and Wall (2003).

The challenge for the insurer is determining how to measure risk and how to include the measure of risk in the insurance assessment. Some of the challenge reflects political or legal decisions that make it difficult for the insurer to charge risk-based premiums. For example, the system created by FDICIA and subsequent legislation in the United States makes it nearly impossible to vary premiums with risk. Instead, deposit insurance premiums are based primarily on maintaining a level of funding in the accounts of the deposit insurer even though such solvency measures make little sense. The FDIC is really backed by the taxing power of the federal government, not by fictional funding in its accounts. We have long recommended changing this arrangement, a position that the FDIC now espouses to at least some degree.[27]

However, most of the challenge in setting risk-based premiums is of a technical nature. Indeed, some analysts have argued that linking deposit insurance premiums to bank risk-taking is close to impossible because the information necessary to evaluate the riskiness of banks is held by the banks themselves and would be expensive to acquire.[28] Although generating deposit insurance premiums that perfectly reflect the riskiness of banks would be prohibitively expensive, there are methods of capturing at least some of the risk-taking of banks in premiums. Some of these methods rely on fairly simple analytical techniques in conjunction with basic financial data.[29]

Because of the favorable attributes of market data (for example, timeliness, forward perspective, and so forth), many analysts use such information in pricing government guarantees such as deposit insurance.[30] Because the methodology is technical, we do not describe it but instead highlight several findings from such exercises.[31] First, estimates of insurance premiums based on market data make it clear that deposit insurance in the United States is, and has been, underpriced. Second, analysts can use market data to make inferences about the riskiness of banks that do not have

27. Feldman (1998); Federal Deposit Insurance Corporation (2001).
28. Chan, Thakor, and Greenbaum (1992). See Prescott (2002) for a related argument.
29. Fissel (1994); Kendall and Levonian (1991).
30. See Thomson (1989) for an example.
31. This discussion is based on papers presented at a conference on deposit insurance sponsored by the Federal Deposit Insurance Corporation and the *Journal of Financial Services Research* in September 2002. Duffie and others (2002), Falkenheim and Pennacchi (2002), and Kuritzkes, Schuermann, and Weiner (2002) are particularly relevant. Laeven (2002c) also discusses methods of pricing deposit insurance.

readily available market signals. Thus market data can influence the pricing of guarantees for all banks. Finally and most important, simulations of the pricing of government guarantees based on market data produce reasonable results.

These results suggest that market information can improve the pricing of deposit insurance in the short term. The FDIC should certainly move in this direction as soon as possible. The largest benefit may still be in the future, however, after reforms putting creditors at a greater risk of loss go into effect.

Future Steps

We endorse two closely related future steps for increasing indirect discipline. The first links supervisory triggers to market data. The second concerns market value accounting.

We have already explained how the existing regulatory system, most notably prompt corrective action, relies on triggers. Risky institutions should automatically face more supervisory scrutiny, higher insurance costs, and more restrictions on activities than do sound institutions. With rare exceptions, the triggers are supervisory measures of risk. Many view supervisory measures as poorly suited for a trigger role because they are the flipside of market data: They are not timely, reflect past rather than future performance, and are easily manipulated by the banks.

We and others agree and believe that policymakers should incorporate market data into the trigger devices.[32] In a fairly simple approach, supervisors could make use of risk-based deposit insurance premiums based on market data to sort banks into various trigger categories. Banks paying a higher market-based premium would face greater strictures on their activities. Alternatively, supervisors could put banks into trigger categories based on their funding costs relative to some benchmark rate, their expected default frequency, or other market measures, such as spreads on credit derivatives.[33] Under a combined regime, regulatory action would be triggered when banks moved from one market-based group to another or from one regulatory category to another.

In contrast to the other indirect uses of market data that we have described, the trigger mechanism could have fairly onerous outcomes, including the shuttering of banks. We therefore view this step as worthy of future

---

32. Stern (1999, 2003) and Lang and Robertson (2002) discuss this reform.

33. Ito and Harada (2003) find that credit derivatives contain information useful in assessing banking conditions.

consideration rather than as something to adopt immediately. Because the cost of closing a bank when it should remain open may be high, it seems reasonable to gain experience with other supervisory uses of market data and simultaneously to enact reforms that would improve the quality of market prices.

That said, we would not make the use of market prices as a trigger contingent on a specific event, such as passing a particular set of reforms. There are other ways to temper the costs of using market data triggers that would raise confidence in this reform. For example, market and supervisory triggers could be used jointly. As another alternative, the market measures could be set at such a high level as to trigger action only against banks in demonstrably poor shape. As experience is gained, the market trigger could be lowered.

In chapter 10 we mention our desire to break the link between prompt corrective action and the book or historic value of assets and liabilities. The logical alternative is to use the market value of assets, or generally accepted fair valuation models when market prices are not available, to determine a bank's level of capital. The pros and cons of market value accounting have been fiercely debated for at least the last fifteen years. Such a long discussion might suggest a certain futility in recommending this accounting treatment again.

However, renewed attention and support have been given to this change in accounting practices. At the end of 2000, the Joint Working Group of Standard Setters, consisting of ten accounting standard setters, including the predecessor to the International Accounting Standards Board, recommended measuring all financial assets and liabilities at fair value.[34] In May 2001, the European Commission issued a directive allowing greater use of fair value accounting by companies based in the European Union; the European Union will require firms to meet International Accounting Standards by 2005.[35] Support for market value accounting, albeit in an indirect and implicit form, has even come from bank supervisors long opposed to the reform. For example, the new capital accord supported by many bank supervisors requires banks to estimate the expected performance of their loans (for example, the chance of default and the losses if default occurs) and to disclose additional information on these estimates. Given the obvious link between the expected performance of a loan and how much an

34. Joint Working Group of Standard Setters (2000); Tweedie (2002).
35. European Commission (2001); International Accounting Standards Board (2002).

investor would pay for it, the new capital accord is at least an implicit endorsement of market value techniques.

We believe this progress reflects both the inherent strength of the arguments for market value accounting and the simple fact that changes in technology make market value treatment a viable option. The core benefit of market value accounting, and the main reason for its adoption, is its superior ability to reflect the financial condition of banks.[36] We have noted that the historic value of an asset may have only a passing relation to its current or future value. Under existing accounting, a bank that appears well capitalized may, in fact, impose significant losses on creditors if it fails and is liquidated. Market valuation of assets would reflect more accurately bank solvency and, hence, the expected cost to creditors at failure. If creditors and supervisors have a better grasp of bank solvency, they can take steps to minimize both losses at failure and the chance of TBTF protection.

Banks and other observers, including bank supervisors, tend to oppose market or fair value accounting (even if they support the capital rules that implicitly endorse market valuations).[37] They argue that most banks hold assets until maturity. The cash generated from these assets and the costs paid to fund them reflect the true economic substance of the strategy. Reporting short-term changes in the value of assets held for the long run, they argue, would provide extraneous and potentially misleading information. They also claim that the artificial volatility of bank assets under market or fair value accounting would lead investors to penalize banks financially (for example, charge a risk premium to hold bank stock). As a result, banks will shift from their traditional role of holding loans to acquiring assets with more stable values, such as government securities. Economies will suffer from the reduction in traditional intermediation without any gain in clarity for bank creditors.

Finally, banks and many observers argue that market prices do not exist for the vast majority of bank assets and liabilities. As a result, banks will have to estimate fair valuations using complex financial formulas. Such valuations could be sensitive to assumptions, open to manipulation, and likely to

36. For short discussions of the pros and cons of market value accounting, see Mondschean (1992); Morris and Sellon (1991); Alan McNee, "Banks Call on Fair Deal for Fair Value," *ERISK.com*, February 2000. A longer, more recent, analysis of market value accounting is found in Joint Working Group of Standard Setters (1999).

37. Joint Working Group of Banking Associations on Financial Instruments (1999) and Board of Governors of the Federal Reserve System (2000c) review the arguments against market value accounting.

obscure cross-bank comparisons. Implementation challenges will further hide the true condition of banks under market or fair value accounting.

We believe that those who oppose market value accounting will lose the debate in the long run because some of their concerns about market or fair value accounting seem wrong in theory and in fact, while others can be managed. Although market or fair value accounting can lead to more volatile bank earnings, it does not lead to more volatile pricing of bank equity. Bank creditors appear able to distinguish between accounting-related noise and true changes in the condition of a bank.[38] In terms of manipulation and fraud, we hardly see the misuse of fair value accounting by Enron and others as disqualifying the reform. Should accountants reject the necessary distinction between capital and operating expense because WorldCom and others have not sorted out their expenses correctly?

Questions about the ability of banks to obtain market values or a reasonable assessment of fair value, in contrast, have merit. Yet, as noted, technology has led to more market pricing of bank assets and even the potential to sell heretofore opaque small business loans. This not only makes mark to market trivial for the assets being traded but also for similar assets on the books of banks. And more generally, advances in technology and computing power have given analysts a more standardized set of tools for determining what market participants are likely to pay for an asset. A number of alternatives exist to address the implementation concerns.[39] In short, we have better information and tools of analysis now, and marking to market in some form is not as daunting as once assumed.

Policymakers can also observe an increasingly lengthy track record of firms that mark their assets to market, even assets that do not trade routinely. Securities firms, which in many cases have exceedingly complex portfolios, routinely run their businesses with market value accounting. It is not surprising that securities firms have been calling for similar accounting for banks. The chairman and chief executive officer of the Goldman Sachs Group, for example, recommended a shift from historical to fair value accounting as a central part of his plan to build investor confidence after the accounting fiascoes of 2002.[40] Certainly some of these calls reflect posturing in response to a competitive threat from banks, but the experience

38. Yonetani and Katsuo (1998) and the citations within.
39. Berger, King, and O'Brien (1991) discuss an alternative. See also Peter Coy, "Accounting: Bringing the Future into Play," *Business Week Online,* March 11, 2002.
40. Paulson (2002). Securities Industry Association (2001) supports increased use of mark-to-market accounting.

of securities firms remains relevant. More to the point, at least some of the largest banks for which TBTF concerns exist already mark their asset portfolios to market. Before its purchase by Chase Manhattan, J. P. Morgan generated a mark-to-market profit and loss statement daily. J. P. Morgan financial engineers opined that other banks could build systems to carry out similar accounting in a year or two.[41] (We would envision market value accounting applying only to the largest banks.)

This is not to say that market or fair value accounting is costless or perfectly accurate. Indeed, some bank asset valuations under a fair market accounting system will, in retrospect, prove wildly off base. As we have noted on several occasions, pointing out that a reform has flaws is no challenge and is in many ways irrelevant. The critical question is whether the flaws of the reform (fair or market accounting) exceed the flaws of the current (historical accounting) system.

We view the major flaw of historical cost accounting as significant and inherent: Historical cost accounting simply does not use most of the major factors that people consider when valuing an asset and thus does not provide a particularly useful picture of the current financial condition of the asset's owner. In contrast, a market or fair value system explicitly tries to capture the valuation process that people undertake when they want to understand a firm's solvency. The fact that banks do not sell their assets daily does not make market valuation extraneous to their decisions. Indeed, when the market valuation is considered adequate, banks sell some or all of their assets. Since entire banks are sold each day in market transactions, we assume that bankers give credence to market valuations and that such valuations influence their decisions. In short, historical cost accounting asks the wrong question and uses the wrong methods for understanding the current worth of a bank. We see market value accounting prevailing as supervisors and accounting standards fall behind firms' behavior on the ground.

We therefore conclude that supervisors should trigger their actions using market values. We include this as a future step in reform because it would threaten banks with closure based on a market signal. It seems worth waiting several years as supervisors and other interested parties gain experience and as others push this accounting reform forward. Waiting would also determine whether technology makes mark-to-market accounting a fait accompli.

41. Steve Burkholder, "FASB Hears from J. P. Morgan about Fair Value Accounting," *BNA Banking Daily,* November 28, 2000.

References

Aggarwal, Raj, and Kevin T. Jacques. 2001. "The Impact of FDICIA and Prompt Corrective Action on Bank Capital and Risk: Estimates Using a Simultaneous Equations Model." *Journal of Banking and Finance* 25 (January–February): 1139–60.

Akhavein, Jalal D., Allen N. Berger, and David B. Humphrey. 1997. "The Effects of Megamergers on Efficiency and Prices: Evidence from a Bank Profit Function." *Review of Industrial Organization* 12 (February): 95–139.

Allen, Franklin, and Douglas Gale. 2003. "Financial Fragility, Liquidity, and Asset Prices." Working Paper 01-37. Wharton School Center for Financial Institutions, University of Pennsylvania, January.

Angbazo, Lazarus, and Anthony Saunders. 1996. "The Effect of TBTF Deregulation on Bank Costs of Funds." Working Paper 97-25. Wharton School Center for Financial Institutions, September.

Athavale, Manoj. 2000. "Uninsured Deposits and the Too-Big-to-Fail Policy in 1984 and 1991." *American Business Review* 18 (2): 123–28.

Ballard, Charles L., John B. Shoven, and John Whalley. 1985. "General Equilibrium Computations of the Marginal Welfare Costs of Taxes in the United States." *American Economic Review* 75 (1, March): 128–38.

Bank Administration Institute. 1996. *Building Better Banks: The Case for Performance-Based Regulation.* Chicago.

Bank for International Settlements. 2001. *Marrying the Macro- and Micro-Prudential Dimensions of Financial Stability.* Basel.

Bank of England. 1998. "Financial Regulation and Incentives." *Bank of England Financial Stability Review* 4 (Spring): 34–56.

Bank of New York. 2002. "Comment on Docket No. R-1122." New York, August 9.

Bankers Roundtable. 1997. *Deposit Insurance Reform in the Public Interest.* Washington.

Barajas, Adolfo, and Robert Steiner. 2000. "Depositor Behavior and Market Discipline in Colombia." IMF Working Paper WP/00/214. Washington: International Monetary Fund, December.

Bartel, Ann, and Ann Harrison. 1999. "Ownership versus Environment: Why Are Public Sector Firms Inefficient?" NBER Working Paper 7043. Cambridge, Mass.: National Bureau of Economic Research.

Barth, James R., Gerard Caprio Jr., and Ross Levine. 2002. "Bank Regulation and Supervision: What Works Best." Unpublished paper. January.

Barth, James R., Daniel E. Nolle, Triphon Phumiwasana, and Glenn Yago. 2002. "A Cross-Country Analysis of the Bank Supervisory Framework and Bank Performance." Economic and Policy Analysis Working Paper 2002-2. Office of the Comptroller of the Currency.

Bartholdy, Jan, Glenn W. Boyle, and Roger D. Stover. 2001. "Deposit Insurance and Market Assessment of Banking System Stability: Evidence from Denmark." Aarhus School of Business.

———. Forthcoming. "Deposit Insurance and the Risk Premium in Bank Deposit Rates." *Journal of Banking and Finance.*

Basel Committee on Banking Supervision. 1992. "The Insolvency Liquidation of a Multinational Bank." Basel, December.

———. 1997. *Core Principles for Effective Banking Supervision.* Basel Committee Publication 30. Basel, September.

———. 1999a. "Intra-Group Transactions and Exposures and Risk Concentrations Principles." Basel Committee Publication 51. Basel, July.

———. 1999b. "Sound Practices for Loan Accounting and Disclosure." Basel, July.

———. 1999c. "Supervisory Lessons to Be Drawn from the Asian Crisis." Working Paper 2. Basel, June.

———. 2001a. "Essential Elements of a Statement of Cooperation between Banking Supervisors." Basel Committee Publication 83. Basel, May.

———. 2001b. "Public Disclosures by Banks: Results of the 1999 Disclosure Survey." Basel, April.

———. 2002a. "Supervisory Guidance on Dealing with Weak Banks: Report of the Task Force on Dealing with Weak Banks." Basel, March.

———. 2002b. "The Third Pillar—Market Discipline." Basel, December.

Bassett, William F., and Thomas F. Brady. 2001. "The Economic Performance of Small Banks, 1985–2000." *Federal Reserve Bulletin* 87 (November): 719–28.

Bell, James, and Darren Pain. 2000. "Leading Indicator Models of Banking Crises: A Critical Review." *Financial Stability Review* 9 (December): 113–29.

Benston, George J., William Hunter, and Larry D. Wall. 1995. "Motivations for Bank Mergers and Acquisitions: Enhancing the Deposit Insurance Put Option versus Earnings Diversification." *Journal of Money, Credit, and Banking* 27 (August): 777–88.

Benston, George J., and George G. Kaufman. 1994a. "Improving the FDIC Improvement Act." In George C. Kaufman, ed., *Reforming Financial Institutions and Markets in the United States.* Dordrecht, the Netherlands: Kluwer Academic.

————. 1994b. "The Intellectual History of the Federal Deposit Insurance Corporation Improvement Act of 1991." In George C. Kaufman, ed., *Reforming Financial Institutions and Markets in the United States*. Dordrecht, the Netherlands: Kluwer Academic.

————. 1995. "Is the Banking and Payments System Fragile?" *Journal of Financial Services Research* 9 (December): 209–40.

————. 1997. "FDICIA after Five Years." *Journal of Economic Perspectives* 11 (Summer): 139–58.

Berger, Allen N., Sally Davies, and Mark Flannery. 2000. "Comparing Market and Supervisory Assessments of Bank Performance: Who Knows What When?" *Journal of Money, Credit, and Banking* 32 (August): 641–67.

Berger, Allen N., Rebecca Demsetz, and Philip E. Strahan. 1999. "The Consolidation of the Financial Services Industry: Causes, Consequences, and Implications for the Future." *Journal of Banking and Finance* 23 (2–4): 135–94.

Berger, Allen N., Kathleen Kuester King, and James M. O'Brien. 1991. "The Limitations of Market Value Accounting and a More Realistic Alternative." *Journal of Banking and Finance* 15 (September): 753–83.

Berger, Allen N., Margaret K. Kyle, and Joseph M. Scalise. 2001. "Did U.S. Bank Supervisors Get Tougher during the Credit Crunch? Did They Get Easier during the Banking Boom? Did It Matter to Bank Lending?" In Frederic S. Mishkin, ed., *Prudential Supervision: What Works and What Doesn't*. University of Chicago Press.

Bernanke, Ben S., Thomas Laubach, Frederic S. Mishkin, and Adam S. Posen. 1998. *Inflation Targeting: Lessons from the International Experience*. Princeton University Press.

Bernard, Henri, and Joseph Bisignano. 2000. "Information, Liquidity, and Risk in the International Interbank Market: Implicit Guarantees and Private Credit Market Failure." BIS Working Paper 86. Basel: Bank for International Settlements, March.

Bhattacharya, Sudipto, Arnoud W. A. Boot, and Anjan V. Thakor. 1998. "The Economics of Bank Regulation." *Journal of Money, Credit, and Banking* 30 (November): 745–70.

Bierman, Leonard, Donald D. Fraser, and Asghar Zardkoohi. 1999. "On the Wealth Effects of the Supervisory Goodwill Controversy." *Journal of Financial Services Research* 22 (Spring): 69–81.

Bigus, Jochen, and Stefan Prigge. 2001. "Subordinated Bonds as an Instrument of Banking Supervision: The Problem of Market Quality and Incentive Problems." Unpublished paper. University of Hamburg, October.

Billett, Matthew T., Jon A. Garfinkel, and Edward S. O'Neal. 1998. "The Cost of Market versus Regulatory Discipline in Banking." *Journal of Financial Economics* 48 (3): 245–82.

Black, Harold, Cary Collins, Breck Robinson, and Robert Schweitzer. 1997. "Changes in Market Perceptions of Riskiness: The Case of Too-Big-To-Fail." *Journal of Financial Research* 20 (Fall): 389–406.

Blaschke, Winfrid, Matthew T. Jones, Giovanni Majnoni, and Soledad María Martínez-Peria. 2001. "Stress Testing of Financial Systems: An Overview of

Issues, Methodologies, and FSAP Experiences." IMF Working Paper 01/88. Washington: International Monetary Fund, June.

Blavarg, Martin, and Patrick Nimander. 2002. "The Riksbank's Approach to Systemic Risk by Monitoring Counterparty Exposures in the Inter-Bank Market." Available at www.bis.org/cgfs/blavarg-nimander.pdf [October 24, 2003].

Blinder, Alan S. 1997. "Distinguished Lecture on Economics and Government: What Central Banks Could Learn from Academics—and Vice Versa." *Journal of Economic Perspectives* 11 (Spring): 3–19.

Bliss, Robert R. 2001. "Market Discipline and Subordinated Debt: A Review of Some Salient Issues." *Federal Reserve Bank of Chicago Economic Perspectives* (First Quarter): 24–45.

————. 2002. "Resolving Large Complex Financial Organizations." Unpublished paper. Federal Reserve Bank of Chicago.

Board of Banking Supervision. 1995. "Inquiry into the Circumstances of the Collapse of Barings." Bank of England, July 18.

Board of Governors of the Federal Reserve System. 1980a. *Semi-Annual Report to Congress.* February.

————. 1980b. *Semi-Annual Report to Congress.* July.

————. 1982. *Annual Report.*

————. 1994. *Commercial Bank Examination Manual.*

————. 1997. "Corporate Business Resumption and Contingency Planning." Supervisory Letter 97-15 (SPE). May 2.

————. 1999a. "Collateralized Loan Obligations." *Trading and Capital Markets Activities Manual.* Section 4353.1. March.

————. 1999b. "Supervisory Guidance Regarding Counterparty Credit Risk Management." Supervisory Letter 99-3 (SUP). February 1.

————. 2000a. "Improving Public Disclosure in Banking." Staff Study 173. March.

————. 2000b. "Lessons Learned from the Year 2000 Project." Supervisory Letter 00-5 (SUP). March 31.

————. 2000c. "Letter to Financial Standards Accounting Board on Reporting Financial Instruments and Certain Related Assets and Liabilities at Fair Value." May 26.

————. 2001a. "Enhancements to Public Disclosure." Supervision and Regulation Letter 01-6 (SUP). March 23.

————. 2001b. "Final Rule on Recourse, Direct Credit Substitutes, and Residual Interest." November.

————. 2002a. "Board Statement on Payments System Risk." August.

————. 2002b. "Working Group on Risk in the U.S. Government Securities Market." November 26.

Board of Governors of the Federal Reserve System, New York State Banking Department, Office of the Comptroller of the Currency, and U.S. Securities and Exchange Commission. 2002. "Summary of Lessons Learned and Implications for Business Continuity." February.

Board of Governors of the Federal Reserve System, U.S. Office of the Comptroller of the Currency, and Federal Deposit Insurance Corporation. 2002. "Bank Regulatory Agencies Find Adversely Rated Syndicated Loans Continue to Increase in 2002, but at Slower Rate Than Previous Years." October 8.

Board of Governors of the Federal Reserve System, U.S. Office of the Comptroller of the Currency, and U.S. Securities and Exchange Commission. 2002. "Draft Interagency White Paper on Sound Practices to Strengthen the Resilience of the U.S. Financial System." August 30.

———. 2003. "Interagency Paper on Sound Practices to Strengthen the Resilience of the U.S. Financial System." April 8.

Board of Governors of the Federal Reserve System and U.S. Securities and Exchange Commission. 2002. "Interagency White Paper on Structural Change in the Settlement of Government Securities: Issues and Options." May 9.

Board of Governors of the Federal Reserve System and U.S. Treasury Department. 2001a. "The Feasibility and Desirability of Mandatory Subordinated Debt." December.

———. 2001b. "Final Rule on an Alternative to the Rated Debt Requirement for Financial Subsidiaries." January 19.

Bomfim, Antulio N. 2001. "Understanding Credit Derivatives and Their Potential to Synthesize Riskless Assets." Finance and Economics Discussion Working Paper 2001-50. Board of Governors of the Federal Reserve System, November.

Bong-Chan, Kho, Dong Lee, and Rene M. Stulz. 2000. "U.S. Banks, Crises, and Bailouts from Mexico to LTCM." NBER Working Paper 7529. Cambridge, Mass.: National Bureau of Economic Research, February.

Bongini, Paola, Luc Laeven, and Giovanni Majnoni. 2002. "How Good Is the Market at Assessing Bank Fragility? A Horse Race between Different Indicators." Journal of Banking and Finance 26 (5): 1011–28.

Bordo, Michael D. 1999. "Comment on 'Can the Financial Markets Privately Regulate Risk?'" Journal of Money, Credit, and Banking 31 (August): 619–22.

Bordo, Michael, Barry Eichengreen, Daniela Klingebiel, and Soledad María Martínez-Peria. 2001. "Is the Crisis Problem Growing More Severe?" Economic Policy 16 (April): 51–82.

Borio, Claudio, and Philip Lowe. 2002. "Assessing the Risk of Banking Crises." BIS Quarterly Review (December): 43–54.

Bovenzi, John F. 2002. "An FDIC Approach to Resolving a Large Bank." In Proceedings of the Federal Reserve Bank of Chicago's 38th Annual Conference on Bank Structure and Competition. May.

Boyd, John H. 1999a. "Comment on 'Can the Financial Markets Privately Regulate Risk?'" Journal of Money, Credit, and Banking 31 (August): 622–23.

———. 1999b. "Expansion of Commercial Banking Powers . . . or Universal Banking Is the Cart Not the Horse." Journal of Banking and Finance 23 (2–3): 655–62.

Boyd, John H., Chun Chang, and Bruce D. Smith. 1998. "Moral Hazard under Commercial and Universal Banking." Journal of Money, Credit, and Banking 30 (August): 426–68.

Boyd, John H., Pedro Gomis, Sungkyu Kwak, and Bruce D. Smith. 2000. "A User's Guide to Banking Crises." Paper presented at the Deposit Insurance Conference, World Bank, June 8–9.

Boyd, John H., and Stanley L. Graham. 1991. "Investigating the Banking Consolidation Trend." Federal Reserve Bank of Minneapolis Quarterly Review 15 (Spring): 1–14.

Breeden, Richard C. 1990. "Answers to Questions. Hearing before the Senate Committee on Banking, Housing, and Urban Affairs on the Issues Surrounding the Collapse of Drexel Burnham Lambert." March 2, pp. 111–54.

———. 1997. "Testimony before the Subcommittee on Finance and Hazardous Materials, Committee of Commerce, U.S. House of Representatives, May 14." Available at www.house.gov/commerce/finance/hearings/051497/bliley.pdf [September 24, 2003].

Brixi, Hana Polackova, and Ashoka Mody. 2002. "Dealing with Government Fiscal Risk: An Overview." In Hana Polackova Brixi and Allen Schick, eds., *Government at Risk: Contingent Liabilities and Fiscal Risk*. Oxford University Press.

Brixi, Hana Polackova, and Allen Schick, eds. 2002. *Government at Risk: Contingent Liabilities and Fiscal Risk*. Oxford University Press.

Broaddus, J. Alfred, Jr. 2000. "Market Discipline and Fed Lending." In *Proceedings of the Federal Reserve Bank of Chicago's 36th Annual Conference on Bank Structure and Competition*. May 5.

Brock, Philip L. 1998. "Financial Safety Nets and Incentive Structures in Latin America." Policy Research Working Paper. Washington: World Bank, Finance, Development Research Group, October.

Bruno, Michael, and Boris Pleskovic, eds. 1993. *Proceedings of the World Bank Annual Conference on Developmental Economics*. Washington: World Bank.

Burnside, Craig, Martin Eichenbaum, and Sergio Rebelo. 2000. "Understanding the Korean and Thai Currency Crisis." *Federal Reserve Bank of Chicago Economic Perspectives* (Third Quarter): 45–60.

———. 2001a. "Government Guarantees and Self-Fulfilling Speculative Attacks." Unpublished paper. September.

———. 2001b. "Prospective Deficits and the Asian Currency Crisis." *Journal of Political Economy* 109 (December): 1155–97.

Bussiere, Matthieu, and Marcel Fratzscher. 2002. "Towards a New Early Warning System of Financial Crises." Working Paper 145. European Central Bank, May.

Cai, Fang. 2003. "Was There Front Running during the LTCM Crisis?" International Finance Discussion Paper 2003-758. Federal Reserve Board, February.

Calomiris, Charles W., and Joseph R. Mason. 1997. "Contagion and Bank Failures during the Great Depression: The June 1932 Chicago Banking Panic." *American Economic Review* 87 (December): 863–83.

Caprio, Gerard, Jr. 1997. "Safe and Sound Banking in Developing Countries: We're Not in Kansas Anymore." In George G. Kaufman, ed., *FDICIA: Bank Reform Five Years Later and Five Years Ahead*. Greenwich, Conn.: JAI Press.

Caprio, Gerard, Jr., James A. Hanson, and Patrick Honohan. 2001. "Introduction and Overview: The Cases for Liberalization and Some Drawbacks." In Gerard Caprio Jr., Patrick Honohan, and Joseph E. Stiglitz, eds., *Financial Liberalization*. Washington: World Bank.

Caprio, Gerard, and Daniela Klingebiel. 2003. "Episodes of Systemic and Borderline Financial Crises." Washington: World Bank, January. Available at wbln0018.worldbank.org/html/FinancialSectorWeb.nsf/(attachmentweb)/Crisistableproduct/$FILE/Crisistableproduct.pdf [October 23, 2003].

Carrow, Kenneth, and Edward J. Kane. 2002. "Event-Study Evidence of the Value of

Relaxing Long-standing Regulatory Restraints on Banks, 1970–2000." *Quarterly Review of Economics and Finance* 42 (Summer): 439–63.

Cartwright, Peter, and Andrew Campbell. 1999. "Deposit Insurance: Consumer Protection, Bank Safety, and Moral Hazard." *European Business Law Review* 10 (March–April): 96–102.

Chan, Yuk Shee, Anjan Thakor, and Stuart Greenbaum. 1992. "Is Fairly Priced Insurance Possible?" *Journal of Finance* 47 (March): 227–46.

Chang, Roberto. 1999. "Understanding Recent Crises in Emerging Markets." *Federal Reserve Bank of Atlanta Economic Review* 84 (2): 6–16.

Christiansen, Hans. 2001. "Moral Hazard and International Financial Crises in the 1990s." *OECD Financial Market Trends* 78 (March): 115–39.

Claessens, Stijn, and Daniela Klingebiel. 2002. "Fiscal Risks of the Banking System: Approaches to Measuring and Managing Contingent Government Liabilities in the Banking Sector." In Hana Polackova Brixi and Allen Schick, eds., *Government at Risk: Contingent Liabilities and Fiscal Risk*. Oxford University Press.

Cole, Rebel, and Jeffrey Gunther. 1998. "Predicting Bank Failures: A Comparison of On- and Off-Site Monitoring Systems." *Journal of Financial Services Research* 13: 103–17.

Coleman, Stacy Panigay. 2002. "The Evolution of the Federal Reserve's Intraday Credit Policies." *Federal Reserve Bulletin* (February): 67–84.

Committee on the Global Financial System. 2000. "Stress Testing by Large Financial Institutions: Current Practice and Aggregation Issues." CGFS 14. Basel: Bank for International Settlements, April.

———. 2001. "A Survey of Stress Tests and Current Practice at Major Financial Institutions." April.

Committee on Payment and Settlement Systems. 2001. "A Glossary of Terms Used in the Payments and Settlement Systems." Basel: Bank for International Settlements, July.

Committee on Payment and Settlement Systems and Technical Committee of the International Organization of Securities Commissions. 2001. "Recommendations for Securities Settlement Systems." Basel: Bank for International Settlements, November.

Contact Group on the Legal and Institutional Underpinnings of the International Financial System. 2002. "Insolvency Arrangements and Contract Enforceability." December.

Cook, Douglas O., and Lewis J. Spellman. 1994. "Repudiation Risk and Restitution Costs: Toward Understanding Premiums on Insured Deposits." *Journal of Money, Credit, and Banking* 26 (August): 439–59.

———. 1996. "Firm and Guarantor Risk, Risk Contagion, and the Interfirm Spread among Insured Deposits." *Journal of Financial and Quantitative Analysis* (June): 265–81.

Cordella, Tito, and Levy Eduardo Yeyati. 1997. "Public Disclosure and Bank Failure." IMF Working Paper 97/96. Washington: International Monetary Fund, August.

———. 1999. "Bank Bailouts: Moral Hazard versus Value Effect." IMF Working Paper 99/106. Washington: International Monetary Fund, August.

Corrigan, E. Gerald. 2001. "Monetary Policy and Financial Market Volatility." Remarks made at the Money Marketeers dinner, New York University, April 4.

Counterparty Risk Management Policy Group. 1999. "Improving Counterparty Risk Management Practices." June.

Crockett, Andrew. 2001. "Statement of the Chairman of the Financial Stability Forum." Meeting of the International Monetary Fund, Board of Governors, International Monetary and Financial Committee, April.

Cull, Robert. 1998. "How Deposit Insurance Affects Financial Depth: A Cross-Country Analysis." Working Paper 1875. Washington: World Bank, January.

Curry, Timothy, Peter J. Elmer, and Gary Fissel. 2001. "Regulator Use of Market Data to Improve the Identification of Bank Financial Stress." Working Paper. Federal Deposit Insurance Corporation, December.

Curry, Timothy, and Lynn Shibut. 2000. "The Cost of the Savings and Loan Crisis: Truth and Consequences." *FDIC Banking Review* 13 (Fall): 26–35.

Dahiya, Sandeep, Manju Puri, and Anthony Saunders. 2001. *Bank Borrowers and Loan Sales: New Evidence on the Uniqueness of Bank Loans.* Research Paper 1746. Palo Alto, Calif.: Stanford University, Graduate School of Business, December.

Davison, Lee. 1997. "Continental Illinois and 'Too Big to Fail.'" In George Hanc, ed., *History of the Eighties: Lessons for the Future.* Federal Deposit Insurance Corporation.

De Bandt, Olivier, and Philipp Hartmann. 2000. "Systemic Risk: A Survey." Working Paper. European Central Bank, November.

DeFerrari, Lisa M., and David E. Palmer. 2001. "Supervision of Large Complex Banking Organizations." *Federal Reserve Bulletin* (February): 47–57.

Dell'Ariccia, Giovanni, Isabel Godde, and Jeromin Zettelmeyer. 2001. "Moral Hazard and International Crisis Lending: A Test." Washington: International Monetary Fund, February.

DeLong, Gayle. 2001. "Stockholder Gains from Focusing versus Diversifying Bank Mergers." *Journal of Financial Economics* 59 (2): 221–52.

Demirgüç-Kunt, Asli, and Enrica Detragiache. 1997. "The Determinants of Banking Crises: Evidence from Developing and Developed Countries." IMF Working Paper 97/106. Washington: International Monetary Fund.

———. 2000. "Does Deposit Insurance Increase Banking System Stability? An Empirical Investigation." Washington: World Bank.

Demirgüç-Kunt, Asli, and Harry Huizinga. 2000. "Market Discipline and Financial Safety Net Design." Washington: World Bank, April.

Demirgüç-Kunt, Asli, and Edward J. Kane. 2002. "Deposit Insurance around the World: Where Does It Work?" *Journal of Economic Perspectives* 16 (Spring): 175–95.

Demsetz, Rebecca S. 1999. "Bank Loan Sales: A New Look at the Motivations for Secondary Market Activity." Staff Report 69. Federal Reserve Bank of New York, March.

Demsetz, Rebecca S., Marc R. Saidenberg, and Philip E. Strahan. 1996. "Banks with Something to Lose: The Disciplinary Role of Franchise Value." *Federal Reserve Bank of New York Economic Policy Review* 2 (October): 1–14.

Demsetz, Rebecca S., and Philip E. Strahan. 1997. "Diversification, Size, and Risk at

Bank Holding Companies." *Journal of Money, Credit, and Banking* 29 (3): 300–13.

De Nicolo, Gianni, and Myron L. Kwast. 2001. "Systemic Risk and Financial Consolidation: Are They Related?" Unpublished paper. April.

Derthick, Martha, and Paul J. Quirk. 1985. *The Politics of Deregulation*. Brookings.

De Swaan, Tom. 2000. "The Changing Role of Banking Supervision." *Federal Reserve Bank of New York Economic Policy Review* 6 (October): 75–79.

Dewatripont, Mathias, and Jean Tirole. 1994. *The Prudential Regulation of Banks*. MIT Press.

DeYoung, Robert, Mark Flannery, William Lang, and Sorin Sorescu. 2001. "The Informational Content of Bank Exam Ratings and Subordinated Debt Prices." *Journal of Money, Credit, and Banking* 33 (November): 900–25.

Diamond, Douglas W., and Philip H. Dybvig. 1983. "Bank Runs, Deposit Insurance, and Liquidity." *Journal of Political Economy* 91 (3): 401–19.

Dionne, Georges, and Scott Harrington, eds. 1991. *Foundations of Insurance Economics*. Dordrecht, the Netherlands: Kluwer Academic.

Downs, Anthony. 2000. "REIT Share Prices and the Declining Relative Importance of Commercial Real Estate." *Wharton Real Estate Review* 4 (Spring): 13–18.

Duffie, Darrell, Robert Jarrow, Amiyatosh Purnanandam, and Wei Yang. 2002. "Market Pricing of Deposit Insurance." Unpublished paper.

Dugger, Robert H. 1984. "Testimony of Subcommittee Deputy Staff Director, Accompanied by Gary Bowser, Senior Auditor, General Accounting Office." Hearings before the Subcommittee on Financial Institutions, Supervision, Regulation, and Insurance of the House Committee on Banking Finance and Urban Affairs, September 18, 19, and October 4.

Edwards, Franklin R. 1999. "Hedge Funds and the Collapse of Long-Term Capital Management." *Journal of Economic Perspectives* 13 (2): 189–210.

Eichengreen, Barry. 2000. "Can the Moral Hazard Caused by the IMF Bailouts Be Reduced?" Geneva Reports on the World Economy Special Report 1. London: Centre for Economic Policy Research.

Eichengreen, Barry, and Carlos Arteta. 2000. "Banking Crises in Emerging Markets: Presumptions and Evidence." Working Paper C00-115. Center for International and Development Economics Research, University of California, Berkeley, August.

Eisenbeis, Robert A. 1997. "International Settlements: A New Source of Systemic Risk?" *Federal Reserve Bank of Atlanta Economic Review* 82 (2): 44–50.

Eisenbeis, Robert A., and Larry D. Wall. 2002. "Reforming Deposit Insurance and FDICIA." *Federal Reserve Bank of Atlanta Economic Review* 87 (1): 1–16.

Ellis, David M., and Mark J. Flannery. 1992. "Does the Debt Market Assess Large Bank Risk? Time-Series Evidence from Money Center CDs." *Journal of Monetary Economics* 30 (December): 481–502.

Ennis, Huberto M. 2003. "Economic Fundamentals and Bank Runs." *Federal Reserve Bank of Richmond Economic Quarterly* 89 (2): 55–71.

ERISA Industry Committee. 1997. "ERIC Applauds PBGC Decision to Consider Dropping Its Misleading and Counterproductive 'Top 50' List." August 29.

Euro Clearing Standing Committee of the Central Banks of the Group of Ten

Countries. 1998. "OTC Derivatives: Settlement Procedures and Counterparty Risk Management." Basel: Bank for International Settlements, September.

European Commission. 2001. "Financial Reporting: Commission Welcomes Adoption of Fair Value Accounting Directive." London, May.

European Parliament and Council of the European Union. 1994. "Directive 94/19/EC of the European Parliament and of the Council of 30 May 1994 on Deposit Insurance Guarantees Schemes."

Evanoff, Douglas D. 2001. "Designing an Effective Deposit Insurance Structure: An International Perspective." Letter 167c. Federal Reserve Bank of Chicago, July.

Evanoff, Douglas D., and Larry Wall. 2001. "Sub-Debt Yields Spreads as Bank Risk Measures." *Journal of Financial Services Research* 20 (October–December): 121–45.

———. 2003. "Subordinated Debt and Prompt Corrective Regulatory Action." Working Paper 2003-03. Federal Reserve Bank of Chicago.

Falkenheim, Michael, and George Pennacchi. 2002. "The Cost of Deposit Insurance for Privately Held Banks: A Market Comparable Approach." Unpublished paper.

Federal Deposit Insurance Corporation. 1984. *Federal Deposit Insurance Corporation: The First Fifty Years.*

———. 1997. *History of the Eighties: Lessons for the Future.* December.

———. 1998. *The FDIC and RTC Experience: Managing the Crisis.* August.

———. 2001. *Keeping the Promise: Recommendations for Deposit Insurance Reform.* April.

———. Various years. *Failed Bank Costs Analysis.*

Federal Financial Institutions Examination Council. 1998. "Guidance Concerning Contingency Planning in Connection with Year 2000 Readiness." Washington, May.

Federal Reserve Bank of New York. 2002. "Meeting Summary on Business Continuity." February.

Feldman, Ron J. 1996. "How Weak Recognition and Measurement in the Federal Budget Encouraged Costly Policy: The Case of Supervisory Goodwill." *Public Budgeting and Finance* 11 (Winter): 81–116.

———. 1998. "When Should the FDIC Act Like a Private Insurance Company?" *Federal Reserve Bank Region* (September): 43–50.

———. 2001. "Improving Control over Fannie Mae and Freddie Mac." In Peter Wallison, ed., *Serving Two Masters, yet out of Control: Fannie Mae and Freddie Mac.* Washington: American Enterprise Institute.

Feldman, Ron J., and Mark Levonian. 2001. "Market Data and Bank Supervision: The Transition to Practical Use." *Federal Reserve Bank of Minneapolis Region* (September): 11–13, 46–54.

Feldman, Ron J., and Arthur J. Rolnick. 1998. "Fixing FDICIA: A Plan to Address the Too-Big-to-Fail Problem." *Annual Report.* Federal Reserve Bank of Minneapolis, March.

Feldstein, Martin. 1997. "How Big Should Government Be?" *National Tax Journal* 50 (June): 197–213.

Ferguson, Roger W., Jr. 2000. "Interview with Roger Ferguson." *Federal Reserve Bank of Minneapolis Region* (June): 24–34.

────. 2002a. "Business Continuity after September 11." Remarks before the SWIFT Sibos World Forum, Geneva, Switzerland, October.

────. 2002b. "Implications of 9/11 for the Financial Services Sector." In *Proceedings of the Federal Reserve Bank of Chicago's 38th Annual Conference on Bank Structure and Competition*. May.

────. 2002c. "Should Financial Stability Be an Explicit Central Bank Objective?" Remarks before the conference Challenges to Central Banking from Globalized Financial Markets, International Monetary Fund, Washington, September.

Ferguson, Roger W., Jr., Angela M. Antonelli, Ronald A. Rosenfeld, Jennifer L. Dorn, and Donald E. Powell. 2001. "Nomination Hearings before the Committee on Banking, Housing, and Urban Affairs." June 13, 21, and 26.

Ferran, Eilís. 2002. "Examining the U.K.'s Experience in Adopting the Single Financial Regulator Model." Unpublished paper. Cambridge University.

Fettig, David. 2000. "Something Unanticipated Happened: Telling Some 'Neo' Stories about the Great Depression of the 1930s." *Federal Reserve Bank of Minneapolis Region* 14 (December): 19–21, 44–47.

Financial Stability Forum. 2001a. "Guidance for Developing Effective Deposit Insurance." Basel, September.

────. 2001b. "Progress in Implementing the Recommendations of the Working Group on Highly Leveraged Institutions." Basel, March.

Fissel, Gary S. 1994. "Risk Measurement, Actuarially Fair Deposit Insurance Premiums, and the FDIC's Risk-Related Premium System." *FDIC Banking Review* 7 (Spring–Summer): 16–27.

Fitch IBCA, Duff, and Phelps. 2001. "Fitch Simplifies Bank Rating Scales." April.

FitchRatings. 2003. "Global Credit Derivatives: Risk Management or Risk." March 10.

Flannery, Mark J. 1999. "Modernizing Financial Regulation: The Relation between Interbank Transactions and Supervisory Reform." *Journal of Financial Services Research* 16 (December): 101–16.

────. 2001. "The Faces of Market Discipline." *Journal of Financial Services Research* 20 (October–December): 107–119.

────. 2002. "No Pain, No Gain? Effect Market Discipline via 'Reverse Convertible Debentures.'" University of Florida, November.

Flannery, Mark J., and Joel F. Houston. 1999. "The Value of a Government Monitor for U.S. Banking Firms." *Journal of Money, Credit, and Banking* 31 (February): 14–34.

Flannery, Mark J., Simon Kwan, and M. Nimalendran. Forthcoming. "Market Evidence on the Opaqueness of Banking Firms' Assets." *Journal of Financial Economics*.

Flannery, Mark J., and Kasturi P. Rangan. 2002. "Market Forces at Work in the Banking Industry: Evidence from the Capital Buildup of the 1990s." University of Florida; Case Western Reserve University, September.

Flannery, Mark J., and Sorin M. Sorescu. 1996. "Evidence of Bank Market Discipline in Subordinated Debenture Yields: 1983–1991." *Journal of Finance* 51 (September): 1347–77.

Fleming, Michael J., and Kenneth D. Garbade. 2002. "When the Bank Office Moved to the Front Burner: Settlement Fails in the Treasury Market after 9/11." *Federal Reserve Bank of New York Economic Policy Review* 8 (November): 35–57.

Freixas, Xavier. 1999. "Optimal Bail-Out Policy, Conditionality, and Constructive Ambiguity." Economics and Business Working Paper 400. Universitat Pompeu Fabra, October.

Freixas, Xavier, and Jean-Charles Rochet. 1997. *Microeconomics of Banking.* MIT Press.

Freixas, Xavier, and Anthony M. Santomero. 2002. "An Overall Perspective on Banking Regulation." Working Paper 02-1. Federal Reserve Bank of Philadelphia, February.

Frydl, Edward J. 1999. "The Length and Cost of Banking Crises." IMF Working Paper 99/30. Washington: International Monetary Fund.

Frydl, Edward J., and Marc Quintyn. 2000. "The Benefits and Costs of Intervening in Banking Crises." IMF Working Paper 00/47. Washington: International Monetary Fund, August.

Fukao, Mitsuhiro. 2003. "Barriers to Financial Restructuring: Japanese Banking and Life Insurance Industries." In Magnus Blomstrom, Jennifer Corbett, Fumio Hayashi, and Anil Kashyap, eds., *Structural Impediments to Growth in Japan.* National Bureau of Economic Research Conference Report. University of Chicago Press.

Furfine, Craig H. 1999. "Interbank Exposures: Quantifying the Risk of Contagion." BIS Working Paper 70. Basel: Bank for International Settlements, June.

———. 2001a. "Banks as Monitors of Other Banks: Evidence from the Overnight Federal Funds Market." *Journal of Business* 74 (1): 33–57.

———. 2001b. "The Costs and Benefits of Moral Suasion: Evidence from the Rescue of Long-Term Capital Management." BIS Working Paper 103. Bank for International Settlements, August.

———. 2002. "The Interbank Market during a Crisis." *European Economic Review* 46 (May): 809–20.

Galati, Gabriele. 2002. "Settlement Risk in Foreign Exchange Markets and CLS Bank." *BIS Quarterly Review* (December): 55–66.

García, Gillian. 1999. "Deposit Insurance: A Survey of Actual and Best Practices." IMF Working Paper 99/54. Washington: International Monetary Fund, April.

———. 2000. *Deposit Insurance: Actual and Good Practices.* IMF Occasional Paper 197. Washington: International Monetary Fund.

García, Gillian, and Matthew Saal. 1996. "Internal Governance, Market Discipline, and Regulatory Restraint: International Evidence." In *Proceedings of the Federal Reserve Bank of Chicago's 32d Annual Conference on Bank Structure and Competition.* May.

Giannetti, Mariassunta. 2002. "On the Causes of Overlending: Are Guarantees on Deposits the Culprit?" Stockholm School of Economics and Centre for Economic Policy Research, February.

Gilbert, Alton R. 1990. "Market Discipline of Bank Risk: Theory and Evidence." *Federal Reserve Bank of St. Louis Review* (January–February): 3–18.

———. 1997. "Comments on Examination and Enforcement." In *History of the Eighties: Lessons for the Future.* Vol. 2: *Symposium Proceedings, January 16, 1997.* Federal Deposit Insurance Corporation, pp. 5–10. Available at www.fdic.gov/bank/historical/history/index.html [October 24, 2003].

Glauber, Robert. 1991. "Testimony before the Subcommittee on Economic Stabilization, Committee on Banking, Finance, and Urban Affairs, United States House of Representatives, May 9." Serial 102-32, pp. 101–30.

Goldman Sachs. 2002. "Fannie Mae, Freddie Mac: Derivative Markets Offer Sufficient Size, Liquidity." March.

Goldstein, Morris, Graciela L. Kaminsky, and Carmen M. Reinhart. 2000. *Assessing Financial Vulnerability: An Early Warning System for Emerging Markets.* Washington: Institute for International Economics.

Golembe, Carter H. 1999. "The Hottest Words in Town." *Golembe Reports,* June 4.

Goodfriend, Marvin, and Jeffrey M. Lacker. 1999. "Limited Commitment and Central Bank Lending." *Federal Reserve Bank of Richmond Economic Quarterly* 85 (Fall): 1–27.

Greenbaum, Stuart I. 1995. "Comment on George J. Benston and George G. Kaufman 'Is the Banking and Payments System Fragile?'" *Journal of Financial Services Research* 9 (December): 299–302.

Greenspan, Alan. 1998a. "Testimony before the Committee on Banking, Housing, and Urban Affairs." U.S. Senate, June 17.

———. 1998b. "Testimony on Private-Sector Refinancing of the Large Hedge Fund, Long-Term Capital Management, before the Committee on Banking and Financial Services, U.S. House of Representatives." October 1.

———. 2002. "Remarks before the Council on Foreign Relations." Washington, November 19.

Gropp, Reint, and Jukka Vesala. 2001. "Deposit Insurance and Moral Hazard: Does the Counterfactual Matter?" Working Paper 47. European Central Bank, March.

Gropp, Reint, Jukka Vesala, and Giuseppe Vulpes. 2001. "Equity and Bond Market Signals as Leading Indicators of Bank Fragility in Europe." European Central Bank, May.

Group of Ten. 2001. "Report of Consolidation in the Financial Sector."

Group of Thirty. 1989. "Clearance and Settlement Systems in the World's Securities Markets." Washington.

———. 1997. "Global Institutions, National Supervision, and Systemic Risk." Study Group Report. Washington.

———. 1998. "International Insolvencies in the Financial Sector." Study Group Report. Washington.

———. 2000. "Reducing the Risks of International Insolvency. A Compendium of Work in Progress: A Reference Guide." Washington.

Guenther, Kenneth A. 2001. "Community Bankers, Deposit Insurance Reform, and Too Big to Fail." In *Proceedings of the Federal Reserve Bank of Chicago's 37th Annual Conference on Bank Structure and Competition.* May.

Gulledge, Robert I. 2001. "Testimony on Behalf of the Independent Community Bankers of America before the Senate Committee on Banking, Housing, and Urban Affairs, Subcommittee on Financial Institutions." August 2.

Gunther, Jeffery W., Mark Levonian, and Robert Moore. 2001. "Can the Stock Market Tell Bank Supervisors Anything They Don't Already Know?" *Federal Reserve Bank of Dallas Economic and Financial Review* (Second Quarter): 2–9.

Gunther, Jeffery W., and Robert R. Moore. 2002. "Loss Underreporting and the

Auditing Role of Bank Exams." Conference series. *Federal Reserve Bank of Boston,* April.

Gup, Benton. 1998. "Too-Big-to-Fail: An International Perspective." In Karl R. Derouen Jr., Joseph Zimmerman, and Benton E. Gup, eds., *Bank Failures in the Major Trading Countries of the World: Causes and Remedies.* Quorum Books, pp. 69–91.

Hahm, Sung-Deuk, Mark Kamlet, David Mowery, and T. Su. 1992. "The Influence of the Gramm-Rudman-Hollings Act on Federal Budgetary Outcomes, 1986–1989." *Journal of Policy Analysis and Management* 11 (2): 207–34.

Hanc, George. 1999. "Deposit Insurance Reform: State of the Debate." *FDIC Banking Review* 12 (December): 1–26.

Harding, Mark. 2002. "The Challenges of Regulating Large, International Financial Organizations." In *Proceedings of the Federal Reserve Bank of Chicago's 38th Annual Conference on Bank Structure and Competition.* May.

Haubrich, Joseph G., and James B. Thomson. 1998. "Large Shareholders and Market Discipline in a Regulated Industry: A Clinical Study of Mellon Bank." Working Paper 9803. Federal Reserve Bank of Cleveland, February.

Herring, Richard. 2003. "International Financial Conglomerates: Implications for Bank Insolvency Regimes." May 2003 draft of paper prepared for Second Annual Seminar on Policy Challenges for the Financial Sector in the Context of Globalization, Washington, June 2002.

Hetzel, Robert. 1991. "Too Big to Fail: Origins, Consequences, and Outlook." *Federal Reserve Bank of Richmond Economic Review* 77 (6): 3–15.

Hills, Bob, and David Rule. 1999. "Counterparty Credit Risk in Wholesale Payment and Settlement Systems." *Financial Stability Review* 7 (November): 98–114.

Hills, Bob, David Rule, Sarah Parkinson, and Chris Young. 1999. "Central Counterparty Clearing Houses and Financial Stability." *Financial Stability Review* 6 (June): 122–34.

Hoenig, Thomas M. 1996. "Rethinking Financial Regulation." *Federal Reserve Bank of Kansas City Economic Review* 81 (Second Quarter): 5–13.

———. 1997. "Banking Regulation: Asking the Right Questions." *Federal Reserve Bank of Kansas City Economic Review* 82 (First Quarter): 5–10.

Hoggarth, Glenn, Ricardo Reis, and Victoria Saporta. 2001. "Costs of Banking System Instability: Some Empirical Evidence." Working Paper 144. London: Bank of England.

Hoggarth, Glenn, and Farouk Soussa. 2001. "Crisis Management, Lender of Last Resort, and the Changing Nature of the Banking Industry." In Richard Brealey and others, eds., *Financial Stability and Central Banks: A Global Perspective.* Centre for Central Banking Studies, Bank of England. London: Routledge.

Honohan, Patrick, and Daniela Klingebiel. 2000. "Controlling Fiscal Costs of Banking Crises." Washington: World Bank.

Hoshi, Takeo, and Anil K. Kashyap. 2001. *Corporate Financing and Governance in Japan: The Road to the Future.* MIT Press.

Hovakimian, Armen, and Edward J. Kane. 2000. "Effectiveness of Capital Regulation at U.S. Commercial Banks, 1985 to 1994." *Journal of Finance* 55 (February): 451–68.

Hovakimian, Armen, Edward J. Kane, and Luc Laeven. 2003. "How Country and Safety-Net Characteristics Affect Bank Risk-Taking." *Journal of Financial Services Research* 23 (June): 177–204.

Hughes, Joseph P., and Loretta J. Mester. 1993. "A Quality and Risk-Adjusted Cost Function for Banks: Evidence on the 'Too-Big-to-Fail' Doctrine." *Journal of Productivity Analysis* 4 (September): 293–315.

Hughes, Joseph P., Loretta Mester, and Choon-Geol Moon. 2001. "Are Scale Economies in Banking Elusive or Illusive? Evidence Obtained by Incorporating Capital Structure and Risk-Taking into Models of Bank Production." *Journal of Banking and Finance* 25 (December): 2169–208.

Huizinga, Harry, and Gaetan Nicodeme. 2002. "Deposit Insurance and International Bank Deposits." International Finance 0302001. London: European Commission, February.

Hunter, William C. 1999. "Bail-Outs for Financial Services Firms." In *Proceedings of the 10th Annual Capital Market Research Center Conference.* June 28. Available at www.msb.edu/prog/cmrc.

Hüpkes, Eva. 2002. "Insolvency—Why a Special Regime for Banks?" Paper presented at the International Monetary Fund Seminar on Current Developments in Monetary and Financial Law, Washington, May 7–17.

Inquiry into Continental Illinois Corp. and Continental Illinois National Bank. 1984. "Hearings before the Subcommittee on Financial Institutions, Supervision, Regulation, and Insurance of the House Committee on Banking Finance and Urban Affairs, September 18, 19 and October 4."

International Accounting Standards Board. 2002. "IASB Chairman Welcomes the EU's Decision to Adopt International Accounting Standards." London, June.

International Financial Institution Advisory Commission. 2000. "Final Report." Washington, March.

International Swaps and Derivatives Association. 2000. "ISDA Collateral Survey 2000." New York.

Ireland, Oliver. 1999. "The Proposed Bankruptcy Reform Act of 1999." Testimony before the Subcommittee on Commercial and Administrative Law, Committee on the Judiciary, U.S. House of Representatives, March.

Ireland, Peter N. 2002. "'Rules Rather Than Discretion' after Twenty Five Years: What Have We Learned? What More Can We Learn?" In Mark Gertler and Kenneth Rogoff, eds., *NBER Macroeconomics Annual 2002,* vol. 17. MIT Press.

Isaac, William M. 1997. "A Former Regulator's Perspective on the Decade of the 1990s." Unpublished paper.

Ito, Takatoshi, and Kimie Harada. 2003. "Market Evaluation of Banking Fragility in Japan: Japan Premium, Stock Prices, and Credit Derivatives." NBER Working Paper 9589. Cambridge, Mass.: National Bureau of Economic Research, March.

Jackson, Patricia. 1999. "Capital Requirements and Bank Behavior: The Impact of the Basel Accord." Working Paper 1. Basel Committee on Banking Supervision, April.

Jagger, Craig, and David Hull. 1997. "Calling the One-Sided Bet: A Case Study of Budget Scoring in the 1996 Farm Bill." *Review of Agricultural Economics* 19 (1): 178–92.

Jaramillo-Vallejo, Jaime. 1993. "Comment on the Role of the State in Financial Markets." In Michael Bruno and Boris Pleskovic, eds., *Proceedings of the World Bank Annual Conference on Developmental Economics.* Washington: World Bank.

Jeanne, Olivier, and Jeromin Zettelmeyer. 2001. "International Bailouts: The IMF's Role." *Economic Policy* 33 (October): 409–32.

Johnson, Steve, and James Lindley. 1993. "The Reaction of Financial Markets to Changes in FDIC Policies on Bank Failures." *Journal of Economics and Finance* 17 (Spring): 43–58.

Joint Working Group of Banking Associations on Financial Instruments. 1999. "Accounting for Financial Instruments for Banks." Memo to the Joint Working Group of Standard Setters on Financial Instruments. London: International Accounting Standards Committee, October.

Joint Working Group of Standard Setters. 1999. "Financial Instruments: Issues Relating to Banks." August.

———. 2000. "Financial Instruments and Similar Items."

Jones, David, and Kathleen Kuester King. 1995. "The Implementation of Prompt Corrective Action: An Assessment." *Journal of Banking and Finance* 19 (3–4): 491–510.

Jones, Jonathan, William W. Lang, and Peter Nigro. 2001. "Recent Trends in Bank Loan Syndications: Evidence from 1995 to 1999." In *Proceedings of the Federal Reserve Bank of Chicago's 37th Annual Conference on Bank Structure and Competition.* May.

Jones, Kenneth. 2001. "Resolving the 'Too Big to Fail' Problem in Banking: A Discussion of Policy Options for the U.S." Paper presented at a meeting of the Southern Economic Association.

Jordan, Cally, and Giovanni Majnoni. 2002. "Financial Regulatory Harmonization and the Globalization of Finance." Policy Research Working Paper 2919. Washington: World Bank, October.

Jordan, John S. 2000. "Depositor Discipline at Failing Banks." *New England Economic Review* (March–April): 15–28.

J. P. Morgan Chase. 2002. "Comment on Docket No. R-1122." August 12.

Kahn, Charles M., James McAndrews, and William Roberds. 1999. "Settlement Risk under Gross and Net Settlement." Working Paper 99-10. Federal Reserve Bank of Atlanta, August.

Kahn, Charles M., and William Roberds. 1999. "The Design of Wholesale Payments Networks: The Importance of Incentives." *Federal Reserve Bank of Atlanta Economic Review* 84 (3): 30–39.

———. 2001. "The CLS Bank: A Solution to the Risks of International Payments Settlement?" *Carnegie-Rochester Conference Series on Public Policy* 54 (June): 191–226.

Kaminsky, Graciela, and Carmen Reinhard. 1999. "The Twin Crises: The Causes of Banking and Balance-of-Payments Problems." *American Economic Review* 89 (June): 473–500.

Kane, Edward J. 1989. *The S&L Insurance Mess: How Did It Happen?* Urban Institute Press.

————. 1991. "Repairing Defects in Regulatory Accountability." Serial no. 102-23, pp. 993–1015. U.S. Congress, House of Representatives, Committee on Banking, Finance, and Urban Affairs, Subcommittee on Financial Institution Supervision, Regulation, and Insurance, Hearings on Restructuring the Banking Industry, April 16, 18, and 25.

————. 1997. "Ethical Foundations of Financial Regulation." *Journal of Financial Services Research* 12 (August): 51–74.

————. 2000. "Incentives for Banking Megamergers: What Motives Might Regulators Infer from Event-Study Evidence?" *Journal of Money, Credit, and Banking* 32 (August): 671–701.

————. 2001a. "Dynamic Inconsistency of Capital Forbearance: Long-Run versus Short-Run Effects of Too-Big-to-Fail Policymaking." *Pacific Basin Finance Journal* 9 (August): 281–99.

————. 2001b. "Using Disaster Planning to Optimize Expenditures on Financial Safety Nets." *Atlantic Economic Journal* 29 (September): 243–53.

————. 2002. "Using Deferred Compensation to Strengthen the Ethics of Financial Regulations." *Journal of Banking and Finance* 26 (September): 1919–33.

Kane, Edward J., and Daniela Klingebiel. 2002. "Alternatives to Blanket Guarantees for Containing a Systemic Crisis." Paper prepared for the second international seminar Policy Challenges for the Financial Sector in the Context of Globalization, World Bank, Washington, June 4–7.

Kaplan-Appio, Idanna. 2001. "Estimating the Value of Implicit Government Guarantees." Paper presented at Asian Crisis II, University of Tokyo, July 17–18.

————. 2002. "Estimating the Value of Implicit Government Guarantees to Thai Banks." *Review of International Economics* 10 (1): 26–35.

Kareken, John H. 1983. "Deposit Insurance Reform, or Deregulation Is the Cart, Not the Horse." *Federal Reserve Bank of Minneapolis Quarterly Review* 7 (Spring): 1–9.

Kareken, John H., and Neil Wallace. 1978. "Deposit Insurance and Bank Regulation: A Partial Equilibrium Exposition." *Journal of Business* 51 (July): 413–38.

Kaufman, George G. 1994. "Bank Contagion: A Review of the Theory and Evidence." *Journal of Financial Services Research* 8 (April): 123–50.

————. 1997a. "FDICIA after Five Years." In George C. Kaufman, ed., *FDICIA: Bank Reform Five Years Later and Five Years Ahead.* Greenwich, Conn.: JAI Press.

————. 2000. "Banking and Currency Crisis and System Risk: Lessons from Recent Events." *Federal Reserve Bank of Chicago Economic Perspectives* 25 (3): 9–28.

————. 2002. "Depositor Liquidity and Loss-Sharing in Bank Failure Resolutions." Working Paper WP-03-2. Federal Reserve Bank of Chicago, September.

Kaufman, George G., ed. 1997b. *FDICIA: Bank Reform Five Years Later and Five Years Ahead.* Greenwich, Conn.: JAI Press.

Kaufman, George G., and Steven A. Seelig. 2002. "Post Resolution Treatment of Depositors at Failed Banks: Implications for the Severity of Banking Crises, Systemic Risk, and Too Big to Fail." *Federal Reserve Bank of Chicago Economic Perspectives* (Second Quarter): 27–41.

Keeley, Michael C. 1990. "Deposit Insurance, Risk, and Market Power in Banking." *American Economic Review* 80 (December): 1183–200.

Kendall, Sarah, and Mark Levonian. 1991. "A Simple Approach to Better Deposit Insurance Pricing." *Proceedings of the Federal Reserve Bank of Chicago's 27th Annual Conference on Bank Structure and Competition.*

Klingebiel, Daniela, Randy Kroszner, Luc Laeven, and Pieter von Oijen. 2000. "Stock Market Responses to Bank Restructuring Policies during the East Asian Crisis." Country Economics Department Paper 2671. Washington: World Bank, December.

Knott, Raymond, and Alastair Mills. 2002. "Modeling Risk in Central Counterparty Clearing Houses: A Review." *Financial Stability Review* 13 (December): 162–74.

Kovacevich, Richard M. 1996. "Deposit Insurance: It's Time to Cage the Monster." *Federal Reserve Bank of Minneapolis fedgazette* (April): n.p.

Kozinski, Alex. 1998. "Should Reading Legislative History Be an Impeachable Offense?" *Suffolk University Law Review* 31: 807.

Krainer, John, and José López. 2002. "Incorporating Equity Market Information into Supervisory Models." Working Paper. Federal Reserve Bank of San Francisco, June.

Kroszner, Randall S. 1997. "Commentary on Institutions and Policies for Maintaining Financial Stability." In *Proceedings of Maintaining Financial Stability in a Global Economy.* Kansas City Federal Reserve Bank.

———. 1999. "Can the Financial Markets Privately Regulate Risk?" *Journal of Money, Credit, and Banking* 31 (August): 619–22.

Krueger, Anne O. 1998. "Whither the World Bank and the IMF?" *Journal of Economic Literature* 26 (December): 1983–2020.

Krugman, Paul. 1998. "What Happened to Asia?" January. Available at web.mit.edu/krugman/www/DISINTER.html [September 17, 2003].

Kuritzkes, Andrew, Til Schuermann, and Scott M. Weiner. 2002. "Deposit Insurance and Risk Management of the U.S. Banking System: How Much? How Safe? Who Pays?" Unpublished paper. June 3.

Kydland, Finn, and Edward C. Prescott. 1977. "Rules Rather Than Discretion: The Inconsistency of Optimal Plans." *Journal of Political Economy* 85 (June): 473–91.

Laeven, Luc. 2002a. "Bank Risk and Deposit Insurance." *World Bank Economic Review* 16 (1): 109–37.

———. 2002b. "International Evidence on the Value of Deposit Insurance." *Quarterly Review of Economics and Finance* 42 (4): 721–32.

———. 2002c. "Pricing of Deposit Insurance." Policy Research Working Paper 2871. Washington: World Bank, July.

Lamm, Richard H. 2001. "The Need for More Definitive Policy for Governmental Intervention in Perceived Market Crises." *Derivatives Quarterly* 7 (Spring): 22–31.

Lang, Richard J. 1996. "Lessons from New Zealand: Banking Supervision Review." *Proceedings of the Federal Reserve Bank of Chicago's 32d Annual Conference on Bank Structure and Competition.* May.

Lang, William W., and Douglas D. Robertson. 2002. "Analysis of Proposals for a Minimum Subordinated Debt Requirement." *Journal of Economics Business* 54: 115–36.

Levine, Ross. 1999. "Law, Finance, and Economic Growth." *Journal of Financial Intermediation* 8 (1–2): 8–35.

Levine, Ross, Norman Loayza, and Thorsten Beck. 2000. "Financial Intermediation and Growth: Causality and Causes." *Journal of Monetary Economics* 46 (1): 31–77.

Levitt, Steven D. 1996. "How Do Senators Vote? Disentangling the Role of Voter Preferences, Party Affiliation, and Senator Ideology." *American Economic Review* 86 (June): 425–41.

Litan, Robert E. 1997. "Institutions and Policies for Maintaining Financial Stability." In *Proceedings of Maintaining Financial Stability in a Global Economy.* Federal Reserve Bank of Kansas City.

Litan, Robert E., and Jonathan Rauch. 1997. *American Finance for the 21st Century.* Report for the U.S. Treasury Department, November. Brookings.

Litvack, Jennie, Junaid Ahmad, and Richard Bird. 1998. *Rethinking Decentralization in Developing Countries.* Sector Studies Series. Washington: World Bank.

Lockhart, James B. 1996. "Counterpart: PBGC's Big Turnaround." *Pensions and Investments,* March 4.

Lokshin, Michael M., and Ruslan Yemtsov. 2001. "Household Strategies for Coping with Poverty and Social Exclusion in Post Crisis Russia." Working Paper 2556. Washington: World Bank.

Lowenstein, Roger. 2000. *When Genius Failed.* Random House.

Mahoney, Christopher. 2000. "The Truth about Bank Credit Risk." Moody's Special Comment. April.

Marino, James A., and Rosalind L. Bennett. 1999. "The Consequences of National Depositor Preference." *FDIC Banking Review* 12 (2): 19–38.

Martínez-Peria, Soledad María, and Sergio L. Schmukler. 1998. "Do Depositors Punish Banks for 'Bad' Behavior? Examining Market Discipline in Argentina, Chile, and Mexico." Working Paper 2058. Washington: World Bank, December.

Mayer, Martin. 1997. "Testimony before the House Banking Committee." May 21.

———. 1999. "Is Everything Too Big to Fail?" *International Economy* (January–February): 24–27.

Mayer, Thomas. 1975. "Should Large Banks Be Allowed to Fail?" *Journal of Financial and Quantitative Analysis* 10 (November): 603–10.

Mayes, David G., Liisa Halme, and Aarno Liuksila. 2001. *Improving Banking Supervision.* Palgrave.

Mayes, David G., and Aarno Liuksila. 2003. *Who Pays for Bank Insolvency?* Palgrave.

McAndrews, James, and John Trundle. 2001. "New Payment System Designs: Causes and Consequences." *Financial Stability Review* 11 (December): 127–36.

McAndrews, James J., and George Wasilyew. 1995. "Simulations of Failure in a Payment System." Working Paper 95-19. Federal Reserve Bank of Philadelphia, June.

McKinnon, Ronald, and Huw Pill. 1999. "International Overborrowing: A Decomposition of Credit and Currency Risks." *World Development* 26 (July): 1267–82.

Medlin, John G. Jr. 1997. "The 1980s in Retrospect." In *History of the Eighties: Lessons for the Future.* Vol. 2: *Symposium Proceedings, January 16, 1997.* Federal Deposit Insurance Corporation, pp. 105–08. Available at www.fdic.gov/bank/historical/history/index.html [October 24, 2003].

Milhaupt, Curtis J. 1999. "Japan's Experience with Deposit Insurance and Failing

Banks: Implications for Financial Regulatory Design?" *Washington University Law Quarterly* 77 (2): 398–431.

Mishkin, Frederic S. 1997. "Evaluating FDICIA." In George G. Kaufman, ed., *Research in Financial Services: Private and Public Policy*. Greenwich, Conn.: JAI Press.

———. 1999. "Lessons from the Asian Crisis." NBER Working Paper 7102. Cambridge, Mass.: National Bureau of Economic Research, April.

———. 2001. "Prudential Supervision: Why Is It Important and What Are the Issues?" In Frederic S. Mishkin, ed., *Prudential Supervision: What Works and What Doesn't*. University of Chicago Press.

———. 2002. "Financial Policies and the Prevention of Financial Crises in Emerging Market Countries." In Martin Feldstein, ed., *Economic and Financial Crises in Emerging Market Countries*. University of Chicago Press.

Mishkin, Frederic S., and Philip E. Strahan. 1999. "What Will Technology Do to Financial Structure?" NBER Working Paper 6892. Cambridge, Mass.: National Bureau of Economic Research.

Mondschean, Thomas S. 1992. "Market Value Accounting for Commercial Banks." *Federal Reserve Bank of Chicago Economic Perspectives* 16 (January–February): 16–31.

Mondschean, Thomas S., and Timothy P. Opiela. 1999. "Bank Time Deposit Rates and Market Discipline in Poland: The Impact of State Ownership and Deposit Insurance Reform." *Journal of Financial Services Research* 15 (3): 179–96.

Moody's Investors Service. 2001. "Bank Credit Research, Monthly Ratings List." December.

Moore, Robert. 1997. "Government Guarantees and Banking: Evidence from the Mexican Peso Crisis." *Federal Reserve Bank of Dallas Financial Industry Studies* (December): 13–21.

Morgan, Donald. 2002. "Rating Banks: Risk and Uncertainty in an Opaque Industry." *American Economic Review* 92 (September): 874–88.

Morgan, Donald P., and Kevin J. Stiroh. 2001. "Market Discipline of Banks: The Asset Test." *Journal of Financial Services Research* 20 (2–3): 195–208.

Morris, Charles S., and Gordon H. Sellon Jr. 1991. "Market Value Accounting for Banks: Pros and Cons." *Federal Reserve Bank of Kansas City Economic Review* (March–April): 5–19.

Moser, James T. 1998. "Credit Derivatives: The Latest New Thing." *Chicago Fed Letter* 130 (June): n.p.

Moss, David A. 2002. *When All Else Fails: Government as the Ultimate Risk Manager*. Harvard University Press.

Moyer, Charles R., and Robert E. Lamy. 1992. "Too Big to Fail: Rationale, Consequences, and Alternatives." *Business Economics* 27 (3): 19–24.

Multidisciplinary Working Group on Enhanced Disclosure. 2001. "Final Report." Basel: Bank for International Settlements, April. Available at www.bis.org/publ/joint01.htm [September 2, 2003].

Mussa, Michael. 2002. "Reflections on Moral Hazard and Private Sector Involvement in the Resolution of Emerging Market Financial Crises." Paper presented at the Bank of England conference Role of the Official and Private Sectors in Resolving International Financial Crises, July.

Nier, Erlend, and Ursel Baumann. 2003. "Market Discipline, Disclosure, and Moral Hazard in Banking." Bank of England, April.

Niskanen, William. 1971. *Bureaucracy and Representative Government.* Chicago: Aldine-Atherton.

Obstfeld, Maurice, and Kenneth Rogoff. 1996. *Foundations of International Macroeconomics.* MIT Press.

O'Hara, Maureen, and Wayne Shaw. 1990. "Deposit Insurance and Wealth Effects: The Value of Being 'Too Big to Fail.'" *Journal of Finance* 45 (December): 1587–600.

Opiela, Timothy P. 2001. "Deposit Market Discipline in Pre-Crisis Thailand: Implications for Modeling the Thai Crisis and Developing a DIS." In *Proceedings of the Federal Reserve Bank of Chicago's 37th Annual Conference on Bank Structure and Competition.* May.

Partnoy, Frank. 1999. "The Siskel and Ebert of Financial Markets? Two Thumbs Down for the Credit Rating Agencies." *Washington University Law Quarterly* 77 (3): 619–712.

Paulson, Henry M., Jr. 2002. "Restoring Investor Confidence: An Agenda for Change." Speech given at the National Press Club, Washington, June 5.

Payments Risk Committee. 2000. "Intraday Liquidity Management in the Evolving Payment System: A Study of the Impact of the Euro, CLS Bank, and CHIPS Finality." April.

Peck, James, and Karl Shell. 2003. "Equilibrium Bank Runs." *Journal of Political Economy* 111 (11): 103–23.

Peek, Joe. 1997. "Comments on Examination and Enforcement." In *History of the Eighties: Lessons for the Future.* Vol. 2: *Symposium Proceedings, January 16, 1997.* Federal Deposit Insurance Corporation, pp. 11–16. Available at www.fdic.gov/bank/historical/history/index.html [October 24, 2003].

Peek, Joe, and Eric S. Rosengren. 1997. "Will Legislative Early Intervention Prevent the Next Banking Crisis?" *Southern Economics Journal* 64 (1, July): 268–80.

———. 2003. "Unnatural Selection: Perverse Incentives and the Misallocation of Credit in Japan." NBER Working Paper 9643. Cambridge, Mass.: National Bureau of Economic Research, April.

Peek, Joe, and James A. Wilcox. 2003. "The Fall and Rise of Banking Safety Net Subsidies." In Benton Gup, ed., *Too-Big-To-Fail: Policies and Procedures.* Praeger.

Penas, María Fabiana. 2001. "Too-Big-to-Fail Policy and Risk-Taking Behavior." Unpublished paper. University of Maryland, August.

Penas, María Fabiana, and Haluk Unal. 2001. "Too-Big-to-Fail Gains in Bank Mergers: Evidence from the Bond Markets." Unpublished paper. University of Maryland, September.

Persaud, Avinash. 2002. "The Political Economy of Basel II." Inaugural lecture as Mercer Memorial Chair in Commerce, Gresham College, October 3.

Persson, Torsten, and Guido Tabellini. 1993. "Designing Institutions for Monetary Stability." *Carnegie-Rochester Conference Series on Public Policy* 39: 53–89.

Petersen, Mitchell A., and Raghuram G. Rajan. 1994. "The Benefits of Lending Relationships: Evidence from Small Business Data." *Journal of Finance* 49 (March): 3–37.

Phaup, Marvin, and David Torregrosa. 1999. "Budgeting for Contingent Losses." In Roy Meyer, ed., *Handbook of Government Budgeting*. Jossey-Bass.

Platts Global Energy. 2001. "S&P Says Enron Collapse Unlikely to Pose 'Systemic' Risk." December 6. Available at www.platts.com/features/enron/exposure.shtml [September 5, 2003].

Polackova, Hana. 1998a. "Contingent Liabilities: A Threat to Fiscal Stability." PREM Notes 9. Washington: World Bank, November.

———. 1998b. "Government Contingent Liabilities: A Hidden Risk to Fiscal Stability." Policy Research Working Paper 1989. Washington, D.C.: World Bank.

Pomerleano, Michael. 1998. "The East Asia Crisis and Corporate Finance. The Untold Micro Story." Working Paper 1990. Washington: World Bank, October.

Poole, William. 2003. "Housing in the Macroeconomy." Remarks before a symposium of the U.S. Office of Federal Housing Enterprise Oversight, Washington, March 10. Available at www.stls.frb.org/news/speeches/2003/3_10_03.html [November 4, 2003].

Poterba, James M. 1997. "Do Budget Rules Work?" In Alan Auerbach, ed., *Fiscal Policy: Lessons from Empirical Research*. MIT Press.

Prescott, Edward S. 2002. "Can Risk-Based Deposit Insurance Premiums Control Moral Hazard?" *Federal Reserve Bank of Richmond Economic Quarterly* 88 (2): 87–100.

President's Working Group on Financial Markets. 1999. "Hedge Funds, Leverage, and the Lessons of Long-Term Capital Management." April.

Quinn, Brian. 1995. "Derivatives and Risk Management: Insight from the Barings Experience." In *Proceedings of the Federal Reserve Bank of Chicago's 31st Annual Conference on Bank Structure and Competition*. May.

Radecki, Lawrence. 1999. "Bank's Payments-Driven Revenues." *Federal Reserve Bank of New York Economic Policy Review* 5 (July): 53–70.

Rice, Tara, and Kristin Stanton. 2003. "Estimating the Volume of Payments-Driven Revenue." Emerging Payments Occasional Paper 2003-1C. Federal Reserve Bank of Chicago.

Rochet, Jean Charles, and Jean Tirole. 1996a. "Controlling Risk in Payment Systems." *Journal of Money, Credit, and Banking* 28 (November): 832–62.

———. 1996b. "Interbank Lending and Systemic Risk." *Journal of Money, Credit, and Banking* 28 (November): 733–62.

Rodden, Jonathan. 2000a. "Breaking the Golden Rule: Fiscal Behavior with Rational Bailout Expectations in the German States." Prepared for the workshop European Fiscal Federalism in Comparative Perspective, Center for European Studies, Harvard University, November 4; second draft, October 26. Available at mit.edu/jrodden/www/materials/brescia2.pdf [October 24, 2003].

———. 2000b. "Decentralization and the Challenge of Hard Budget Constraints." PREM Notes 41. Washington: World Bank, July.

Rodden, Jonathan, Gunnar S. Eskeland, and Jennie Litvack. 2002. "Introduction and Overview." Unpublished introduction to a book. Massachusetts Institute of Technology.

Rogoff, Kenneth. 1985. "The Optimal Design of Commitment to an Intermediate Monetary Target." *Quarterly Journal of Economics* 100 (November): 1169–89.

Rolnick, Arthur J. 1987. "The Benefits of Bank Deposit Rate Ceilings: New Evidence on Bank Rates and Risk in the 1920s." *Federal Reserve Bank of Minneapolis Quarterly Review* (Summer): 2–18.

———. 1999. "In This Issue." *Federal Reserve Bank of Minneapolis Quarterly Review* 23 (Winter): 1.

Rossi, Marco. 1999. "Financial Fragility and Economic Performance in Developing Economies: Do Capital Controls, Prudential Regulation, and Supervision Matter?" IMF Working Paper. Washington: International Monetary Fund, May.

Saidenberg, Marc R., and Philip E. Strahan. 1999. "Are Banks Still Important for Financing Large Businesses?" *Federal Reserve Bank of New York Current Issues in Economics and Finance* 5 (July).

Santomero, Anthony, and David Eckles. 2000. "The Determinants of Success in the New Financial Services Environment." *Federal Reserve Bank of New York Economic Policy Review* 6 (June): 5.

Santomero, Anthony M., and Paul Hoffman. 1998. "Problem Bank Resolution: Evaluating the Options." Wharton Financial Institutions Center 98-05-B. October.

Santos, J. A. C. 2001. "Bank Capital Regulation in Contemporary Banking Theory: A Review of the Literature." *Financial Markets, Institutions, and Instruments* 10 (2): 41–84.

Saunders, Anthony, and Berry Wilson. 1999. "The Impact of Consolidation and Safety-Net Support on Canadian, U.S., and U.K. Banks: 1893–1992." *Journal of Banking and Finance* 23 (2–4): 537–71.

Schick, Allen. 2002. "Budgeting for Fiscal Risk." In Hana Polackova Brixi and Allen Schick, eds., *Government at Risk: Contingent Liabilities and Fiscal Risk*. Oxford University Press.

Securities Industry Association. 2001. "Letter to the Federal Reserve Board on 'New Basel Capital Proposal.'" May.

Seidman, L. William. 1991. "Testimony on 'The Implications of Too Big to Fail' before the Subcommittee on Economic Stabilization, Committee on Banking, Finance, and Urban Affairs, United States House of Representatives, May 9." Serial 102-32.

Shadow Financial Regulatory Committee. 1989. "An Outline of a Program for Deposit Insurance and Regulatory Reform." Statement 41. February.

———. 2001. "Requiring Large Banks to Issue Subordinated Debt." Statement 168. February.

Shleifer, Andrei. 1998. "State versus Private Ownership." *Journal of Economic Perspectives* 12 (Fall): 133–50.

Silverberg, Stanley C. 1985. "Resolving Large Bank Problems and Failures." *Issues in Bank Regulation* (Winter): 12–15.

Sironi, Andres. 2000. "Testing for Market Discipline in the European Banking Industry: Evidence from Subordinated Debt Spreads." Working Paper. Universita Commerciales Luigi Cocconi, July.

Soussa, Farouk. 2000. "Too Big to Fail: Moral Hazard and Unfair Competition." In Maximilian Fry, ed., *Financial Stability and Central Banks—Selected Issues for Safety Nets and Market Discipline*. Bank of England.

Spiegel, Mark M. 1999. "Moral Hazard under the Japanese 'Convoy' Banking System." *Federal Reserve Bank of San Francisco Economic Review* 3: 3–13.

Spiegel, Mark M., and Nobuyoshi Yamori. 2000. "The Evolution of Bank Resolution Policies in Japan: Evidence from Market Equity Values." Pacific Basin Working Paper PB00-01. Federal Reserve Bank of San Francisco.

Standard and Poor's. 1999. "Support Factors in Bank Ratings."

———. 2002. "Bank Survivability Assessment." September 12.

Stern, Gary H. 1999. "Managing Moral Hazard with Market Signals: How Regulation Should Change with Banking." Remarks before the 35th Annual Conference on Bank Structure and Competition, Federal Reserve Bank of Chicago, May 6.

———. 2001. "Taking Market Data Seriously." *Federal Reserve Bank of Minneapolis Region* 15 (September): 8–10.

———. 2003. "Using Market Data in Supervision." Remarks before the 39th Annual Conference on Bank Structure and Competition. Chicago, May.

Stiglitz, Joseph E. 1993. "The Role of the State in Financial Markets." In Michael Bruno and Boris Pleskovic, eds., *Proceedings of the World Bank Annual Conference on Developmental Economics.* Washington: World Bank.

Stiroh, Kevin, and Jennifer Poole. 2000. "Explaining the Rising Concentration of Banking Assets in the 1990s." *Federal Reserve Bank of New York Current Issues in Economics and Finance* 6 (August): 1–6.

Stone, Pierce. 2002. "Testimony before the Financial Institutions and Consumer Credit Subcommittee, House Financial Services Committee, April 25th."

Study Group on Subordinated Notes and Debentures for the Federal Reserve System. 1999. "Using Subordinated Debt as an Instrument of Market Discipline." Staff Study 172. December.

Swary, Itzhak. 1986. "Stock Market Reaction to Regulatory Action in the Continental Illinois Crisis." *Journal of Business* 59 (July): 451–73.

Temzelides, Ted. 1997. "Are Bank Runs Contagious?" *Federal Reserve Bank of Philadelphia* (November–December): 3–14.

Thompson, John. 2002. "Have REITs Helped Tame Texas Real Estate?" *Federal Reserve Bank of Dallas Southwest Economy* (November–December): 13–18.

Thomson, James B. 1989. "The Use of Market Information in Pricing Deposit Insurance." *Journal of Money Credit and Banking* 19 (4): 528–37.

Todd, Walker F., and James B. Thomson. 1990. "An Insider's View of the Political Economy of the Too-Big-to-Fail Doctrine." Working Paper 9017. Federal Reserve Bank of Cleveland, December.

Tornell, Aaron. 2001. *Financial Liberalization, Bailout Guarantees, and Growth.* Cambridge, Mass.: National Bureau of Economic Research, September.

Tweedie, David. 2002. "Memorandum." Submitted to the U.K. Select Committee on Treasury, September.

U.S. Code. 1991. "Congressional and Administrative News." 102 Cong. 1 sess. West.

U.S. Congressional Budget Office. 1991a. "Budgetary Treatment of Deposit Insurance: A Framework for Reform." May.

———. 1991b. *The Cost of Forbearance during the Thrift Crisis.* June.

———. 1992. "The Economic Effects of the Savings and Loan Crisis."

U.S. General Accounting Office. 1984a. *Guidelines for Rescuing Large Failing Firms and Municipalities.* GAO/GGD-84-34. March.

————. 1984b. "Statement for the Record by the Comptroller General of the United States Concerning the Federal Rescue of Continental Illinois National Bank." Submitted to the House Committee on Banking, Finance, and Urban Affairs, December 14.

————. 1989. "Thrift Failures: Costly Failures Resulted from Regulatory Violations and Unsafe Practices." AFMD-89-62.

————. 1996. "Bank and Thrift Regulation: Implementation of FDICIA's Prompt Regulatory Action Provisions." GAO-GGD-97-18. November.

————. 1997a. "Budgeting for Federal Insurance Programs." GAO/AIMD97-16. September.

————. 1997b. "Financial Crisis Management: Four Financial Crises in the 1980s." GAO/GGD/97-96. May.

U.S. House of Representatives. 1990. "Leveraged Buyouts and Bankruptcy." Hearings before the House of Representatives Subcommittee on Economic and Commercial Law of the Committee on the Judiciary.

————. 1991. "House Report 102-330." *U.S. Code Congressional and Administrative News*, vol. 3. 102 Cong. 1 sess.

U.S. House of Representatives, Committee on Banking and Financial Services. 1998. "Hedge Fund Operations." October.

U.S. Office of the Comptroller of the Currency. 2001. *An Examiner's Guide to Problem Bank Identification, Rehabilitation, and Resolution.* January.

————. Various years. *Quarterly Derivatives Fact Sheet.*

U.S. Office of Federal Housing Enterprise Oversight. 2003. "Systemic Risk: Fannie Mae, Freddie Mac, and the Role of OFHEO."

U.S. Office of Management and Budget. 1992. *The Budget of the United States Government, Fiscal Year 1993.*

U.S. Senate. 1982. "Senate Report 97-536." *U.S. Code Congressional and Administrative News*, vol. 3. 97 Cong. 2 sess.

U.S. Treasury Department, Federal Reserve System, and Federal Deposit Insurance Corporation. 2001. "Risk-Based Capital Guidelines, Final Rule." *Federal Register,* November 29.

Vittas, Dimitri, and Yoon Je Cho. 1995. "Credit Policies: Lessons from East Asia." Policy Research Working Paper 1458. Washington: World Bank.

Vittas, Dimitri, and Akihiko Kawaura. 1995. "Policy-Based Finance, Financial Regulation, and Financial Sector Development in Japan." Policy Research Working Paper. Washington: World Bank.

Vives, Xavier. 2001. "Restructuring Financial Regulation in the European Monetary Union." *Journal of Financial Services Research* 19 (February): 57–82.

Wall, Larry D. 1993. "Too-Big-to-Fail after FDICIA." *Federal Reserve Bank of Atlanta Economic Review* 78 (January–February): 1–14.

————. 1997. "Taking Note of the Deposit Insurance Fund: A Plan for the FDIC to Issue Capital Notes." *Federal Reserve Bank of Atlanta Economic Review* 82 (1): 14–31.

Wallace, Neil. 1990. "A Banking Model in Which Partial Suspension Is Best." *Federal Reserve Bank of Minneapolis Quarterly Review* 14 (Fall): 1–14.

Walsh, Carl E. 1995a. "Is New Zealand's Reserve Bank Act of 1989 an Optimal Central Bank Contract?" *Journal of Money, Credit, and Banking* 27 (November): 1179–91.

————. 1995b. "Optimal Contracts for Central Bankers." *American Economic Review* 85 (March): 150–67.

————. 2002. "When Should Central Bankers Be Fired?" *Economics of Governance* 37: 1–21.

Ward, Jonathan. 2002. "The Supervisory Approach: A Critique." Working Paper 2. Cambridge Endowment for Research in Finance.

Whalen, Gary. 1997. "The Competitive Implications of Safety Net–Related Subsidies." Working Paper 97-9. U.S. Office of the Comptroller of the Currency, May.

Wildasin, David. 1997. *Externalities and Bailouts: Hard and Soft Budget Constraints in Intergovernmental Fiscal Relations.* Policy Research Paper 1843. Washington: World Bank, November.

Wilmarth, Arthur J. 2002. "The Transformation of the U.S. Financial Services Industry, 1975–2000: Competition, Consolidation, and Increased Risks." *University of Illinois Law Review* 2: 215–476.

World Bank. 2002. "Building Institutions for Markets." In *World Development Report 2002.* New York: Oxford University Press.

Yonetani, Tatusya, and Yoko Katsuo. 1998. "Fair Value Accounting and Regulatory Capital Requirements." *Federal Reserve Bank of New York Economic Policy Review* 4 (October): 33–43.

Zhou, Ruilin. 2000. "Understanding Intraday Credit in Large Value Payment Systems. Federal Reserve Bank of Chicago." *Federal Reserve Bank of Chicago Economic Perspectives* 25 (3): 29–44.

Index

Accounting methods: cash-based accounting, 102–03; cost-accounting shortcomings, 196; market value accounting, 145, 193–96. *See also* Budgeting

Accrual budgeting, 104–09

African American ownership of small banks and government bailout, 75

American Bankers' Association's proposal on coinsurance, 129

Appointment of conservative bank regulators, 92, 95

Asian financial crisis, 28, 57, 76, 172

Asset-backed securities market, 181

Asset holdings: distribution among largest banks, 61–63; residual, 183; technological advances making easier to understand, 182

Audience intended, 5–6

Bailouts: aligning with stability in case-by-case determinations, 22; and coinsurance, 128–30; commitment to and credibility of, 146, 147–48; government's unwillingness to support, 80, 85; government's willingness to support, 75–77; and IMF loans, 76–77; international comparisons of, 40; investigation data to be publicly disclosed, 162; negative consequences from, 22; policy of "no bailouts ever," 3, 19, 20, 147; tax on large banks to recoup cost of, 78, 79

Bank failure: and government takeover, 12; insufficient past data to evaluate effects of, 50–51; interbank failures, 45, 50, 61, 138, 147; multinational, 118–19; and rapid recapitalization, 128; and shared exposures of banks, 46; shutting down insolvent banks, 124–28, 148; significance of, 1; timing of, 130–31

Bank financial strength ratings, 34–37

Banking crises: analysis of costs of, 40; extenuating circumstances surrounding, 177; increase in number worldwide, 75; misinformation about, 56; from *1985* to *1992,* 152

Bank of England, 81, 85, 137

228   INDEX

148; restricting spillovers in, 132–40; spreading of risk, 135. *See also* Securities; Settlement system and possibility for bank failure; Technology

PCA (prompt corrective action), 125–27

Policymakers: contracts to enforce performance of, 142, 160–61, 165, 167; imposing costs on supervisory agencies, 161–62; imposing costs on via disclosure, 162–63, 165–66; imposing direct costs on supervisors, 159–61; logic of, 45–52; penalizing of, 141, 142, 159–67; personal gain of, 43–44, 52–56, 58–59; reservations about increasing costs to, 163–64; third-party pressure on, 163–66. *See also* Uncertainty of policymakers

Prompt corrective action (PCA), 125–27

Public disclosure. *See* Disclosure

Purchase and assumption method of FDIC to deal with failing banks, 151–54

Railroads and government support, 15

Rapid payment to creditors, 122–23

Rapid recapitalization, 128

Real-time payments, 135, 136, 139

Recession: of *1980-82,* 92; resulting from government need to bailout banks, 28; resulting from significant bank failure, 46–47, 50; and supervisory reactions, 176; true causes of, 49

Reforms, 87–88, 148; appointment of conservative bank regulators, 92, 95; budgeting, 98–110; dominant payment providers, targeted reforms for, 119–22; improved accounting of federal guarantees, 58; legal and regulatory changes, 116–19; limited discretion of supervisors, 59; limiting creditor losses, 124–31; of

market discipline, 179–96; market value accounting, 145, 193–96; of payment system, 135–37; penalizing policymakers, 159–67; planning for bank failure, 112–16; rapid payment to creditors, 122–23; reduction of forbearance, 58; of S&R, 142–43, 168–78; spillover control, 132–40; transparency increased due to changes in technology, 145, 180–83. *See also* Discipline

Regulation F, 138

Reputation of decisionmakers as factor in TBTF coverage, 54–55

Resona Holdings, 54

Risk assessments, 17, 169–70; risk-focused exams, 175, 178; systemic risk needed for bailouts, 81–83; transparency increased due to changes in technology, 183

Risk-taking: and CD rates, 41; deposit insurance premiums to vary with, 190–92; excessive by banks, 18, 23–26, 27, 169–70; forbearance policy encouraging, 54; government credit allocation encouraging, 56–57; of larger banks, 64–65; practical evidence of, 171–72; reforms aimed at, 138; uninsured creditors' pricing of, 29, 40–42, 162. *See also* Risk assessments; Supervision and regulation (S&R)

Russian financial crisis, 40

Safety and soundness regulation, 24, 125; failure to enforce (forbearance), 53–54

S&R. *See* Supervision and regulation

Savings and loan crisis: Federal Home Loan Bank board failure in, 161; forbearance during, 53; and government bailout costs, 23–24

Scenario planning by policymakers, 112–16; public disclosure of, 115–16

Scope of TBTF problem, x, 11–22, 29–42

Granato

K Hoover
R Droyer
D. Coates
Chappell